'This COCAP volume is a profound and timely contribution. Psychoanalytic under-
standings of compulsive disorders expressed through the body in infants, children,
and adolescents – including psychosomatic disorders in infants, repetitive behavioral disorders in young children, and emotional disorders in adolescence that underlie addiction, self-harm, and suicide – are discussed in lucid theoretical and clinical
terms. Given the epidemic proportions of addiction and self-harm in adults today,
this book demonstrates possible early life roots of pathology and offers a crucial
foundation for therapists, educators, and members of the public devoted to alleviating self-destructive disorders in those whom they serve and/or love.'

Harriet L. Wolfe, M.D., *Past President,*
International Psychoanalytical Association

'This book tackles in a truly courageous, in-depth, and innovative way the theme
of a ubiquitous psychosocial macro-phenomenon that characterizes our era, which
dramatically endangers the development of new generations and which, until now,
has not found adequate tools for understanding and community responses.

It is the most advanced contemporary theoretical-clinical text on this subject,
thanks to the contributions of an interregional scientific network of the highest
excellence, and offers fundamental help to all those who deal with these scenarios
of suffering and who want to acquire useful and substantial tools for understanding
and working.'

Stefano Bolognini, *Past President,*
International Psychoanalytical Association

'This new volume in the COCAP series brings together leading psychoanalytic perspectives on compulsion, addiction, self-harm, and suicidal states in infancy, childhood, and adolescence. Grounded in clinical material and theoretical elaboration, it
explores early bodily experience, failures of symbolization, and the pathways from
autoerotic regulation to destructive repetition. Contributors show how trauma, narcissistic fragility, and the digital environment shape new forms of suffering in the
young. By linking early psychic organization to later psychopathology, this indispensable book speaks not only to clinicians but to all professionals working with
children and adolescents across diverse fields of care and education.'

Virginia Ungar, M.D., *Past President,*
International Psychoanalytical Association

'In this remarkable volume the editors bring a series of deeply insightful and clinically rich chapters written by leading specialists in child and adolescent psychoanalysis from around the world, exploring some of the most urgent and complex
issues facing families today.

With empathy and depth, the contributors address themes such as compulsion, psychosomatic manifestations, anorexia, substance abuse, self-harm, suicide, societal pressures, destructiveness and masochism—examining how these painful manifestations speak to deeper psychic realities. A central focus of the book is the nuanced exploration of the libidinization of the body as a protective mechanism against self-destruction.'

Catalina Bronstein, M.D., *Training Analyst,*
British Psychoanalytical Society

The Body and Compulsion from Infancy to Young Adulthood

The Body and Compulsion from Infancy to Young Adulthood: New Perspectives on Addiction, Self-Harm and Suicide examines the complex interplay between early childhood experiences and the development of compulsive behaviours across the lifespan, with a focus on how these compulsions present from infancy to young adulthood.

A diverse group of international psychoanalysts from a range of theoretical perspectives and clinical experiences examine the severe bodily symptoms and syndromes often seen in young patients. They provide profound insight into the metapsychological foundations of repetition and destructiveness. Through compelling clinical vignettes and theoretical explorations, the contributors demonstrate how early trauma and neglect can disrupt the psyche, leading to damaging behavioural and emotional pathologies. Conditions such as eating disorders, depression, anxiety, violent behaviour, suicidality, and addiction are explored in detail, with the contributors highlighting the challenges they pose in the therapeutic setting and offering guidance on how to navigate sessions with those suffering from them.

This essential volume provides invaluable insights for psychoanalysts, psychotherapists, and mental health professionals working with patients struggling with compulsive patterns, while also offering theoretical depth for scholars interested in early development, trauma, and the foundations of psychic structure.

Christine Anzieu-Premmereur is a psychiatrist and psychoanalyst based in New York City, USA. She is the series editor of the Routledge Child and Adolescent Psychoanalysis Book Series and the co-editor of *A Psychoanalytic Exploration of the Contemporary Search for Pleasure* (2023), *The Infinite Infantile and the Psychoanalytic Task* (2022) and *A Psychoanalytic Exploration of the Body in Today's World* (2017).

Mary T. Brady is an adult and child psychoanalyst in San Francisco. She is the author of *Psychoanalysis with Adolescents and Children: Learning to Surf* (2024) and the editor of *Braving the Erotic Field in the Treatment of Children and Adolescents* (2022), as well as author of *Analytic Engagements with Adolescents* (2018) and *The Body in Adolescence* (2015).

Christine Franckx is a child psychiatrist and training (child) analyst in the Belgian Psychoanalytic Society. She is the EU co-chair of COCAP. She works in private practice in Antwerp with adults, children, and infants.

Fernando M. Gómez is a pediatrician, psychiatrist, and child and adolescent psychoanalyst of the Asociación Psicoanalítica Argentina (APA), FEPAL, and IPA. He is the Latin America Co-Chair of COCAP and works in private practice in Buenos Aires with adults, children, and infants.

The Routledge Child and Adolescent Psychoanalysis Book Series

Editor: Christine Anzieu-Premmereur
Co-Editors: Mary T. Brady
Christine Franckx
Fernando M. Gómez

The Routledge Child and Adolescent Psychoanalysis Book Series is devoted to manuscripts that illuminate the creative and challenging work of child and adolescent psychoanalysis and psychoanalytic psychotherapy. While we believe that the study of child psychoanalysis is relevant to all psychoanalysts – as the study of the unconscious is essential to all psychoanalysts – the particularities of child and adolescent work require that the setting adapt itself to the child and adolescent, not the other way around. We also see children and adolescents as quite sensitive to cultural and societal changes and catastrophes. Children and adolescents are like the canaries in the coal mine – particularly vulnerable to the presence of gases. For that reason, our Book Series is dedicated to excellent and creative clinical technique and theoretical work, writing that is sensitive to the setting, and writing that is perceptive of societal and cultural changes that affect children and adolescents.

The series editors are especially interested in selecting books which enhance the understanding and further expansion of infant, child, and adolescent psychoanalytic thought. Part of the mission of this international series is to nurture communication amongst psychoanalysts working in different models, in different languages, and in different regions of the world.

Series Editor Biographies

Christine Anzieu-Premmereur is a psychiatrist and psychoanalyst in New York City who works in private practice with adults, children, parents, and their babies. A member of the Société Psychanalytique de Paris, she is on the faculty of the Columbia Psychoanalytic Center for Training and Research and is Assistant Clinical Professor in Psychiatry at Columbia University. She is the chair of the IPA Committee for Child and Adolescent Psychoanalysis (COCAP). With Vaia Tsolas, she is the co-founder of Pulsion Institute. She recently published *The Process of Representation in Early Childhood* and *Attacks on Linking in Parents of Young Disturbed Children*. She co-edited with Vaia Tsolas *A Psychoanalytic Exploration of the Body in Today's World: On the Body* (2017) and *A Psychoanalytic Exploration of the Contemporary Search for Pleasure: The Turning of the Screw* (2023).

Dr. Mary T. Brady is an adult and child psychoanalyst in private practice in San Francisco, USA. She is on the faculties of the San Francisco Center for Psychoanalysis and the Psychoanalytic Institute of Northern California. She is the editor of

Braving the Erotic Field in the Treatment of Children and Adolescents (2022). Her books, *Analytic Engagements with Adolescents* and *The Body in Adolescence,* were published by Routledge in 2018 and 2016, respectively. She is the North American Co-Chair for the Committee on Child and Adolescent Psychoanalysis (COCAP) of the IPA. She co-leads a Psychoanalysis and Film group.

Dr. Christine Franckx is an adult and child psychoanalyst and psychiatrist. She works in Antwerp in private practice for adult analysis, and she has created an analytic psychotherapeutic center for early development (0–6 years). She is a Training Analyst of the Belgian Psychoanalytic Society, of which she has been the President (2016–2020). She is the editor of two books *Eros op de scene* (2021) and *Het kinderlijk trauma* (2023). She is a trainer in infant observation (Esther Bick). She is the European Co-Chair for the IPA Committee on Child and Adolescent Psychoanalysis (COCAP).

Dr. Fernando M. Gómez is a child and adolescent psychoanalyst, psychiatrist, and pediatrician. He works in Buenos Aires in private practice for children, adolescents, and adults analysis. He was trained at the Asociación Psicoanalítica Argentina (APA), where he is a Training Analyst, and has served as Director of the Publications Committee (2016–2020) and of the Department of Children and Adolescents "Arminda Aberastury" (2020–2023). He is the Latin American Co-Chair for the IPA Committee for Child and Adolescent Psychoanalysis (COCAP). He is a former member of the Advisory Council of the General Directorate of Mental Health of the Government of the City of Buenos Aires. He edited a 4-volume collection: *Pilares del Psicoanálisis Contemporáneo* (2017, 2018, 2019, 2020), *Psicoanálisis Contemporáneo Latinoamericano* (2017, coedited with FEPAL), and *Clinica e Investigación en el Psicoanalisis de bebés, niños y adolescentes. Nuevos horizontes, nuevos desafíos* (2025).

The Body and Compulsion from Infancy to Young Adulthood

New Perspectives on Addiction, Self-Harm and Suicide

Edited by
Christine Anzieu-Premmereur,
Mary T. Brady, Christine Franckx
and Fernando M. Gómez

Routledge
Taylor & Francis Group

LONDON AND NEW YORK

Designed cover image: 123 RF, 211423645, *Portrait of a beautiful woman underwater.*

First published 2026
by Routledge
4 Park Square, Milton Park, Abingdon, Oxon OX14 4RN

and by Routledge
605 Third Avenue, New York, NY 10158

Routledge is an imprint of the Taylor & Francis Group, an informa business

For Product Safety Concerns and Information please contact our EU representative GPSR@taylorandfrancis.com. Taylor & Francis Verlag GmbH, Kaufingerstraße 24, 80331 München, Germany.

Trademark notice: Product or corporate names may be trademarks or registered trademarks, and are used only for identification and explanation without intent to infringe.

British Library Cataloguing-in-Publication Data
A catalogue record for this book is available from the British Library

ISBN: 978-1-041-08879-0 (hbk)
ISBN: 978-1-041-08878-3 (pbk)
ISBN: 978-1-003-64731-7 (ebk)

DOI: 10.4324/9781003647317

Typeset in Times New Roman
by codeMantra

Contents

Series foreword

The Committee on Child and Adolescent Psychoanalysis (COCAP) is delighted to present this new book in our new Series – *The Body and Compulsion from Infancy to Young Adulthood: New Perspectives on Addiction, Self-Harm and Suicide,* edited by four COCAP members who have gathered a list of international analysts for their expertise on the severe issues we observe now in the young population, negativeness, depression, psychosomatic issues, addiction, destructiveness, and self-injuries. This book includes the clinical work and the understanding of unconscious dynamics of eminent psychoanalysts coming from different analytic perspectives. Written with rigor and experience, all chapters offer a view on the diversity of techniques with serious clinical issues. It will make this new book of great interest for psychoanalysts and mental health clinicians seeing patients of all ages.

The COCAP Book Series is devoted to manuscripts that illuminate the creative and challenging work of child and adolescent psychoanalysis and psychoanalytic psychotherapy. While we believe that the study of child psychoanalysis is relevant to all psychoanalysts - as the study of the unconscious is essential to all psychoanalysts – the particularities of child and adolescent work require that the setting adapt itself to the child and adolescent, not the other way around. We see children and adolescents as quite sensitive to cultural and societal changes and catastrophes. Children and adolescents are like the canaries in the coal mine – particularly vulnerable to the presence of gases. For that reason, our Book Series is dedicated to excellent and creative clinical technique and theoretical work, writing that is sensitive to the setting, and writing that is perceptive of societal and cultural changes that affect children and adolescents.

The series editors are especially interested in selecting books which enhance the understanding and further expansion of infant, child, and adolescent psychoanalytic thought. A mission of this international series is to nurture communication amongst psychoanalysts working in different models, in different languages, and in different regions of the world.

Series Editor: Christine Anzieu-Premmereur
Chair, Committee on Child and
Adolescent Psychoanalysis

Contributor biographies

Laura Accetti is a full member of IPA, member of the Italian Psychoanalytic Society (SPI) and IPA-recognized expert on children and adolescents psychoanalysis. She serves as the Scientific secretary of the Specialization Program on Developmental Age at the Winnicott Institute in Rome. She is Professor of Psychotherapy with Adolescents in the Winnicott Institute Specialization Program and leads a research program on gender incongruence in the Winnicott Institute. She is the author of numerous papers on Adolescence published in journals and books. She is a member of the Forum on Adolescence Committee of the EPF and the author of numerous articles on adolescence published in journals and books. She lives and works in Rome, Italy.

Paula Guadalupe Cerutti Agelet is a psychologist and analyst in training at the Argentine Psychoanalytic Association (APA). She holds a Bachelor's degree in Psychology (UBA). She is a graduate of the specialization program in psychoanalysis with children (UCES). She serves as the COCAP Representative of the International Psychoanalytical Studies Organization – IPSO (2023–2024) and is a member of the Candidates Scientific Committee – Argentine Psychoanalytic Association (APA). Additionally, she is the liaison representative candidate with the Department of Children and Adolescents "Arminda Aberastury" at the Argentine Psychoanalytic Association (2021–2024). She lives and works in Buenos Aires, Argentina.

Panos Aloupis, MD, PhD, is a psychiatrist and psychologist, a full member of the Paris Psychoanalytic Society (SPP), a correspondent member of the Hellenic Psychoanalytic Society (HPS), a training and supervising member of the Paris Psychosomatic Institute (IPSO Pierre Marty), and a member of the editorial committee of the Revue française de Psychosomatique. Last paper: *ALOUPIS P. (2023) Enemies of unpleasure in A psychoanalytic exploration of the contemporary search for pleasure, NY, Routledge, 123–132.*

Christine Anzieu-Premmereur is a psychiatrist and psychoanalyst in New York who works with adults, children and babies. A member of the Société Psychanalytique de Paris and of the American Psychoanalytic Association, she chairs the IPA Committee for Child and Adolescent Psychoanalysis, COCAP. She is the co-founder of Pulsion Institute. She has published on child psychoanalysis, motherhood, the symbolization process, psychosomatics, and addiction. She co-edited with the COCAP *The Infinite Infantile and the Psychoanalytic Task: Psychoanalysis with Children, Adolescents and their Families*. With Vaia Tsolas, she co-edited "A Psychoanalytic Exploration of the Body in Today's World: on the Body", and in 2023, "A Psychoanalytic Exploration of the Contemporary Search for Pleasure: The Turning of the Screw".

Heribert Blass, Dr. med., is a full member of the International Psychoanalytical Association – IPA and a training and supervising psychoanalyst for adults, children, and adolescents. He is a member of the German Psychoanalytical Association (DPV). He is President elect of the IPA (2025). He was the President of the European Psychoanalytic Federation – EPF (2020–2024). He was the Vice President of the EPF (2016–2020). He was the Chair of the EPF group "Exploring Training Process and Practice" (ETPP) from 2014 to 2017 and staff member of the EPF Forum "End-of-Training-Evaluation-Project" (ETEP) from 2004 to 2014. He was the Training Director at the DPV from 2010 to 2016. He is the author of various publications, for instance on fatherhood, male identity and sexuality, on gender dysphoria and transgender issues, and others. He lives a work is in private practice in Düsseldorf, Germany.

Mary T. Brady, Ph.D., is an adult and child psychoanalyst in San Francisco. She serves on the faculties of the San Francisco Center for Psychoanalysis and the Psychoanalytic Institute of Northern California. She is recipient of the American Psychoanalytic Association's Roughton Paper Award. Her book, *Psychoanalysis with Adolescents and Children: Learning to Surf,* was published by Routledge in 2024. She is the editor of *Braving the Erotic Field in the Treatment of Children and Adolescents* (Routledge, 2022). She is also the author of *Analytic Engagements with Adolescents* and *The Body in Adolescence* (Routledge 2018 and 2016, respectively).

Mónica Cardenal is a training analyst of APdeBA and former Scientific Coordinator. She is Associate Professor in Clinic Psychology and Infant Psychiatry Postgraduate Training and Coordinator of the Infant Observation Seminar (Bick's method) at the University Institute, Italian Hospital, Buenos Aires. She is Chair IPA Committee on Psychoanalytic Assistance in Crises and Emergencies and a consultant to the IPA Committee on Child and Adolescent Psychoanalysis. She is Academic Advisor and supervisor of the work program with street children and young refugees in Puebla, Mexico, Fundación JUCONI. She is the co-editor of the books: "Territorios postkleinianos. Una actualización de la tarea Psicoanalítica", Teseo, Buenos Aires, 2020 and "The Infinite Infantile and the Psychoanalytic task. Psychoanalysis with Children, Adolescents and their Families" IPA, COCAP and Routledge, London and New York 2022.

She was the co-editor of the Journal "Revista Internacional de Observación de bebés", Buenos Aires, from 2000 to 2023.

Germain Dillenseger is a psychiatrist and psychoanalyst in training at the Societe Psychanalytique de Paris, working in private practice and in a parents-and-infant unit in Alsace, France. He is an IPSO representative at COCAP and a candidate at the Société Psychanalytique de Paris.

Kristin Fiorella is a psychoanalyst in San Francisco where she sees children, adolescents, and adults in psychotherapy and psychoanalysis. She is on the faculty at Psychoanalytic Institute of Northern California (PINC) and San Francisco Center for Psychoanalysis (SFCP). She writes and publishes about the intersection between Buddhism and psychoanalysis.

Silvia Flechner is a medical doctor, psychologist, and Master in Psychoanalysis. She is a full member of IPA and a child and adolescent training analyst of the Uruguayan Psychoanalytic Association (APU). She served as Past President of the Uruguayan Psychoanalytic Association (2012–2014 APU); and the Past Co-Chair for Latin America of the IPA International New Groups between 2017 and 2021. She is a psychoanalyst in private practice specialized in working with adolescents. She is the author of several publications in journals and books and has published widely in Spanish, English, and Portuguese. Routledge published *The Astonishing Adolescent Upheaval in Psychoanalysis*, edited by her and R. Cassorla. She is the former Chair of the Publications Committee of the IPA (2021–2025). She lives and work in Montevideo, Uruguay.

Christine Franckx is a child psychiatrist and training (child) analyst in the Belgian Psychoanalytic Society. She is EU co-chair of COCAP and a member of editorial board of the *Dutch Journal of Psychoanalysis*. She works in private practice in Antwerp with adults, children, and infants. She is an Infant Observation trainer. She co-edited Eros op de scene (2021) on Joyce Mc Dougall and Kinderlijk Trauma (2023) on Sandor Ferenczi. She has published and lectured on child analysis, infant–parent psychoanalytic psychotherapy, and contemporary psychoanalysis related to societal changes.

Patricia Gherovici, Ph.D., is a psychoanalyst, analytic supervisor, and co-founder of Pulsion: The International Institute of Psychoanalysis and Psychoanalytic Psychosomatics, New York. She received the Sigourney Award for her clinical work with Latinx and gender variant communities (2020). She is the author of the book *The Puerto Rican Syndrome*, winner of the Gradiva Award and the Boyer Prize (2003). She is the author of several publication in journals and books, as "Transgender Psychoanalysis", and the co-author of the book *Psychoanalysis in the Barrios: Race, Class, and the Unconscious*, winner of the Gradiva Award for Best Edited Collection and the American Board and Academy of Psychoanalysis Book Prize; Routledge (2019); and also the book *Psychoanalysis, Gender and Sexualities: From Feminism to Trans*, winner of the Gradiva Award for Best Edited Collection; Routledge (2023). She works in Philadelphia and New York, USA.

Dr. Fernando M. Gómez is a medical doctor, pediatrician, psychiatrist and child and adolescent psychoanalyst. He is a training (child and adolescent) analyst of the Argentine Psychoanalytic Association (APA). He is a full member of Latin America Federation of Psychoanalysis – FEPAL, and of the International Psychoanalytic Association – IPA. He is the Co-Chair for Latin America – COCAP (2021–Present). He was the former Director of the Child and Adolescent Department "Arminda Aberastury"– APA (2020–2023). He was Former Member-General Directorate of Mental Health of the Government of the City of Buenos Aires (2021–2024). He was the Chair of the "1st International Virtual Congress on Babies, Children and Adolescents Psychoanalysis Research" – APA (2022). He has received APA Baranger-Mom Award (2007) and APA – "Dr. Luis Alberto Storni" Prize (2024). He was an observer in Child Psychiatry Department, Hospital For Sick Children, Toronto-Canada (1996). He is the editor of several books and author of many papers in Spanish, English and French. He is Professor of the Angel Garma Institute – APA, and in seminars offered in Brazil, Mexico, Spain and Ukraine. He is Supervisor in Argentina and in Brazil (SOS Brazil). He lives and works in Buenos Aires, Argentina.

Howard B. Levine is a member of PINE, the Contemporary Freudian Society, and Pulsion. He serves on the Editorial Board of the IJP and Psychoanalytic Inquiry and Editor-in-Chief of the Routledge Wilfred Bion Studies Book Series and in private practice in Brookline, Massachusetts. He is the editor of many books and the author of *Transformations de l'Irreprésentable* (Ithaque 2019) and *Affect, Representation and Language: Between the Silence and the Cry* (Routledge 2022).

Jeanne Magagna, PhD., is a Tavistock Clinic trained Child, adult, and family psychotherapist who was the Head of Psychotherapy Services at Great Ormond Street Hospital for Children in London. Her commitment to the Tavistock Clinic method led to the development of a specialized nursery in Rome. She teaches and publishes internationally. Jeanne is the joint editor of various books including *Intimate Transformations: Babies with their Families*, *Being Present for Your Nursery Age Child* and editor of *The Silent Child: Communication without Words* (2012), and also the author of *The Psychotherapeutic Understanding of Children with Eating Difficulties* (2021).

Ann Martini is an adult and child analyst in private practice near San Jose, California, with a special interest in early childhood and parent work. She is on the faculty of the San Francisco Center for Psychoanalysis where she is a training and supervising analyst, as well as a member of COCAP.

Anouk Meurrens, PhD, is a clinical psychologist and advanced candidate in the Belgian Psychoanalytic Society, representing IPSO. She works with adolescents and adults and is very interested in artistic media and group work. She has published papers in the Revue Belge de Psychanalyse and in the Revue Française de Psychanalyse. Her areas of research interest include psychosis, art, and language.

Humberto Lorenzo Persano, is a psychiatrist at the School of Medicine in the University of Buenos Aires, Argentina. He is a professor of Mental Health and Psychiatry, and Psychology of Nutrition as well as holding the position of Director of the Institute of Clinical Psychiatry and Mental Health. He is a member of the Argentine Psychoanalytic Association, and a training analyst, supervisor, and child and adolescent psychoanalyst at the IPA.

René Roussillon, from the Paris Psychoanalytical Society, is Professor emeritus of clinical and psychopathological psychology, Lyon 2 University Director of the clinical psychology department 1989–2012. He is the Director of the research team Lyon2 University and Training Psychoanalyst at the Société Psychanalytique de Paris and the Groupe Lyonnais. He received Bouvet Prize in 1991, and Sigourney award in 2016. He published many books, the recent one being on the Deconstruction of Narcissism.

Clara R. Schejtman is a member of the Argentine Psychoanalytic Association, and Chair of the children and adolescent department, Permanent Professor and Research Director in Buenos Aires University and Belgrano University. She is a faculty member in Research Training Program (RTP) and a member of the OPA Research Grants Subcommittee. She is the author of numerous publications and books (Routledge, Akadia).

Claudia Spadazzi, MD, is a Full Member Italian Psychoanalytic Society (SPI) and International Psychoanalytic Society (IPA). She is a clinical psychologist, gynaecologist, and sexual therapist. She is the co-founder of the Italian Psychoanalytic Dialogues (IPD). She was the member of IPA in Health Committee and was the Europe Co-Chair of the Cartagena IPA Conference 2023.

José Alberto Zusman, MD, PhD, is Chair of the IPA Addiction Subcommittee, a Full Member of the IPA Health Committee, a Training Analyst of the Rio de Janeiro Psychoanalytic Society, Professor in the Psychiatry and Mental Health Department (Federal University of Rio de Janeiro – UFRJ). He earned his PhD in Psychoanalysis under the mentorship of Dr. Portella (UFRJ) and completed a postdoctoral degree in addiction under the mentorship of Dr. Khantzian (UFRJ/Harvard).

Introduction

Christine Anzieu-Premmereur

Child and adolescent psychoanalysts working as a team in the IPA Committee COCAP have put together their knowledge, experience, and energy to treat young people in distress. The figures of depression in the young population all over the world were already of serious concern by the end of 2019, when the 2020 pandemic put on the scene dramatic mental health issues in the young generation.

Infants were showing psychosomatic symptoms, young children showed repetitive behavioral issues, and teenagers suffered from either depression and destructive features or presented dissociation/disorganization. We are facing now an epidemic of addiction with such a huge number in young and older population that it is an international health emergency and a source of concern for future generations.

Negative emotion, extreme defenses that limit contact with others, pain, and destructiveness manifested through a range of symptoms that all limited the freedom to think and be alive in a social environment. All those behavioral and emotional pathologies have in common their bodily expressions and their irrepressible repetitions.

Psychoanalysts work at containing and treating those disorders. Giving them a symbolic form instead of bodily symptoms is to try to restore more internal freedom and a sense of integration. Addictive social media, automatic electronic systems creating neediness, and dependency were already in the social landscape. Now it's the same with childhood, even toddlerhood. Parents addicted to screens need children to be quiet, silent in their own virtual life.

Dependency toward biological needs, repetition of pain, and relief is daily human life. A more specific form of repetition is the compulsion to repeat: compulsion to get rid of tension and anxiety, in a never-ending system of rituals or dependency toward external means: food, sex, drugs, games…

This book originally began in the September 2024 COCAP Conference, "Compulsion and the Body," an online international series of panels with translation in four languages. More than 20 international speakers presenting on a diversity of theories and clinical techniques made that scientific event a big success.

We thank all the COCAP members and those amazing presenters, as the IPA team for its technical support.

Early experiences, bodily, sensorial, and emotional are the sources of psychic processes that develop with repetition. Staying alive requires the cyclic repetition in balance with body needs. Freud observed how 'Being' precedes 'Having' the object and living in a Self: a psyche that observes external reality while creating a symbolic succession of mental representations and a flow of unconscious fantasies.

Instincts and drives, bodily needs and the psyche associating satisfaction with pleasure and pain with anxiety, form the background of our psychosomatic balance. Repetition is a fundamental part of it, and one of the first visible experiences is that children play. Freud observed his grandson's actively throwing a reel and having it back, while trying to master his separation anxiety and his aggression. The repetitive compulsion of this was for Freud the sign of a fundamental part of human life, what he labeled the death drive, as the tendency to deconstruct and to go to the Nirvana principle, like feeling nothing and being quiet.

We start our lives with the compulsive need for mastering anxiety, and playing is the most powerful way to do it. Then it can be transformed from repetition into a flow of associations where pleasure is experienced, and not lonely quieting the anxious mind. "Why do Children Play?" asked Winnicott, observing the pathology of those who cannot play, as on adolescents who need repetitive masturbation without daydreaming.

"Play is an alternative to sensuality" wrote Winnicott (p. 145), but when bodily sensuality is compulsive, play becomes impossible.

The art of psychoanalysis, through free association, is to promote the integration of the personality. Trauma, terrors, interfere with the capacity to play or to associate. Child and adolescent psychoanalysts know well how children and adolescents can stay dependent upon their bodily needs, when compulsion is the constraint to mechanically contain anxiety, when the ability for communicating the distress has been lost.

The role of the body is thus a central issue in the psychopathology of our time, like the clinical vignettes in this book will show the damage inflicted on the body in childhood and adolescence.

Now that screens, flows of images, and the virtual spaces have invaded the social space as the interrelations, the body is limited at nonmoving but only virtually experiencing sensations. Meanwhile, the subject is then overwhelmed by compulsive sensorial or muscular activities that are disconnected from relationships with others. Captured in the virtual, children as adults seem to lose daydreaming and thinking ability. The omnipresence of screens in parents as in children seems to modify imaginary constructions and the relationship between body and connection with the environment.

We are seeing more young patients suffering for the lack of transitional space, losing the capacity for playing, but using of fetish instead of autoerotic play with transitional objects. An inability to wait creates an urge for immediate relief of pain and tension, whatever the means.

In the 1924 economic problem of masochism, Sigmund Freud introduced the notion of primary or erotic masochism. Beyond masochistic perversions, there should be, at the very early processes of life, a solution, in a constant work in progress, to the tendency of self-destruction.

In "Beyond the Pleasure Principle," Freud addresses the rhythmic character of pleasure-unpleasure. He speculates that in infancy, the sensations of pleasure and unpleasure depend not on "any directly proportional ratio," but on "the amount of increase or diminution in the quantity of excitation in a given period of time." When working on painful repetitive dreams in traumatic neuroses and on unpleasurable experience in the wooden reel play of his grandson, as models of masochism, Freud suggests a continuity between the negative/unpleasurable experience of tolerable frustration, inflicted by the object, that leads to symbolization and, at the other end of the spectrum, excessive and painful experience that produces pathology. This was a new perspective on masochism and its tendency to endlessly resurface in life, which we can discuss today.

Early sensations of pleasure and unpleasure are described by Freud not only as quantities to be regulated, but as qualities of experience dependent upon a factor of rhythm. The dyadic relationship with the maternal object is rhythmic.

Is it the pleasure that is repeated many times a day at the breast, or painful frustrations? Freud thinks the instinct for mastery meets eventually in infancy with the libido, in sadistic wishes toward the so needed object. He thought that a part of the destructiveness that cannot be driven toward the maternal object remains inside, "libidinally bound. It is in this portion that we must recognize the original, erotogenic masochism." Freud wrote about the phases into which primary masochism plays a part, at oral, anal, and phallic stages, in the fear to be eaten, and to be beaten. For Freud, this new masochistic solution is a fundamental protection.

This narcissistic cathexis of the pain that is the last resort when facing unbearable object loss seems to start very early in life.

I would like to share briefly two different kinds of experience with infants and their parents, when a baby is amazingly repressing hunger now to be fed.

Some infants seem to get through time a sense of waiting, tolerating the pain of hunger, and developing some capacity to get pleasant sensations by themselves when frustrated, when others withdraw into a narcissistic bubble, ignoring the maternal object after intense suffering.

Max is a four-month-old baby desperately refusing the breast, arching to avoid the contact with the mother's body. At first, when hungry, he was in rage when the mother wasn't ready to feed him. She had a lot of anxiety and ambivalence toward a child born from a donor's egg and her husband's sperm; she felt like facing a stranger into whom she couldn't recognize herself. Max has avoided her eyes when frustrated. This very painful situation finally ended up with Max sleeping nonstop, never ready to eat, not interested by the outside world. His father had to wake him up to feed him by forcing the bottle into his lips. It was as if the infant had found a way to integrate the pain of hunger and lack of communication. He didn't have any pleasurable use of his body nor self-soothing activity.

In contrast, Lou was three-month-old when she reacted by arching her body away from the breast few weeks after her mother had been disturbed by acute anxieties. The lack of mental availability of the mother and her panicking reactions when the baby was in distress have created a new pattern of Lou waiting to suck the nipple only when she was able to get a firm holding of her back by her mother looking at her. At the age of five months, Lou was carefully observing her environment, reproducing the rhythm of frustration and relief by accepting the breast only after a long time. This capacity for waiting had developed with Lou finding her thumb in an autoerotic activity as replacement of the breast, and rapidly as a self-soothing system when alone.

A year later, Max was obviously presenting a developmental delay. In therapy, he took months to be able to play. Finally, he enjoyed making the analyst miming extreme frustration when Max was offering a bottle to her, abruptly taking it away with a sadistic joy, in a post-traumatic repetitive play. When frustrated, he tended to hurt his head into the floor. Pain was a way to discharge rage in a non-symbolic way.

But Lou became an acute observer of others, a precocious child, smart talker, and playful toddler. She had a transitional object, and her aggression was not difficult to contain, since she found playful ways to express it. She became able to make compromises. Her finger-sucking was at the service of autoerotic pleasure.

In Winnicott's elaboration on the illusion of omnipotence and creation of a transitional space, he includes the "optimal frustration" a mother is inflicting to her baby to associate with the faith in a good enough object, reliable, even if coming a little too late.

The libidinization of the body functions is a protection against self-destructiveness. This explains the intensity of aggressiveness turned against the outer world as the subsequent increase of narcissistic feelings. Infantile narcissism is a protection against self-destructiveness. Max, the non-welcome child, to paraphrase Ferenczi, "the unwelcomed child and his death instinct," had developed a cathexis toward pain at waiting for the breast resulting in a destructive defensive system of withdrawal into a narcissistic state, avoiding his mother and denying any feeling the distress at losing her. The masochistic discharge of his aggression was a sign of his inability at making links with objects, in a displacement of his affects.

I think it is important to differentiate how we see aggression: the distinction must be held between aggression in the service of life and that which is harnessed to more hateful or destructive purposes. Self-destructive and self-mutilating behaviors may, by their very excess, be seen as palliative in relation to the failure of the initial masochistic nucleus. In the intensity of the transferential relationship, as in Sarah's case, we can see that a new libidinal dimension has been found. When the analyst knows how to meet these very young patients in great suffering, almost at the end of their vital resources, the most tenuous libidinal trace can find its way, even in a masochistic protective way.

The capacity to wait is at first a masochistic cathexis of displeasure that allows for a space into which the hallucination of pleasure can take place. This plays an important role in the analytic space.

Body pleasure is one of the best sources of representation in childhood, since through infantile sexuality and autoeroticism the child can develop a figurative power. Later in life, when genital adult sexuality had been organized, the fantasy world is again supported by the quality in object relations. When the differed action (Après-Coup) gives a sexual meaning to the childhood events, the narcissistic issues that the child has faced will make the adult feeling again the sense of emptiness of life. The importance of addictions that is part of the modern society seems to be associated with those early troubles in the process of representation.

The frenetic need to use pictures or videos on the Internet to stimulate sexual fantasies, for example, and the intensive masturbation developed instead of relationship with a partner, could be understood as an equivalent of lack of a good level of representation. Early narcissistic failures can later in life be replayed in a sexualized way, to get fixed.

This leads to intolerance toward absence and separation. The need for staying dependent on a real object like food, drugs, or sexuality, or denying the dependence like in anorexia. Early therapeutic intervention in childhood could be a prevention of the many faces of depression and addiction later in life.

The book is divided into four sections.

Compulsive repetition with the body in infancy, consequences in adolescence and adulthood

The first chapter opens with Christine Anzieu-Premmereur and René Roussillon each presenting on early psychic forces and defenses that support creative capability for daydreaming and recreating pleasure or form the basis for repetition and addiction to external objects.

Christine Anzieu-Premmereur explores how early disorders can lead to addiction and compulsive behaviors in adulthood. Early therapeutic intervention is described as crucial to prevent addiction and foster creativity and free association in patients. Autoerotic fantasmatic and bodily activities facilitate the associativity between of sensations and representations; so, the role of the environment at keeping regular pattern of care and the attunement between an infant and the caregiver can allow for mental and physical ability in the child for pleasurable self-soothing: daydreaming and autonomy are in their way. The "Eat, Sleep, Console" approach for neonatal opioid withdrawal demonstrates the psychosomatic effects of repetitive care in a well-structured environment. Early trauma and neglect can disrupt the psyche's ability to represent and symbolize, leading to narcissistic issues and addictive behaviors in adulthood.

Clara Schejtman brings forth a rich discussion on the relation between autoeroticism in babies and self-regulation, and destructiveness, in the Freudian meaning, as part of the creative process. Clinical cases support that discussion.

René Roussillon writes on destructiveness, melancholy, and the death drive, from the Freudian concepts on the life and death drive and their functions in depression and melancholia, to Winnicott's discussion on early narcissistic trauma that led to specific disorders. Roussillon proposes that destructiveness stems from the psyche's inability to integrate early experiences, leading to a threat of "psychic death" and the need for specific primitive defenses. Negative therapeutic reactions arise from the maintenance of the "logic of perception," which prevents the subject from detaching and symbolizing experiences, leading to a paradoxical transfer and the unleashing of destructiveness.

Freud's later ideas about hallucination and repetition suggest that the repetition of earliest experiences is driven by a constraint to integrate them into the psyche. The Winnicottian theory of the survival of the object when facing the destructive rage, can help the psychoanalyst in the negative and destructive reactions in the patient, knowing that the construction of the psyche is there at stake.

Howard Levine wrote on the role of primary narcissism and early issues in object relations. In providing containment and psychic regulation for the patient, the psychoanalyst keeps an unconscious communication that often involves the patient's attempt to evoke emotional involvement.

Early experiences that carry extreme threats to the psychological survival of the subject can leave non-ideationally represented traces that continue to "haunt" the psyche, leading to the development of excessive, often chaotic, or destructive forces in need of containment and transformation.

Discussing both Anzieu-Premmereur and Roussillon's papers, Germain Dillenseger develops on the different types of compulsion, either leading to destructiveness or the capacity for creating links. Clinical vignettes follow this development of early relational experiences and repetitive compulsion.

Facing the pain: from substance abuse to human dependence

Mary Brady introduces the three clinical experiences with dissociated young patients, showing the use of drugs and additive substance to recreate and at the same time to fight early dissociative states when facing traumatic environment.

– Substance abuse in an adolescent boy: waking the object

Mary Brady writes on the analysis with an adolescent dependent upon alcohol and drugs and putting himself in big danger. The analyst understanding the abuse as an effort to communicate a mental state that couldn't be recognized nor symbolized: an identification with a dead object, as his parents had been neglectful and their destructiveness introjected by the patient.

– Substance use as part of a pathological organization

Kristin Fiorella reports the analysis of a psychotic adolescent girl who was abusing marijuana and Xanax as a defense against a psychotic anxiety that were finally expressed by the patient to the analyst, when dissociation led to a severe psychotic breakdown. Eventually the patient was able to reconnect with early violent traumas. This girl entered treatment in a dissociative state that we were gradually able to speak about. By the time she revealed extensive drug use, she was ready to stop. When she did, she quickly plummeted into a psychotic state that led to hospitalization and eventually, she recovered the ability to talk about her being numb and 'not existing' when facing a destructive cruel parent.

– A shelter of numbness

Claudia Spadazzi gives a history of the many theories on addiction and looking for numbness. Using psychoanalytic thinking with knowledge of neurological formations during alterations of consciousness, she shows in the interactive mechanisms between looking for numbness and neurotransmitters unbalanced, with the analysis of regressive states and dependency. The case of a young adult in a painful cycle of regressive states with misperception of the body, shows the circle of primitive emotional systems and the increasing of self-medication.

– Jose Zusman brings a rich documented discussion of the three cases of addiction in adolescence

Self-harming, a challenge to patients and to analysts

Christine Franckx introduces the chapter on self-harming, a challenging issue for therapists, which is now of increase in the young population.

– Self-harming in early life and the difficulty in living for some infants

Monica Cardenal discusses the complex mental states and the vicissitudes of the primary object relationships in babies and young children who are at a high psychological or vital risk. Self-harming in an infant does not present the same evidence or happens in the same way as can be observed in an adolescent or an adult. They have to find a way to support and integrate the Self through repetitive self-harming behavior and as they have not yet been able to construct or trust an internal containing object. This is a possible vortex to understand the predominant compulsion. These young children "exist" outside themselves, immersed in a world of sensations. Through the clinical material presented, early depressive aspects that can invade the Self are demonstrated, with the use of concepts related to the organization of a second skin. The symbolic capacity of the mind has become impoverished for these infants, just like their relationship with the world.

– The silenced scream: 'under anorexia nervosa'

Jeanne Magagna describes how fight-flight comatose states are a baby's survival mechanisms, protections used to help avoiding primitive agonies. She demonstrates how adhesive identification when overused becomes part of the omnipotent destructive anorectic symptomatology which masks 'a basic fault'.

Drawings, poems, and clinical vignettes illustrate ways of working therapeutically with anorectic children and the importance of therapeutic work with parents to help them understand their children's emerging from previously repressed split-off feelings of hurt, hate dependence, and longing. A clinical case of anorexia illustrates the author's theory on communication without words in young severely ill patients.

– Self-harm behaviors in adolescents: psychoanalytic understanding

Humberto Persano discusses the link between an increasing of self-harming in adolescents and young adult, thinking it could be related to features of our contemporary lifestyle. It reveals a deep malaise among young people and is a predictive indicator of suicidal behavior, especially in vulnerable populations. The phenomenon of replication through social networks may be one of the factors of this increase.

It often involves an unconscious attack on one's own sexuality and emerging femininity. It is not related to a specific condition, although more common in patients with a multiplicity of clinical symptoms, such as borderline and narcissistic personality organizations, eating disorders, substance abuse, different forms of depression, and psychosis.

Self-destructive aggression is almost exclusively limited to human beings; the most extreme case is suicide. Also called malignant aggression – considered intrinsically human – it is related to destructiveness and cruelty. In some narcissistic personalities, dysregulation of the self, difficulties regulating self-esteem and unbearable affective states lead to self-harm. In contemporary society, the recognition of violence plays a crucial role in understanding self-harming behaviors.

– Discussion of self-harming from a French psychoanalytic perspective

Panos Aloupis discusses the presentations about self-harming processes, in connection with the emergence of compulsive destructive processes faced to the presence of trauma. In all cases, trauma affects the body, when psychic transformation processes fail to integrate deeply experienced affects and representations into unconscious fictions and fantasies.

In cases of traumatic object relations, sensory-motricity and passivity are difficult to invest with pleasure, and the death drive is used more to exhaust internal and external destructiveness than to transform excitation into drive and tolerate otherness and conflicts.

When pleasure is inhibited by traumatic traces, when passivity is experienced as intrusion, active aggression of the body becomes a compulsive and punitive act of paradoxical verification of a self that wants to triumph and survive beyond destructiveness.

– A 'superstructure' for holding on to or for self-destroying?

Anouk Meurrens explores through two intersecting clinical vignettes, the development of an internal structure of hyper control that serves a paradoxical double objective: survival, and self-destruction. It is a kind of hollow hyper-skeleton, both rigid and fragile. This mechanism is sometimes described by these patients as a black, rotting wooden structure, sometimes as impressive and indestructible ruins. It aims to control the body and mind by imposing a quasi-permanent, codified, and painful relationship with food, physical exercise and the body. The transferential-countertransferential movements in these two clinical encounters plunged us into the depths of chaotic and fusional primary relationships.

Suicide and masochism in adolescence today

Fernando Gomez introduces the very actual critical clinic that society, parents, and psychoanalysts are working on.

– An endless tragedy: attempts and suicide in childhood and adolescence.

Silvia Flechner shows how symbolic and real death seem to be intertwined during adolescence. While symbolic death implies a radical change that dramatizes the Oedipal conflict typical of this period, the pursuit of death through suicide is one of the most painful and challenging situations we face. On many occasions, adolescent suicide does not give us the possibility of appeasing this impulse expressed fundamentally in the suicidal act, while on others, supported by the transference–countertransference axis, we manage to appease these impulses. A deep knowledge of the foundation of the psychic structure from the subject's birth can give us some valuable tools to understand the possible failures in maternal and paternal psychism. And a deep knowledge of transgenerational family, social, and cultural history will be essential. The presentation of a clinical case in which we can observe the deployment of some of the variables mentioned above in the analytic field, can expand the understanding of suicide in such early stages of life.

– Are the kids alright? Why is life unlivable? Suicidal tendencies in gender disorders and trans identity

Patricia Gherovici *wrote on* the "gender trouble" experienced during adolescence, when it links sexuality, mind–body nexus, taboos, lineage, ego ideals, and consumerism, will reveal that gender transition, often, is a question of life or death. The clinical vignette of a teenager who claimed to be "oppressed by gender" after making a spectacular suicidal gesture, makes the author exploring a path toward figuring out how to live with the death drive, which, paradoxically renders life possible. Here death emerges not as the opposite of life but rather as a condition for life. When the wish to change one's gender is not seen as a strategy of eluding sexual difference but entails a heightened concern for sexual difference.

The author proposes an ethics of embodied desire capable of fundamentally rethinking sexuality by taking seriously the question of mortality inscribed in sexuality. If pre-transition, trans persons feel not fully alive, the strategy of finding a livable life goes from a first birth to a second birth through death.

– Hosting strangeness: self-harm and suicide in adolescence

Laura Accetti observes how the suicide attempts in adolescence seem to be related to the body being felt as persecutory. This leads us to think that in the primitive and primary phases of individual development, constitutive of the self and the sense of oneself, which deal with those basic maturational processes that, facilitated or obstructed by the environment, concern integration, and primary non-integration, pseudo-integration, something has 'gone wrong'. This risk is greatly increased in the case of transgender adolescents, in whom the body is precociously experienced as foreign, alien, not belonging to the self. A research group observed how in some cases transgender children and adolescents perpetuate a relationship with a fantasmatic body, different from the one they possess, in order to avoid disintegration, collapse. A clinical exemplification of a 12-year-old trans adolescent allows to observe how in the mother–child relationship the development of male genitalia during puberty has returned to constitute a 'traumatic situation' of early sexual differentiation, experienced by the mother in relation to her son, already in the first months of pregnancy.

Then Heribert Blass and Paula Cerutti present a rich discussion on the papers of suicide and masochismadolescence today.

To conclude

This book offers a multifaceted comprehension of the contemporary disorders in the young population. The diversity of psychoanalytic perspectives opens a field that enriches our understanding of such complex pathology that interferes with the integration of a form of harmonious adulthood taking responsibility of the always changing world, while experiencing liveliness. Psychoanalysis now faces those psychic, social, and environmental transformations. We assembled your experience and creativity for understanding and offering therapeutic interventions at any age of life.

Part 1

Introduction

Compulsive repetition with the body in infancy: consequences in adolescence and adulthood

Christine Anzieu-Premmereur

As psychoanalysts, we were already grappling with complex situations involving numerous young adult patients presenting with blank depression, psychosomatic problems, states of body/mind dissociation, or addictive solutions to their anxiety and neediness.

Observing the profound impact of pessimism and catastrophic anxieties not only on our patients but also on the parents of young children, we provide a platform for clinicians to exchange their concerns.

Freud's malaise in culture ends with a rather somber observation, questioning the future.

The profound cultural changes affecting both our relationships with social spaces and intimate connections necessitate a return to the foundational work of psychoanalytic thought. In this context, how does the question of the alliance of life and death arise? Certain conditions can foster aggression and its destructive potential, while others may provide alternative escape routes.

The topic "Compulsion and the Body" is the core of the multifaceted symptoms and emotional issues we have observed in our patients over the past years. Repetitive neediness, regardless of its destructive nature, never provided lasting solace.

The compulsion to repeat serves as a defense mechanism against unpleasurable and traumatic experiences, from the infant's integration of pain into a psychosomatic equilibrium to the destructiveness observed in dysregulated adolescents and addicted adults.

Is it self-soothing repetition or a movement toward daydreaming autoerotism?

The destructive potential of the drives poses a significant risk when post-traumatic solutions are developed in emergency to preserve the psyche. Fragility in confronting primitive anxieties, confusion between internal and external reality, and self-directed violence can be interpreted as a search for an object that can withstand the attacks that already cause unbearable guilt. The role of the object and its survival will be explored in this chapter.

Similarly, as we are today, it was when confronted with clinical masochism, negative therapeutic reactions, traumatic nightmares, and symptoms that compelled Sigmund Freud to recognize a destructive aspect within the mind. This led him to develop a novel theory of the drives.

The concept of repetition holds immense importance in Freud's work and warrants our attention in contemporary clinical practice.

DOI: 10.4324/9781003647317-1

Freud introduced the notion of repetition in 1919 in his seminal work "Remembering, Repeating, and Working Through," marking a pivotal moment in his drive theory.

As Roussillon postulated, "repetition acquired drive status" upon recognizing the dominance of the unconscious mind by a "compulsion to repeat." This compulsion, originating from instinctual impulses and likely inherent in the very nature of instincts, possesses the power to override the pleasure principle, often perceived as uncanny.

The compulsion to repeat is described for the first time as a primordial tendency to repeat destructive and distressing events experienced by a subject. It becomes an elemental quality of the drive, characterized by the inclination to return to an earlier state and the expression of the struggle against this tendency.

In his seminal work "Beyond the Pleasure Principle" published in 1920, Sigmund Freud introduced the concept of the death drive. Drawing upon the analysis of the compulsive repetition observed in traumatic neurosis and the child's "reel game," Freud elucidated the existence of psychic acts that transcend the sole influence of the pleasure principle. The child actively reenacted the traumatic loss of their mother, attempting to process and work through the emotional turmoil associated with her absence. Freud's theory underscored the fact that psychic processes can be driven by forces other than mere pleasure seeking.

Freud's insights extended to the significance of rituals and plays in children's lives. These practices serve as a means of reinforcing the notion that tomorrow will be similar to today, providing a sense of stability and security amidst the uncertainties of life. Furthermore, Freud's emphasis on the binding force of ceremonial occasions and commemoration resonates with the concept of the death drive.

Freud envisioned the death drive as a force that seeks to sever ties and strive for a return to an earlier state. He harbored a suspicion that the compulsion to repeat may be a fundamental aspect of instincts and, potentially, even organic life in general. This urge to restore an earlier state of being could be seen as a universal attribute of the human psyche.

Benno Rosenberg's seminal work on primary masochism, published in 1988, further elucidated the role of the death drive in human behavior. Rosenberg demonstrated that the death drive serves as a mechanism that contains the libido, thereby serving the ego's interests. However, if left unchecked, the libido can become an uncontrollable force, seeking to merge all aspects of existence and posing a significant threat. Consequently, a derivation of the death drive can be seen as a mechanism that "contains" the libido, thereby reducing its strength.

From a clinical perspective, the understanding of the life drive and the death drive becomes crucial in comprehending the experiences of ecstasy, suicidal tendencies, and repeated acting out exhibited by patients. Each of these drives pursues its own path, potentially leading to self-destructive outcomes.

If we consider all actions that deviate from the object-related aim of the life drive to be driven by the death drive, then decathexis, disavowal, denial, and the splitting of the ego can be understood as manifestations of the sense of emptiness left by a denied object.

In psychosomatic clinical practice, the early insomnia of the infant (Kreisler, Fain, & Soulé, 1974) serves as an exemplary model of the manifestations of the death drive. It is postulated that there is a lack of integration of fantasy in the mother, who engages in a series of unbound, contradictory, and antithetical movements in an attempt to calm a state of excitation she has provoked. It is crucial to distinguish this sought-after calm from that engendered by the satisfaction of desire.

The first section of the chapter, entitled "Baby and Compulsion," is authored by Christine Anzieu-Premmereur. In this section, she explores the phenomenon of babies left alone in self-soothing repetitive patterns. She delves into the role of a solid and rhythmic containment in infants born addicted to their mother's drug, and she further develops associations between the human need for repetitive rhythms and the creative capacity for making associative modifications to repetition. She examines the connection between infant mental health and the ability to confront loss and depressive feelings without experiencing breakdown.

Anzieu-Premmereur's work is complemented by Clara Schejtman, an expert in infant research. Schejtman contemplates the infant's vulnerability and the significance of emotional and physical relatedness. She explores the concept of structural autoerotism and its relationship to self-regulation. Additionally, Schejtman examines the destructive aspect of the intimate bond when libidinal resources are available.

René Roussillon, a French psychoanalyst, delves into the realm of primary experiences and the role of the object in his writings. His insights shed light on unconscious stakes in destructiveness and the survival of the object, providing a theoretical foundation for our contemporary mental health crisis. By offering colleagues working with adolescents and adults a framework for thinking and managing the psychological tolls associated with psychoanalysis, Roussillon aims to facilitate the recognition of countertransference and unconscious tensions and cathexis within the analytic space. This framework encourages the analyst's "survival" of the patient's destructiveness and fosters the co-construction of a shared space for association and thought, resulting in a recovered liveliness.

Howard Levine initiates the discussion on compulsion to repeat from the positive perspective of the defense against unpleasurable or traumatic experiences. Drawing parallels with Freud's work on eroticism, he establishes connections with the clinical experience of contemporary psychoanalysts overseeing borderline personalities and narcissistic disorders. From Andre Green and Bion's perspectives on symbolization, he further develops analytic techniques tailored to patients' constraints to repetitive, lifeless patterns.

Germain Dillenseger, an IPSO representative at COCAP, who works in a parents-and-infant unit in France, engages in a discussion on Christine Anzieu-Premmereur and Rene Roussillon's contributions to the understanding of early interactions and dysfunctions. Drawing upon his own clinical experience, he establishes connections between adult vulnerable patients and mother–baby dyads experiencing pain.

Reference

Kreisler, L., Fain, M., Soulé, M., & Lebovici, S. (1978). *L'enfant et son corps: études sur la clinique psychosomatique du premier âge*. PUF, Paris.

Chapter 1

Baby and compulsion

Christine Anzieu-Premmereur

Psychoanalysts explore the role of compulsion in early childhood, particularly in relation to death drive and Eros. They examine how early relationship disorders can lead to addiction and compulsive behaviors in adulthood. Early therapeutic intervention is crucial to prevent addiction and foster creativity and free association in patients.

Autoeroticism facilitates the association of sensations and representations, leading to the development of infantile sexuality. The "Eat, Sleep, Console" approach for neonatal opioid withdrawal demonstrates the psychosomatic effects of repetitive care in a well-structured environment. Early trauma and neglect can disrupt the psyche's ability to represent and symbolize, leading to narcissistic issues and addictive behaviors in adulthood.

Autoerotic capacities emerge within an intermediate space that fosters creativity and self-awareness. Repetition is a fundamental concept in Freudian metapsychology, serving both subjective appropriation and compulsive de-symbolization. The depressive position begins with the mourning of omnipotence and the renunciation of boundless desire, leading to the development of thought and the establishment of a secure connection with the world.

Infants experience transient depressive anxieties that can be resolved through quality care. However, neglect or trauma can lead to withdrawal reactions, psychosomatic disorders, and negative responses to social interactions. Early therapeutic intervention can prevent addiction and promote healthy development.

Since psychoanalysts today are increasingly working with processes of decathexis, they are considering situations where psychic economy no longer succeeds in establishing the necessary regulation for the pleasure principle. In this chapter, we discuss situations in which patients encounter conflicts that transcend the traditional dichotomy between the pleasure principle and the reality principle, instead involving Eros—the principle of excitation—and the unbinding Freud termed the death drive.

Given the alarming rise in addiction issues and autistic disorders during childhood and adolescence, it is imperative to examine the early stages of life during which these challenging processes were embedded.

DOI: 10.4324/9781003647317-2

The compulsion to repeat is a mental pressure that compels the subject to act or think under the influence of unconscious impulses. Freud postulated that this coercive power serves as a manifestation of the insurmountable drive activity.

In "Beyond the Pleasure Principle" (1920), Freud observed that the repetition of painful traumatic experiences functions as an ego defense to bind and assimilate undesirable experiences. It introduced the theory of the death drive, opposing the libidinal cathexis as an energy to go back to an inorganic state.

Associated with primary masochism, repetition can be understood as an early step to subjugate the libido. It also serves as a means of discharging painful affects and trying to give them meaning. For Lacan, this is expressed through jouissance—enjoyment in the repetition, while for Melanie Klein, it represents a fundamental narcissistic phenomenon. We repeat what had been internalized during the earliest relationships.

This chapter is about infancy and repetition, whether as a source of compulsive discharge of unassimilated pain or as an effort to integrate destructiveness into a more libidinal space in which repetition can open onto creativity.

Research on infancy—including psychoanalytic infant observation and clinical work with parents and infants—offers valuable insights into the nature of early relationship disorders.

Classical and contemporary Freudian concepts help clinicians understand these disorders. For instance, the assumption of primary narcissism, the drive theory associating self-preservation needs and pleasurable satisfaction as the source of the libido, and conflicts, anxieties, and defense mechanisms are all relevant. The infant's primitive internal organization is understood as a complex unconscious dynamic system.

The profound impact of early disappointments with the feeling of helpless abandonment has been extensively studied by psychoanalysts, who emphasize that a disturbance in the relationship with the caregiver can lead to a psychic economy focused on avoiding anxiety, resulting in a diminished capacity for development.

In psychoanalytic theory, the economic perspective underscores the significance of the quantity of emotions and affects experienced in daily life. Babies may experience both excess and lack from the maternal object, leading to psychosomatic consequences.

Adult patients have also been observed expressing feelings of excess and lack—for example, a lack of intimacy with their partner while simultaneously being unable to tolerate reconciliation, resulting in a preference for self-soothing and addiction.

The process of opening to the external world through libidinal fantasies that make it desirable has failed. The transitional object becomes fetishized in a continuous disavowal of depressive anxiety. There is a failure to integrate self-soothing functions while remaining in a stage of full dependency on an object.

We observe the lack of reciprocity in infant relationships, as seen in their reliance on self-soothing objects, similar to adults' compulsive use of technology and even adult-sized dolls for comfort without a partner. This trend suggests an increasing need for therapeutic interventions to create transitional spaces.

Addiction provides neither long-term satisfaction nor a structure for the psyche. Mastering the object becomes the sole means of avoiding emotional pain.

We can apply the concept of the transitional object to contemporary psychosocial trends while examining pertinent aspects of the parent–infant relationship.

The capacity to establish a novel boundary between the self and the maternal object is contingent upon the quality of attunement within the parent–infant dyad; this, in turn, has implications for the analytic process. Specifically, it facilitates the development of genuine transitional objects, which can be distinguished from the compulsive utilization of concrete objects or repetitive body actions as a means of mitigating anxieties and tensions.

Similarly, caregivers can support the development of transitional capability in children, while analysts can assist patients in cultivating creativity and free association. This can be contrasted with infants' excessive reliance on self-soothing objects as well as older children and young adults' compulsive reliance on technology as a source of comfort, which may reflect a lack of mutual understanding within their internal relationships. In such instances, therapeutic interventions centered on the creation of a transitional space have become increasingly crucial.

Addictive behavior and autoeroticism

Autoeroticism is a central concept in Freud's theory of human sexuality. It involves the satisfaction of sexual desires without the presence of an external object. This can be achieved through self-induced sensorial activity, such as masturbation, without mental representation, or as an autoeroticism inhabited with representations of libidinally invested internal objects. When the need for the presence of another person arises due to the internalization of love objects being deficient, the search for satisfaction becomes imperative.

Any deficiency in the autoerotic capability leads to self-soothing activities associated with the need for strict mastery over a concrete object. However, this does not provide internal satisfaction and must be repeated compulsively.

The profound impact of early disappointments, particularly the sensation of being helplessly abandoned, has been extensively studied by psychoanalysts. They emphasize that a disruption in the relationship with the caregiver can lead to a psychic economy focused on avoiding anxiety, resulting in a diminished capacity for development. Sandor Ferenczi delved into the intensification of destructiveness in unwelcome children who experienced primary physical rejection. This hinders the transformation of violence into ambivalence. Failures in primary satisfaction often escalate violence, as envy manifests as constant dissatisfaction. The release of repressed drives can lead to increased violence against oneself and others.

In cases of early relational deficiency, it has been observed that infants develop mechanistic self-stimulation for painful physical sensations. I had a therapy session with a 13-month-old toddler who severely damaged her skin by compulsively pulling her hair while facing a lifeless and depressed mother, who was herself in an impossible mourning of her own mother.

Absence and separateness appear to be the starting point of the psychoanalytic observation. Modern patients demonstrate that the construction of the primitive link between the absent object and its trace in psychic representation is not a given. When the creative process of associating an equivalence between presence and sensorial and symbolic equivalences is not available, the subject becomes susceptible to the vicissitudes of social encounters. We observe autistic, melancholic, or antisocial traits in such cases.

Early therapeutic intervention in childhood should be aimed at preventing addiction later in life. Constant breastfeeding or the use of pacifiers can create a state of perpetual neediness in children, hindering their ability to differentiate between pain, fear, sensations, and emotions. The drive for love becomes a need for short-term oral satisfaction. Pacifiers can become objects of addiction, associated with a new need: eating and sucking as the sole means of calming down, regardless of the underlying cause of distress. Some mothers may inadvertently replicate their own calming system and, when faced with challenges such as introducing the father or promoting separateness, may favor quick, mechanical solutions for their children. As we have observed, the widespread availability of smartphones, videos, and social media provides convenient ways for parents to be distracted from anxiety. Technology has insinuated itself into our intimate lives.

Excessive dependence can never be abruptly terminated; it can transform into an acute form of support that becomes indispensable for navigating through crises, particularly adolescence. However, the encounter with the object of dependence can be overly immediate and excessively satisfying to the extent that it becomes a means of avoiding the frustration of external reality. Dependence provides a shortcut to evade the challenges of external reality, magically liberating the subject from the need for critical thinking. Consequently, there is no room for the development of an adapted action to transform external reality. We find ourselves in the opposite process compared to the original capacity for mourning, which is crucial for the development of symbolic equivalences and ambivalent emotions toward the lost object.

Autoeroticism, with its boundless potential to recreate memories, facilitates the association of sensations and representations, thereby facilitating further displacements. In the absence of the mother, the subject develops a sense of identity not only with her but also with her maternal qualities. This allows the psyche to modify its relationship with itself. When body sensations, feelings, and actions are experienced as belonging to the subject, there is a transformation of the relationship with the body and emotions, as they are recognized as "mine" and subsequently represented. Autoeroticism serves as a background upon which the image is being represented. Infantile sexuality originates from this process.

The reel game that Freud observed in his grandson and described in "Beyond the Pleasure Principle" provides a unique perspective on the nature of representation.

The child who conceived the play by concealing the reel beneath his bed not only performed the act of discarding a representation of his absent mother but also identified himself with her departure in a tangible manner. In this manner, the absence was portrayed as an action that simultaneously signified the mother's return. The relationship with the mother was manifested through this dynamic process. Acting and speaking "Oo, Aa" (translating to "fort und da," or "away and here") represented the internal play with the object and symbolized the mother's absence. A psychologically active mind engages in creative variations, forming associations and identifying similarities, while a less active mind merely repeats identical copies. This concept aligns with Freud's fundamental insight in "Beyond the Pleasure Principle." However, the French psychoanalyst Michel de M'Uzan challenges the clear distinction between repetitions with variations and identical repetitions, which he categorizes as "the same." He associates these identical repetitions with the death instinct and repetition compulsion.

In essence, everything exists on a spectrum between these extremes. Repetition compulsion is central to the play of childhood. When confronted with painful passivity, the young child actively seeks to recreate the mother's presence in their play, thereby becoming a creator. Instead of merely repeating a sad event's memory, the child engages in creative recreation, allowing for the introduction of differences and novelties. Repeating can provide a sense of comfort, while repeating to craft a new narrative is fueled by unconscious libidinal fantasies.

The paradox of narcissism posits that to be one's authentic self, one must draw nourishment from others. This entails incorporating and introjecting objects, necessitating a certain level of passivity. If pleasure is absent, passivity becomes perilous. When left alone without care or affection, a child is precociously confronted with its helplessness. Consequently, the pleasure of satisfaction clashes with the pleasure of control and mastery over the object. However, remaining in constant neediness risks being overwhelmed with violence in a self-destructive pursuit of sensation. Paradoxically, the more insecure and dependent a child becomes on external intervention, the less it can receive from others. The object becomes vital for the infant's survival, but is experienced as a source of envy when perceived as having a separate existence.

In instances of early trauma, neglect, or excessive engagement with an object, violent emotions may be discharged, potentially disrupting the psyche's ability to represent and symbolize. Consequently, early defenses such as splitting, denial, decathexis, expulsion of the psyche from the body, somatic reactions, and foreclosure may interfere with any representational process.

Furthermore, the impact of early and trans-generational trauma on the functioning and psychic organization of the individual is a subject of inquiry. The role of the pleasure principle in the psychic elaboration and potential representation of the aftermath of such trauma is also of interest.

Eat, sleep, console approach for neonatal opioid withdrawal

A 2023 study conducted in the United States involving infants born to mothers with opioid addiction presents a compelling model for the psychosomatic effects of repetition within a well-structured environment that aligns with biological needs. This environment provides repeated care of essential needs, fostering satisfaction and security while also managing emotions and affects.

The study compares the "Eat, Sleep, Console" approach with the more conventional neonatal scoring method for assessing the severity of withdrawal symptoms. This standard approach may inadvertently overestimate the necessity for medications, particularly morphine. Notably, the "Eat, Sleep, Console" method significantly reduced the duration of hospitalization for infants experiencing neonatal opioid withdrawal syndrome before they were medically ready for discharge. This approach focuses on an infant's ability to consume food, sleep, and receive comfort, ensuring the close proximity of the baby and mother. The protocol emphasizes maintaining a consistent sleep-feeding-play-sleep rhythm, with caregivers encouraged to provide soothing measures such as gentle rocking, skin-to-skin contact, and soft talking to calm the infant in a quiet environment.

This intriguing experiment on the biological repercussions of repetitive containment serves as an apt model for the early subject–object interactions that orchestrate rhythms of frustration and satisfaction, containment, and appeasement. This concept closely aligns with Freud's exploration of masochism, emphasizing the necessity for rhythmic, integrated experiences that alternate between frustration and satisfaction.

Since Rene Spitz's description of depressed infants, we have observed that in early childhood, the manifestations of a lack of rhythm and attention from the caregiver appear. These infants exhibit self-balancing, repetitive movements, indifference toward external stimuli, and withdrawal into systematic body usage, such as pulling hair, regurgitation, or less noticeable symptoms that are always repetitive and lack any indication of pleasure or daydreaming activity.

The consequences of the disparity between physical and emotional maternal contact have been extensively studied in Spitz's observations of inconsistent maternal behavior among the mothers of rocking infants. These mothers alternated between outbursts of hostility and tender love toward their infants.

Among the rocking infants, 63% exhibited developmental retardation. Spitz proposed that the abrupt swings in maternal behavior hindered or even prevented the infants from forming a secure attachment to their mothers, leading to a disruption of their libidinal balance. Consequently, their object relations shifted toward an overinvestment in narcissism, which manifested in their rocking behavior.

The rhythmic movement itself provides a physical sensation of vitality that persists as long as it continues. However, when it ceases, a profound sense of longing and distress inevitably returns.

Child analysts have observed infants who rocked for months during their first and second years and were subsequently brought for assistance due to motor disturbances, such as tics, hyperactivity, and impulsivity, as well as intense fears of object loss. These observations suggest that such behaviors often originate during infancy.

Consider the body self-representation of infants who are engrossed in an iPad while their caregiver is captivated by an iPhone. Despite not directly interacting with each other, these infants mirror a virtual figure, always maintaining the same emotional state. Initially, the experience evokes pleasure and curiosity, but after a brief period, it becomes a matter of losing attention. The fear of neglect could potentially lead to a fragmentation of the sense of attachment to oneself and the parent. Body pleasure serves as an exceptionally effective source of representation during childhood, facilitating the development of figurative power through auto-eroticism. Later in life, when genital adult sexuality has been organized, the fantasy world is once again supported by the quality of object relations. When the differentiated action (Après-Coup) imbues childhood events with a sexual meaning, the narcissistic issues that the child has encountered resurface, leading to a renewed sense of emptiness in adulthood. The prevalence of addictions in contemporary society seems closely associated with these early troubles.

The intense reliance on visual stimuli, particularly images and videos, to stimulate sexual fantasies and the subsequent development of compulsive masturbation instead of nurturing a romantic relationship can be interpreted as a manifestation of inadequate representation. Early narcissistic failures can later manifest in a sexualized manner, serving as a means of seeking validation and resolution. These addictive behaviors reveal the underlying damage to the process of representation creation and the pressing need for concrete bodily stimulation in the absence of a tangible object.

During childhood, young individuals may compensate for a lack of emotional fulfillment by engaging in aggressive overstimulation of their skin and bodies. These manifestations indicate the disintegration of instinctual drives and the failure of psychological integration. The vehement self-injury behavior exhibited by the hair-pulling toddler underscores the vulnerability of her psyche to disorganization.

The observations presented here align with Winnicott's theory, which distinguishes between the fetishization of an object and its playful role in the transition between the infant's body and the maternal breast.

Autoerotic capacities emerge in an intermediate space that fosters creativity and self-awareness. Conversely, compulsive self-soothing behaviors may lead to fetishistic and addictive tendencies.

Observing infants after the feeding process, psychoanalyst Willy Hoffer (1949) noted how babies utilized their fingers to maintain oral pleasure. Some engaged in playful experimentation, introducing one finger into their mouths, while others sought touch and caressing through the skin. Winnicott was grateful for these observations to screen infants capable of replaying oral pleasure with calmness, distinguishing them from those still in need of intense arousal, akin to a state of frustration.

Pain and pleasure are both sources of addiction. As seen in the toddler case, the search for any sensation, particularly painful ones, serves as a potent source of compulsion. In contemporary societies, we observe that the lack of meaning often exacerbates masochistic, painful behaviors; the "work of pain" is closely associated with trauma and depression. It serves as a physical fixation for an object psychologically unrepresentable. Like self-harming adolescents, there is a lack of capacity for symbolizing psychic suffering. Consequently, the perception of pain becomes the sole indicator of mental distress.

We acknowledge that the satisfaction of basic needs, such as hunger, is insufficient to leave a trace that facilitates the emergence of thought. However, it may also compel the child into a clinging relationship with a substitute object. An infant must develop its hallucinatory potentialities, establish a sense of self, and facilitate the transitional phase.

Addictive behaviors attempt to recreate the mother as an object for the infant's needs, ensuring complete dependency.

Repetition

Repetition is a fundamental concept in Freudian metapsychology. It is essential for achieving a cure, as transference occurs through repetition. However, repetition operates at various levels of psychic functioning and addresses diverse and even potentially antagonistic issues. In some instances, repetition appears to serve subjective appropriation and symbolization in the clinic. Conversely, it may exhibit a compulsive character, leading to the de-symbolization of the repeated content, giving it the appearance of true automatism.

In 1920, Freud recognized that certain forms of repetition do not provide satisfaction and are beyond the pleasure principle. These forms reveal a more fundamental aspect of the psychic life.

We repeat past experiences, regardless of their emotional content, indicating a primitive constraint on the psychic life. If we engage in pleasurable rehearsals, it suggests that the repeated content has become an integral part of our self.

In contrast, we frequently reiterate the concept of "beyond the pleasure principle," which implies repeating what cannot be integrated, repeating the non-appropriate narrative, repeating what cannot be symbolized, repeating the non-occurrence of oneself, the unrealized potential, and so on. We no longer repeat to seek the "lost object" but to bring about the non-appropriate potentials, to make appropriate what could not previously yield satisfaction, those that lie "beyond the pleasure principle." These experiences remain stagnant in the psyche and, consequently, tend to repeat themselves to the extent of their psychic non-integration, the splitting that affects them in this manner.

On the other hand, while we often discuss the potential dangers of children's excessive exposure to digital screens, we tend to overlook the issue of parents' excessive connectivity, which can leave toddlers isolated and prone to compulsive self-soothing behaviors.

Pediatricians consider the overexposure of young children to digital screens as a public health concern. However, what about children who experience their hyperconnected parents? The shared pleasure with parents contributes to the vitality of the toddler, libidinal energy, and the dynamics of their thought. The energy circulating in interactions between babies and adults serves as an instinctual fuel that nourishes all the child's investments, fosters their creative abilities, enhances their relational capacities, builds their language, and augments their intellectual prowess. The omnipresence of digital tools in the hands of adults can adversely affect the child–parent relationship. A parent who is hyperconnected to their laptop risks becoming a parent who is disconnected from their child, potentially impoverishing the toddler's desire for physical contact. This constant presence of digital tools can serve as a propelling force for the child's psychic growth, a precious and vital force.

The depressive position

Traditionally, the depressive position begins with mourning the loss of omnipotence in satisfying one's needs, accompanied by the renunciation of boundless desire. Partial renunciation is a well-known concept. However, before being deprived of the fantasy of omnipotence, one must first have experienced it. Winnicott demonstrated that the initial months of life are characterized by the construction of the object relationship based on an external world that facilitates action and exchange. The mother maintains the child's illusion of limitless power over the world. This narcissistic investment in the world, a source of gratification, leaves traces in the child's confidence in their own ability to act and think. This belief is fundamental to the development of thought in the face of reality. Thus, establishing a secure connection with both the real and objective world is paramount at the outset of life.

The inevitable failures and discontinuities in maternal care are perceived as narcissistic losses. The child learns that the maternal container possesses flaws and limitations, which pose real threats to an infant's vulnerability in their original state of distress. Observations of mother–infant interactions reveal that many mutual adjustment defects can be rectified, with dyads often finding the capacity to find suitable agreements after misunderstandings. The adjustment between needs and satisfactions, desire and gratifications, is never perfect. The mother may err by anticipating too much or delaying gratification, and she can only be considered "good enough." Consequently, the child's daily life is permeated with disappointments, unfulfilled expectations, and the tensions and conflicts inherent in their natural journey toward individuation. The maternal excitation shield remains partial. These repeated events can accumulate and assume a traumatic value.

Infants frequently experience transient depressive anxieties, as observed in their natural environments. These anxieties typically resolve due to the quality of the psychological and physical care they receive. However, when such care is lacking—due to specific reasons involving the mother or the infant—withdrawal reactions, psychosomatic disorders, and negative responses to smiling and eye contact may emerge.

During the initial months of life, infants do not experience the loss of an object because their relationships are still too fragile. However, the impact becomes evident only during the gradual differentiation between themselves and the object, as well as the quality of the investment made in the object, which remains precarious. This is why the frequency of sessions is crucial for maintaining the construction of a secure bond. Anaclitic depression, in particular, provides insufficient mental stimulation for the child, leading to the cessation of autoerotic games and the activation of functional behaviors. These serious infants often exhibit a constant state of unease, lack vitality, and frequently engage in repetitive self-calming behaviors.

As Bowlby and Winnicott independently elucidated, it is not the separation that causes depression in infants, but rather the loss of hope. Objects that disappear and become inaccessible— whether due to rapid weaning, interactions with an inanimate mother without vocalizations or expressions, illnesses, surgical interventions, and other factors—can sever the infant's connections to these objects, leaving the body and psyche destitute. Infants may exhibit sluggishness, withdrawal, slowed development, and psychosomatic disorganization. They may present pathological defenses, such as avoidance of visual contact, paralysis of behavior, or freezing, as well as transformed emotions, such as noisy joy and disorganized excitement, instead of displaying distress or anxiety. Self-aggression is also common.

During the perinatal period, between 0 and 6 months, the reactions we commonly associate with depression in infants are more accurately understood as reactions of a collapsed life force and a loss of investment potential rather than as reactions to the loss of an object that is not yet fully formed. We observe infants with frozen faces, devoid of laughter, smiles, or joyful expressions, rather indifferent and rarely surprised. They may look away, vocalize minimally, and exhibit sluggish gestures and a lack of postural anticipation when we take in an infant who has lost their skills, detached from others and themselves. Illness, pain, and fatigue, as well as the loss of internal connections, can trigger these reactions. At the beginning of life, the body's envelope remains fragile, and maintaining sensations and the experience of being alive through movements and bodily actions is crucial. Interactions with others contribute to the physical unity of the body and the individual's sense of self, through touch, holding, and eye contact, leaving internal traces that hold the body and oneself together. A failure to establish these connections constitutes a failure of the subject's constitution. Reestablishing bodily dialogue is an urgent necessity.

The economic aspect of maternal psychic functioning is communicated to the child through the dance of preverbal games. The prosody, rhythm of enunciation, carrying, intensity of looks, and voice are essential signals to which the baby responds with its own primitive register.

However, it is crucial to acknowledge that depression does not exist without hatred. Hatred is necessary to create an object in its absence, akin to the envy experienced for an object. It is an early rage rather than an organized emotion, as Winnicott demonstrated. Furthermore, Freud classified indifference as a specific case of hatred. This intense and early organization of negative movements necessitates the active mobilization of life movements by those around the child. Consequently, early therapies often arise as emergencies.

The impact of intersubjectivity on the psychological development of the child and the genesis of the sense of self, the foundational element of the Self, is paramount. It can provide guidance to the analyst working with infants. Intervening directly with a baby when the mother permits access to her child is immediately effective. If we consider that the emergence of initial representations and the establishment of symbolization processes occur during interactive play, we can assist a mother in providing the baby with the physical anchoring of shared experiences and guiding her attention to the sensations the baby experiences without always enabling integration. Babies' innate desire for contact with others facilitates the therapist's work. At the outset of life, play is gestural and serves as the foundation for emotional and affective sharing, organizing the child's future communication possibilities.

Primary depression is often associated with early trauma. Infantile sexuality and its auto and heteroerotic investments are no longer appropriate when we no longer feel assured of our survival. The risk is libidinal loss, the loss of the connecting quality of the libido, leading to a de-sexualization of psychic functioning. This results in the disappearance of the joy of successful acts and the pleasure derived from autoerotic investments.

Early therapeutic intervention in childhood could potentially prevent addiction later in life. A flaw in the organization of the primary relationship can disrupt sufficient harmony between mother and child, leading to excessive frustration, gratification, and dysrhythmia in exchanges.

When the encounter is unsuccessful, and during the maternal absence, the child is unable to easily develop their autoeroticisms in connection with the representation of the absent object. Consequently, they resort to alternative means, such as self-calming processes and neo-needs, which provide the release of tension but are not linked to libidinal activity.

Investing in a paternal third party becomes challenging due to the existing mother–child bond. However, a father who is absent, fleeing conflicts, falsely egalitarian, or violent is perceived as weak, unable to penetrate the narcissistic dyad, yet also too violent, reinforcing elements of reality that contribute to a disorganized oedipal fantasizing. As a result, the father cannot serve as a pole of identification or a symbolic third. The work of mourning regarding omnipotent illusions is hindered, and the child remains attached to the maternal object. Difficulty in grieving impedes object change, perpetuating the ideal ego.

Addiction and repetitive solutions, therefore, attempt at self-healing, soothing the identificatory conflict, existential distress, and providing a transient anxiolytic appeasement.

In the field of psychopathology involving early traumas, maintaining a reference to the après coup is a crucial aspect of psychoanalytic practice while caring for young infants. A young woman, who exhibited a strong inclination toward drugs, shared in her analysis of dreams of agonies associated with falling for a reef, accompanied by a panic that led to a dissociation from her body. She had experienced an infant stay in the Neonatal Intensive Care Unit (NICU) and was subsequently cared for by a mother who was apprehensive about holding her and would abruptly detach herself from her child in a cold and hostile manner.

Patients provide detailed accounts of their dreams during analytic sessions with adolescents or adults, allowing us to delve into the bodily sensory memories of their early experiences.

To conclude

This collective book explores the manifestations of destructive narcissism, specifically through the lens of destructiveness, evacuation, and the absence of psychic space.

Over the past decade, particularly during the pandemic, we have witnessed an increasing prevalence of repetitive addictive behaviors among patients. This has made it challenging for them to engage in free association and creative activities during sessions. Consequently, their libidinal capacity has diminished, hindering their ability to develop pleasurable pursuits.

Psychoanalysts can benefit from recognizing the connection between adolescent and adult addiction as well as their early experiences that are replicated in the transference. This allows for a new interpretation of the Après Coup, a productive analytic session.

Deep cultural shifts, impacting both social interactions and intimate relationships, necessitate a return to psychoanalytic thought. In this context, the question of how life drives and death drives arise. Certain conditions can foster aggression and its destructive potential, while others provide alternative escape routes.

Repetition serves as the driving force behind drive activity, when transformed into an opening for transformation, malleability, and a constant movement towards associativity, pleasure, and creativity emerge. Playfulness should be a fundamental aspect of adult psychoanalysts, akin to their childhood counterparts.

Traumatic experiences can disrupt transitional spaces, prompting their reconstruction. The analytic space can maintain this existence, but it may be fragile and subject to ownership by the subject. Alternatively, it can be refueled, drawing from the complicity of the maternal object and later cultural experiences. Art and creative expression serve as a royal road to preserving and sustaining this fluid space, ensuring its vitality.

References

Freud S. 1920, Beyond the Pleasure Principle, SE, 18, 14–17.
Hoffer, W. 1949 Mouth, hand and ego-integration. In: *The Psychoanal. Study Child*, Vol. III/IV New York: International Press, Inc., pp. 49–56.
Winnicott D.W. 1953, Transitional Objects and Transitional Phenomena, *International Journal of Psychoanalysis*, 34, 89–97.
Young L.W and Coll. 2023, Eat, Sleep, Console Approach or Usual Care for Neonatal Opioid Withdrawal, *New England Journal of Medicine*, April 30.

Chapter 2

Early psychic co-constructed structure in a hyperconnected world

New challenges for parents and for clinicians: discussion of Christine Anzieu-Premmereur chapter

Clara Schejtman

In this communication, I will present some ideas inspired by Christine Anzieu's paper.

The states of neediness and anxiety in infants

Primary helplessness and its consequent vulnerability are human birthmarks. Vulnerability, from Latin, *"vulnus,"* or wound, defines the state that makes us susceptible to being injured. Christine points out that the failure to cope with the states of neediness and anxiety may bring blank depression, psychosomatic problems, states of body/mind dissociation, or addictive solutions.

Shared pleasure between the infant and the adult is a strong libidinal input and a source of vitality, which produces a feeling of exuberance and amplification of the self. But, as Laplanche (1980) proposes, close relationships may have the paradoxical potential to produce both a feeling of being sustained and being hurt by the significant other. Fear of loss and separation anxiety are always implicit in all loving and supportive bonds.

Christine suggests that hyperconnected parents may engage in less shared pleasure, which could diminish the libidinal connection, impoverishing the child's appetite for contact and vitality.

Why are some children more affected than others, and how do different parents deal with their hyperconnection in more or less addictive ways?

Bernard Golse (2013) explores the polifactorial nature of development. He studies the primary inter-sensorial and inter-affective channels, noting that while innate channels may be more closed, the presence of hypersensitivity increases vulnerability without necessarily creating pathology. The environment constitutes a secondary decompensation factor, which can either amplify or mitigate the effects of the primary factors in producing higher psychic suffering and potential psychopathology. This epigenetic model is key to understanding the complex interaction between constitutional factors and the crucial impact of early relationships, even in infants who suffer physical health conditions and neurodevelopmental disorders.

DOI: 10.4324/9781003647317-3

Laplanche (1975) and other authors differentiate between traumatism and trauma. From this point of view, traumatism can be understood as an excessive input that disrupts the energetic balance, potentially leading to transformation, whereas trauma is an intromission that can produce a kind of wound that needs to be darned but leaves a scar.

This foundational and normal traumatism caused by the primary caregiver arises not only from bodily arousal but also from the unconscious conflicts and representations within the parents, which are part of their investment in their infant's body.

Development, in itself, can be seen as a form of healthy trauma, where new stimuli destabilize the child and lead to continuous reorganization of both the internal and external worlds. This model is especially useful in these times of permanent cultural changes.

Christine points out that the paradox of narcissism lies in the fact that, in order to be oneself, the subject must nourish oneself and, in some way, be penetrated by the other. If pleasure is absent, passivity becomes dangerous.

How does parental input function in this process?

Psychoanalysis and infant research have offered multiple theories on the parent–infant primary bond, and I suggest addressing these theories from two simultaneous perspectives: Asymmetry and Bidirectionality.

1 The asymmetrical perspective emphasizes the impact of the mature psychic structure on the vulnerable, developing infant. This perspective considers the role of adults' psychic structure, their own infant history, and their mental health state. The sexualizing, seductive adult may implant drives, unconscious desires, projections, and representations, whose excess (intromission) can hinder the process of binding affects with representations in the child, potentially leading to traumatic effects (Laplanche, 1989).
2 Bidirectionality refers to the mutual, permanent affective transformation between the infant and the parent.

    A bidirectional relational matrix, continuously co-constructed and transformed by experience, can be thought of as a unit of analysis in itself and as a motivator and organizer of psychic life (Dio Bleichmar, 2005).

Through infant research, we know that babies are born with the potential capacity for intersubjectivity and the ability to organize their internal world through a proto-representational system, which interacts with the environment in a unique way.

Intersubjectivity refers to a state of mutual understanding and reciprocity, where each personal identity is formed through permanent transactions between subjects, in an inextricable relationship between the individual and his or her social relations. Seligman points out that the "relational baby" has been discovered, thanks to the immense contributions of observational research on early interactions.

In our 20-year research program,[1] funded at various stages by the University of Buenos Aires, which aims to establish bridges between research and psychoanalytic concepts, we found that early dyadic interactions are not as synchronized or reciprocal as an idealized view might suggest. Rather, dyads are engaged in a complex interplay of matches and mismatches (Schejtman & Vardy, 2022).

An embryonic, singular regulatory capacity present at birth elicits interaction and fosters a strong emotional connection with the infant's environment. The parental environment provides intersubjective scaffolding that promotes the development of the infant's affective, psychomotor, social, and cognitive potential. Tronick (1989) suggests that the Mutual Regulation Model enables the child to modulate increasingly complex states of mind and to scaffold the achievement of self-regulation. Negative affect and persistent dysregulation, not sufficiently repaired by the adult, may perpetuate feelings of neediness and fear of being hurt, increasing the risk of isolation and withdrawal. Parental failure may also be linked to withdrawal and depression. It is important to address not only maternal perinatal depression but also paternal depression, which is often underdiagnosed. Traumatism, in this sense, implies coping with novelty, enigma, messiness, pain, and separation anxiety. Mourning narcissistic omnipotent positions, both in the infant and the parents, contributes to the building of symbolic resources that help integrate unpleasure and pain while reducing the risks of trauma and decathexis.

Some depressed babies may react with more passive, decathectized, and withdrawn behaviors (sometimes exhibiting autistic-like signs, even if they are not actually autistic), while others, on the contrary, may react with frequent dysregulations and intense tantrums that disrupt functions such as sleeping and eating. These babies can be particularly difficult for parents and educators to manage, and this situation may perpetuate a feeling of being rejected and lonely, leaving a deep tear in the child's subjectivity. This wound may drain pain continuously and often lead to rigid defenses and addictive or compulsive self-soothing behaviors to alleviate the suffering. Nevertheless, the "noisy" babies have a greater chance of receiving help.

By acknowledging the inevitable moments of the infant's unintended disconnection and extreme sensitivity, the caregiver can help develop a protective envelope. The adult is part of the infant's protective system, transforming affects. However, if parents feel they are unable to regulate their infant's emotions and frequently offer them colorful and noisy screens, the libidinal process can become disrupted. The protective envelope may then turn into a rigid shield and the use of screens may become compulsive and fetishistic. These sensory-overload stimuli, which are difficult to metabolize, may intensify tendencies and diminish the child's demand for closeness and consolation from the adult. As Christine points out, the risks include the activation of helplessness, splitting, and a sense of fragmentation in the feeling of being attached to both oneself and the parent.

This leads us to the second point: the role of autoerotism in the psychic structure and its relation to self-regulation

Autoerotism may be defined as the infant's attempt to bind surplus arousal without adult assistance, protecting the subject from overwhelming trauma. Anzieu (2022) links the autoerotic, creative, and healthy capacities in the baby to the fantasy of plenitude during the mother's absence.

In our research, we found that babies who engage in oral self-comforting with toys are developing self-regulated, pre-symbolic resources that help them calibrate the distance and closeness to the object. We relate the connection between self-regulation and autoerotism to Winnicott's (1965) concept of the capacity to be alone in the presence of another.

By observing and microanalyzing interactions, we were able to differentiate subtle signs of self-regulation, displayed as a libidinal resource, from more defensive and withdrawn engagement in oral self-comforting. Occasionally, oral self-regulation through sucking their own finger, toys, or a pacifier can serve as autoerotic alternatives that allow the discharge of oral drives in an active way. The use of pacifiers is controversial, but in my opinion, when used for short periods, they can facilitate oral discharge while helping to build the representation of the libidinal object during its brief absences, thereby preserving the continuity of investment and engagement. In contrast, when screens are offered for consolation, this representational process may be disturbed.

We can relate to Christine's proposal about the difference in self-induced sensorial autoerotic activity, like masturbation in adolescence, when these activities are accompanied by mental representation of an invested object or without mental representations.

On the other side, very dedicated mothers may find it difficult to tolerate the infant's self-engagement and can become quite intrusive, constantly offering the breast or a pacifier without perceiving the infant's communicative signals, which indicate a desire for pleasurable self-exploration in their presence.

From our research and clinical work, we found that when parents are emotionally attuned, available, and reflective, both positive and negative affects are more integrated, and self-regulation is achieved, reducing traumatic separation anxieties.

We also found that dysregulated displays in infants and toddlers are strong, detectable signals of psychic suffering that may lead to psychoanalytic consultations.

This brings us to the third point: the destructiveness in the intimate bond

Intimate relationships are complex and ambivalent. The narcissistic perspective of significant bonds is marked by a love–hate polarity. Feeling the possible interruption or distancing of the object of love may activate hate through regression to the previous sadistic stage. Hate, Freud (1915) postulates, is prior to love; it arises from the narcissistic repulsion of the awareness that the loved object is external to the ego. This primitive early love pattern may be actualized in rivalry and possessive relationships and can be linked to eruptions of domestic marital violence.

Winnicott (1969) proposes that the adult must survive the impact of the infant's destructive impulses without retaliation in order to establish healthy relationships. In this sense, in her paper, Christine suggests considering repetition as an effort to integrate destructiveness and pain into a libidinal space that may open to creativity, rather than serving as a source of compulsive discharge.

Parents overwhelmed by highly idealized demands of professional and economic success, often engaged in non-stop home office work, may not always be aware of their own ambivalence when dealing with their child´s states of neediness.

Have the upheavals of our century changed the way new generations are constructing intimacy?

Are they sufficiently aware of the conflicts between pleasure and unpleasure, hate and love, self and alterity?

Are parents less available to address negative affects and conflicts while trying to regulate their children?

Do parents feel unable to modulate increasing amounts of affective display, failing in their capacity to regulate both their own and their children's negative and positive affects and offering electronic devices too quickly?

Detecting even mild signs of suffering or partial withdrawal in normal development is crucial for referring the family to brief psychoanalytically oriented early interventions within a flexible setting.

The analyst, as a third person invested in the process, supports the child, the parents, and the relationship, transforming compulsive solutions into creative, interactive play. Additionally, community programs offered by public institutions are critical for addressing affective deprivation and preventing violence.

Clinical case

Julian was four years old, born prematurely at six months, weighing 1.3 kg, and spending three weeks in the Neonatal Intensive Care Unit (NICU). He did not suffer any lasting damage. Very irritable, he needed his mother's contact or hand to fall asleep, as he had in the incubator.

At second-and-a-half years old, his brother, E., was born.
Father:

> Julian is terribly jealous of his brother. He sticks his finger in his eye, squeezes him, and feels good only when he is given exclusive attention. We get angry with him, but he doesn't stop until we shout at him. Then he cries and looks very miserable, and afterwards he beats himself. He is very thin, eats "only two things," frequently vomits and we still feed him.

The mother seems depressed; she doesn't eat either.

Julian has fallen several times, had fractures and needed to be immobilized. He also suffers from respiratory problems. He does not connect with teachers or other children at kindergarten; his language is very poor, and the kids do not understand him. He tries to approach them, but he is disruptive, hits them, and is rejected, and then, he withdraws into his own shield. Sometimes, rocking is observed.

Although toilet training was achieved, he had episodes of prolonged constipation.

In the second session with Julian, I noticed that one of his lips was badly damaged, something his parents had not reported. When I asked them about it, they told me that Julian had developed a 'tic' of sucking his lip to the point of biting himself and bleeding, which had been happening frequently since his admission to the NICU, due to the tubes.

I conducted sessions with the parents together and separately, with Julian and his parents, and with Julian alone. In the joint sessions with the father, I noticed that the father was always 'teaching' Julian something in a rather intrusive and hostile way, asking him to repeat letters, numbers, and words. Julian 'complied' to satisfy his father but displayed his self-affirmation through dysregulation, refusing to eat, speak fluently and showing uncontrolled aggression toward himself and his brother.

We can infer a deficit of parental narcissization and a lack of primary shared pleasure due to the traumatic potentiality of the hospitalization and the difficulties in the early relationship. The parents were terrified of this vulnerability and the possible after-effects of prematurity, and they do not appreciate his progress.

Julian was a very dysregulated baby, and the parents failed to create attunement and mutual satisfactory affective transformation. The precarious constitution of the psychic envelope became a defensive shield against the overwhelming stimuli and against the parents' permanent rejection.

The stressful experience in the NICU was not sufficiently repaired due to a poor libidinal exchange with the parents, and the over-engagement with his mouth linked intense pleasure with pain. This can be related to a failure in the development of a healthy autoerotic self-regulation and to the emergence of more compulsive defensive autoerotism, with a risk of withdrawal.

The bleeding mouth showed that the link between physical and psychic pain was still present, with the risk of splitting and a feeling of fragmentation in the sense of being attached to oneself and to the parent.

Early painful psychic experiences produce a trace of primitive anxieties that may interfere with the psyche-soma entanglement and self-integration. These experiences may become a traumatic, non-representable inscription that can be linked to self-harming and a poor capacity for symbolization and mentalization at different points in life, especially during adolescence.

I was surprised by the quick connection he made with me in the individual sessions, happily shouting my name from the corridor.

Julian defined the therapeutic setting. The joy and affective amplification he displayed in the individual sessions indicated that this was the facilitated "port of entry" for the therapy, as paternal intrusiveness was very strong in the family sessions. In the individual sessions, Julian engaged in rich play and create a strong connection with me. It was clear that he did not have developmental or cognitive impairments. After a few sessions, his lip healed definitively, and more words and smiles of happiness appeared in his face.

An intense focus on reflective functioning and emotional availability was conducted with the parents, centering on their mourning process and their own depression. In the work with the parents, we addressed the narcissistic wound caused by the traumatic birth, and they could associate with other hard, significant situations in their lives and with unconscious conflicts.

They became aware of their own hostility toward each other and toward Julian, as well as their difficulty in sustaining and transforming his affective needs and anxiety. They were able to reflect on the differences they felt regarding his brother, who reached developmental milestones at almost the same time as Julian. The father's rigid, authoritarian, and impulsive position reflected his own depression and anxiety about Julian's development. Research shows (Keren, 2022) that paternal perinatal depression is underdiagnosed, especially when the newborn is problematic. Nurses at the NICU address more to mothers than to fathers. Men often have difficulty expressing their depression and asking for help, tending to engage in avoidance, splitting, and discharging through aggression and addiction.

We can infer that a poor autoerotic capability linked to a poor representation of the libidinal object could lead to a compulsive self-soothing need to avoid pain. The protective shield that Julian built also limited his openness to the external world, including language and development (Schejtman & Vardy, 2022).

Julian presented signs that could be interpreted as part of the autistic spectrum, although he was not autistic. The therapeutic intervention was conducted in a flexible setting at different levels, addressing the primitive anxieties of both the parents and Julian.

After an initial period, I introduced an intersubjective setting in which we could work on amplifying affective circulation between the child and the parents, and enhancing awareness of the messages Julian was conveying with his body and his compulsive defenses. This intense work brought remarkable changes in a short time and opened Julian to be emotionally available for other interventions, both in school and with a speech therapist, without feeling so threatened.

To conclude

Today, awareness of early psychic suffering is central to mental health policies, and psychoanalysis plays a crucial role in prevention. Compulsive autoerotism, dysregulation, and partial withdrawal in normal development are key signs of psychic suffering in infants, and we believe that early psychoanalytic interventions with an intersubjective perspective can reduce the risks of engaging in addictive solutions.

Brief clinical early interventions can have a critical impact on enriching the growing infant's capacity to handle increasing levels of emotional intensity – both positive and negative – allowing them to build meaningful, close relationships.

Working with babies, young children, and their families has taught me very much and has also transformed my analytic practice with adolescents and adults by:

- Increasing libidinal and playful exchanges
- Actively fighting against processes of decathexis and loneliness, offering an engaged libidinal position while maintaining neutrality and abstinence

- Listening to subtle body sensory signs and memories, not always easily seen
- Promoting the search for meaningful symbolic relationships in patients

The shared pleasure of thinking together with implicated and reflective colleagues and exploring new psychoanalytic knowledge helps to create new conceptual networks to better understand our patients in these changing and chaotic times. May the analytical space remain a refuge for subjectivity and inter-human commitment in this age of technologically mediated relationships.

Note

1 The members of this research program are: Clara Schejtman (Director), Constanza Duhalde (Co-director), Vanina Huerin, Pía Vernengo, Inés Vardy, Sandra Casabianca, Milagros Maurette, Malvina Escalera, Federico Bernao, Emilia Villalba, and Paula Adelardi.

Bibliography

Anzieu-Premmereur, C. (2022). Early Depressions: Loss of liveliness, withdrawal, psychosomatic issues and risk of developmental delay. In Leuzinger-Bohleber, M. and coll. (eds.) *Early depressions. On the Dark Side of Chronic Depression* (pp. 112–120). London: Routledge.

Dio Bleichmar, E. (2005). *Manual de psicoterapia de la relación padres e hijos.* Buenos Aires: Paidós.

Freud, S. (1915). Instincts and their vicissitudes. *SE*, 14, 109–140.

Golse, B. (2013). *Mon combat pour les Enfants Autistes,* Editeur Odile Jacob, Paris.

Keren, M. (2022). Diagnosticar síntomas clínicos en bebés: ¿Por qué y cómo? In Schejtman, C. R. (comp.) *Primera Infancia y Psicoanálisis II: Investigación – Clínica – Prevención.* Buenos Aires, Argentina: Akadia.

Laplanche, J. (1975). *Problematiques III. Sublimation.* Paris: Presses Universitaires de France.

Laplanche, J. (1980). *La sublimation.* Paris, France: Presses universitaires de France.

Laplanche, J. (1989). New Foundations for Psychoanalysis. Translated by David Macey. Cambridge, MA: Oxford: Basil Blackwell, Ltd., 176 pp.

Schejtman, C. R. & Vardy, I. (2022). Diagnósticos en primera infancia. Problemáticas y propuestas. In Schejtman, C. R. (comp.) *Primera Infancia y Psicoanálisis II.* Akadia.

Tronick, E. Z. (1989). Emotions and emotional communication in infants. In *American Psychologist, Vol. 44* (pp. 112–119). Wimmer: University of Massachusetts.

Winnicott, D. W. (1965). *The Family and Individual Development.* London: Tavistock Publications.

Winnicott, D. W. (1969). The use of an object. *The International Journal of Psychoanalysis, 50* (4), 711–716.

Chapter 3

Destructiveness, melancholy and the death drive

René Roussillon

The analysis of destructiveness and its effects has been a major problem in psychoanalytical clinical research since 1915, when it first appeared in the clinical pictures of narcissistic pathologies in Freud's article "Mourning and Melancholia." The movement that Freud then initiated led, in 1920, to the proposal of the hypothesis of a death drive's underlying forms of destructiveness, representing a kind of watershed in Freud's thinking on the relationship with death.

Indeed, in Freud's 1913 article "The Theme of the Three Caskets" in which he examines and analyzes the hidden reasons behind the choice of the third box representing death, whether in metaphorical or more explicit form. Freud's central hypothesis is that what represents death finds its meaning in the reversal that turns the inevitability of death into the effect of a choice. If death is chosen, then it is no longer the effect of a destiny – a constraint – from which there is no escape.

With the introduction of the death drive in 1920, Freud seems to have forgotten the wisdom of his 1913 analysis, or else he is confronted with a point of metapsychological complexity that he is not yet able to address, and which rests on a paradox that I shall try to formulate.

*Freud stressed that there could be no representation of death in the unconscious, insofar as we had no experience of our own death.

*The experience of the death of another, a loved one, for example, provokes the experience of a loss, a disappearance, which is part of the series of losses that punctuate human life, but not the experience of the death of oneself. It is about the biological death.

*The return to an anterior state, a state prior to life, which Freud put forward in 1920, also eludes the hypothesis of a representation arising from lived experience.

Or else, this hypothesis would open the question of a death that, present in previous generations, would fall on the cradle of the newborn as soon as he or she is born, but then it would be "a death from elsewhere."

The war and massacres of 1914–18, which also affected Freud – war traumas – form one of the clinical supports for Freud's 1920 article and the bereavements Freud himself was directly confronted with, are said to have produced a form of "thought disorder."

DOI: 10.4324/9781003647317-4

Do the social forms of destructiveness with which humans are inevitably confronted cause a form of "acted penetration" into the clinical position of psychoanalysts, prompting a form of disruption in clinical thinking to the point of producing a halt on the value of manifest content and its impact?

If manifest destructiveness stems directly from a destructive drive, then there is no longer any gap between the expression of the drive and the manifest, no longer any unconscious, latent stakes, and the gap necessary for thinking and symbolizing is crushed.

A clinical example, which has left a deep impression on me, will perhaps help us to understand this difficulty better and open the way to an initial alternative proposal.

I'm called upon to supervise a team in a child psychiatry department whose "specialty" is receiving children rejected by the various services that have previously taken them in. This team has just taken in an 11-year-old child who "breaks everything." The team's initial efforts to get to grips with this child have been in vain, and the head of the clinic is considering tying him to his bed. The head of department feels that this is not a "care solution" and, faced with the impasse in which the team finds itself, resolves to attempt supervision.

The boy is immobilized by relatively tight sheets, and a clinician lies next to him and is wrapped. He must formulate "double" what he feels or what he thinks the child feels, another clinician stands and offers meaning to what is said. The session lasts between an hour and an hour and a half. Three sessions are scheduled during the week. Gradually what emerges from this device is an intense anxiety in the young boy, an anxiety of bursting, of explosion. Anxiety, or better terror, which, progressively and from what is formulated and the reactions of the child, is linked to experiences of an encounter with an external object and the behaviors and responses of this object (experiences reconstructed "by groping" and based on what the team had also been able to observe about the mother's behavior). Gradually the child calms down. His behavior also changes between sessions, and he becomes more and more capable of requesting a body wrap session himself. The sessions decrease and then are only implemented at his request, and the context which provoked his request is then used to construct hypotheses about what caused the terrifying anxiety. I came out of that experience of this clinical work with the conviction that the "destructiveness" enacted in this boy had to be linked to the internal invasion in him of a terror of bursting: he "broke everything" trying to escape the anxiety of being all broken himself.

I then linked this hypothesis with the description of the basic instinctual opposition proposed by Freud in 1925 in his article devoted to (de)negation: "I want to eat this" or "I want to spit it out." When a subject is undergoing an experience he can either integrate it, or he must reject it if he cannot integrate it. But rejecting it does not make it disappear because it is recorded at a primary level (somatic probably) and continues to harass the subject when the current context activates it.

When the young child cannot integrate the experience he had live early on, it threatens his integrity, and his psychic organization and therefore his being with annihilation. The produces an affect of terror that is not representable. Integration does not allow an appropriate representation: it is the affect that represents it and just the affect itself. And the affect of terror is linked to the experienced threat of self-disappearance, of death.

This leads me to a proposition that may underlie the difficulties that I noted above in Freud's thought.

Death is not like itself; death in the existential experience is not similar to biological death, the experience of a threat of "psychic death" is not similar to biological death: the hypothesis of a "death drive" tends to confuse the two, it results from a time where representation and the thing are not differentiated.

Winnicott, in the article he devotes to "The Fear of Collapse," seems to me to be very close to the idea of experiencing "psychic" death without actual death.

We are then led to the following hypothesis: certain early experiences carry an extreme threat to the psychological survival of the subject; they are unintegratable and are rejected by the psyche, but they continue to "haunt" it in search of integration and attack the psychic organization that rejects them. Destructiveness results from this attack or from the defenses that the psyche puts in place.

Primary narcissistic deception

For developing my thinking, I would like to return to Freud's work and the different clues he left us to continue the construction of a more complete model.

First: if, in 1925, he proposed, as I pointed out above, two antagonistic issues in the reactions of the psyche to the lived experiences with which it is confronted – integrate/ reject –, he also underlines that the two instinctual reactions can /must amalgamate, become entangled. The unleashing of destructiveness therefore appears linked either to the significant failure of entanglement or to the domination of rejection processes over integration processes.

The question then is that of the circumstances and processes which govern and accompany the drive entanglement. The definition of the drive implicit in the 1925 article closely links the reaction of the psyche to the subjective experience lived. It is expressed in the following terms: "a work requirement imposed on the psyche due to its contact with the soma."

If we keep in mind that experiences – whether they come from outside and from the encounter with significant external objects or from within with somatic modifications (like the somatic modifications of puberty for example, or indeed from a somatic suffering) – are first received and recorded at a somatic level, it clearly appears that we can only think of the drive in connection with the lived experience, and only as a reaction to it: the drive is not an "in itself" which would exist independently of the history of the subject and its psychological impact.

In 1920, Freud proposed the hypothesis according to which the different organs of perception "bury themselves" secondarily in the depths of the psyche to form "the cores of the Ego;" he thus describes the first "core envelopes" of the Ego.

In 1923, he placed the id, the basis of the psyche, as the first "psychic system" in contact with the soma, and he specifies that the contents of the Id are not "capable" of becoming conscious in this primary form. They must therefore be transformed to continue their integration into the Self.

It is therefore the role of the "core envelopes" of the Self to carry out the work of transformation necessary for psychic integration. In 1924, in the article he devoted to the magic slate, and which he proposed as a metaphor for both the psychic recording of lived experience and its conservation, he described a process made up of a dialectic between a process of inscription, a "gluing" of the envelopes together, and a process of conservation, a process of "peeling off" them.

It therefore proposes a glued/detached dialectic. The glued is an interface process which combines the impact of the outside and the trace it produces within, the detachment is the effect of the transformation carried out by the envelope. The envelopes of the Self are not simple outlines or simple containers; they are processes of transformation.

Freud thus anticipates the proposals of the Chilean neuroscientist F. Varela – the bodily inscription of the mind – which underlines the fundamental role of bodily envelopes conceived as a system of transformation of what comes from outside into a form compatible with the biological functioning of humans and even more generally living things. What applies to the biological also applies to this aspect of the biological, that is, psychic functioning.

These remarks open the question of the processes and conditions which govern the transformation necessary for psychic integration or, conversely, its pronounced failure.

The "borderline situations" of destructiveness

First, it is the first stage of the dialectic that Freud proposed in 1924; it must "stick," but it must stick in such a way that it can also come off afterwards. In "Mourning and Melancholy" Freud underlines that the first psychic inscription is carried out by a process (memory) which he calls "identity of perception" – it fits – which must normally be followed by a process which he calls "identity of thought," which takes off and allows integration through symbolization. It is the transition to the identity of thought which then appears to him as a failure in melancholy, a failure which prevents the melancholic subject from being able to detach himself from the object to begin the work of mourning. But he also underlines an uncommon remark in his work on melancholy, that the maintenance of the search for identity of perception comes from a disappointment in the encounter with the object. The transformation fails because the encounter with the object was disappointing, because a fundamental psychic need was absent from this encounter, a fundamental need whose lack hinders the process of symbolization. The "logic of the whole," which characterizes the identity of perception necessary for psychic inscription, cannot be transformed into a more partial form, which characterizes the work of symbolization and can only be carried out "part by part," at the center of the mourning process (Freud 1915).

Maintaining the "logic of perception" locks the subject into a form of paradoxality and hinders access to psychic conflict. The effects of this "entrapment" in "the logic of everything" are undoubtedly one of the underlying causes of negativism and negative therapeutic reactions as the following clinical sequence highlights.

During psychoanalysis treatment, the paradoxicality that I have just mentioned produces a "limit situation" of the analyzing space, which results in a paradoxical transfer and the domination of reversal processes. It produces forms of negative therapeutic reactions, in which the further the treatment progresses, the worse the patient appears to be.

The processual forms of the negative therapeutic reaction and the "unleashing" of destructiveness and negativity (negativism), which goes with it, are especially pernicious variants of the "all or nothing" processes, which characterize the clinical forms of maintaining the search for an identity of perception. Some samples of the forms of expression of negativism will allow us to clearly understand how negativity proceeds; they will allow us to highlight the "paradoxical logics" that they produce within secondary processes.

I would start first with an example of "awareness" of the acuteness of the process being analyzed. In the preceding sessions, the processes of the patient's negativism began to be addressed, the work led to the famous formulation on which J. Bergeret was able to emphasize: "faced with a glass half full, (the patient) sees it half empty." During the following session, the patient wants to bring up this formula to challenge it, and she ends up saying: "Ah yes that's it, when there is a full glass, I see it half empty." She stops and bursts out laughing when she hears herself modifying this formula, thus radicalizing it, instead of contesting it as she wanted to do.

In my 1983 article devoted to the negative therapeutic reaction, I began to note certain particularly characteristic clinical forms, some of the "paradoxical logics" of this type of process, which attack the possibilities of psychic functioning and integration. Here are some samples taken from the work of the time.

"What you say is good and just. But it's worthless, and it's bad because it wasn't me who thought it up alone."

"What I receive from others is worth nothing because I receive it from others, and only what I produce myself is good and acceptable."

Or even "receiving something from the other means that I could not produce it myself, which then means that I am worthless."

We recognize here forms of self-generation, which imply the refusal of all dependence.

"What I have is worth nothing because I have it, only what the other has and which I do not have is good, only what I do not have is worth."

We owe to one of the Marx Brothers a particularly telling expression of the opposite position: "I would never agree to be part of a club that would accept people like me." "What I have is bad because I have it, and everything I have is bad or worthless because I have it." "Everything that touches me becomes bad."

Finally, this series of formulations unfolded according to the forms delivered by the treatment clinic.

"What I receive is fair and "good," but it is worthless because (it is "bad") or because:

*I didn't receive it at the right time (when I was a child, before, when I needed it so much). It's the opposite of the famous "better late than never."

*I did not receive it from the right person (from my mother, from my father from whom I expected it, only what I receive from them can be good, but I received nothing from them…).

*I did not receive it in the right way, as it should, exactly as I expected…"

Such processes, we readily imagine, burden the work of clinical elaboration and the work of integrative recovery of the vagaries of the history of historical failures and traumas. What is thought and understood in the space of the session is ipso facto invalidated by the fact that it was not there historically or previously. Even better, the current revelation increases the suffering of not having previously received what is now possible. Where the subject had begun a process of forced mourning, he discovered that what he had thought he had to give up, as something intrinsically impossible for him, was in fact possible and relative to the intersubjective context of the moment.

The historical impasse experienced by the subject is transferred to the psychoanalytic space, and it is the psychoanalyst who now experiences it, since the more "relevant" he is, the less the patient can grasp what he is offering! The transfer does not take place in a mode of movement, as classically described, but in a mode of reversal, or even in both modes at the same time, but separated from each other and structuring a form of "double bind" at the center of paradoxicality.

Hope, and the risk of suffering linked to the possibility of disappointment that all hope implies, is thus actively counter-invested: "Better known despair than hope and its attendant unknown and potential suffering." Evil is more "certain," more predictable than good and good, evil is therefore better than good, which is more random.

The subject places himself in a position of "foreclosure": it is too late, what could not have happened in childhood and with the parents, can never again be produced or can never take place again. The transfer and the necessary "illusion" which establishes its analyzable forms, is thus stunned at the base, there is nothing to expect from the analysis insofar as what was to take place in its time did not take place…

These logics of course also evoke envy and its forms described by M. Klein and H. Rosenfeld regarding the negative therapeutic reaction. However, the continuation of the analysis beyond the procedural forms that we have noted reveals a "subjective position" which is the core of the problem, and which is maintained by the failure of the current therapeutic effort.

"If I did not receive what was 'due' to me when I was a child, it is because I am inherently bad, it is my fault alone and not also the fact of those around me first or context." If what has happened historically is the result of an inevitable destiny, if it is linked to the "evil" which inhabits the subject, then he cannot blame his historical objects, and he finds himself protected from any violent effect on his part. Violent affects are then turned against the self and contribute to fueling the feeling of a "bad self". He is thus also protected from his feelings of infantile helplessness in the face of the inadequacy or failures of his primary objects.

Rather guilty, rather "bad," than helpless and being restricted.

In the debate between Winnicott and M. Klein about the primary source of the forms of destructive envy, Winnicott emphasizes that they are not intelligible without reference to the primary narcissistic traumas underlying them.

These few clinical data, which are only there to facilitate the representation of certain forms of "primary narcissistic disappointment" that hinder the primary entanglement– the primary amalgamation – of the two primary reactions of the psyche to the lived experience.

In his article on melancholy, Freud emphasizes that the disappointing object is a "narcissistic" object. Many current works, I am thinking of Winnicott's proposals concerning the mirror role of the maternal face – but undoubtedly it is the entire behavior and mode of communication of the mothering environment which is involved, and not just the face – which lead to considering that "narcissistic" objects are treated by the infant as reflections, doubles of himself, and are not differentiated as "others."

It is a characteristic of the primary archaic environment to obey this "narcissistic" characteristic. G. Gergeli, a Hungarian researcher who has worked extensively on modes of communication and early exchanges, was able to demonstrate that the adjusted responses of the mothering environment, – those which took into account both the functioning "in double" of the baby and at the same time the threat of confusion which weighs on it – were characterized by a mirror representation of the states and affects of the very little one and at the same time in a transmodal and "played" form which signifies to the new born that the reflected affect is not that of its author, that the latter "makes the mirror." The environment thus opens the possibility of a possible "detachment" to come, opens the potential game of the glued/detached dialectic.

Negative therapeutic reactions and negativity are encountered in psychoanalysis cures but there are more "extreme" forms of destructiveness which are hardly encountered on couches or in adult analyzing systems but to which clinicians, whether they are concerned of those who work with early childhood or those who venture "outside the walls," may be confronted, and which must also be investigated.

We remember the article by S. Ferenczi "The Unwelcome Child and His Death Drive" in which the author underlines the link between the forms of clinical destructiveness and the conditions of the first reception of the newborn.

In the article he devoted in 1916 to "Some Characters Identified by Psychoanalysis," Freud evokes the major disturbing element in *Richard III*, Shakespeare's play, which declares, from the first scene of the first act, that he was born "a midget" without the capacity to be loved and condemned forever to rejection, and therefore since good is impossible: "let evil be its good," which astonishes the functioning of the principle of essential pleasure/displeasure in the psychic integration of the experience. A careful reading of the text of the play draws attention to what his mother says about the birth and reception of the baby Richard III: she underlines her anguish when she was pregnant with Richard, an anguish in which she saw the sign that the future child would be a "poop daemon" dedicated to evil and disgusting. Richard was born in an atmosphere of primary maternal rejection, undoubtedly accompanied by a touch taboo.

An article by J. Hopkins focuses specifically on the taboo of the mother's primary touch and its effect on the child. Based on various clinical materials, J. Hopkins puts forward the hypothesis that the absence of maternal touch or a touch accompanied by a certain repulsion on the part of the latter, transmits to the child a representation of him that we could represent waste as "a bag of shit": "a poop daemon" to use the words of Richard III's mother.

Hovering over the birth of newborns is not only a simple insufficiency of "ego needs" but also a representation of the baby, which represents a greater threat to its development, and which threatens its very identity. Because in the place of the first representation of self, identity in Freud's thought, first form of basic identification – I am the breast – a first opposing representation of self is put in place: "I am evil," the bad, the "villain," the basis of melancholy, negativism and, therefore, forms of destructiveness.

We must therefore add to the lack of considering the need of the fundamental Ego the alternative hypothesis in extreme situations of a threat concerning the construction of a viable identity.

Extreme situations and destructiveness

In the most extreme cases, and beyond the simple narcissistic disappointment, those who have been subjected to early violence and to the terror of being destroyed by it, the return of the primary traumatic experience will occur in a hallucinatory mode, which will only be curbed in a murderous criminal reversal. These clinical situations can make it possible to explore this hypothesis.

In the clinical research that I carried out with Mr. Ravit concerning crime and the processes of its functioning – these are long-term clinical explorations carried out in prison with subjects who have committed crimes – therefore a form of "extreme" destructiveness, we were gradually led to propose the following clinical hypothesis. In the moments preceding the murderous act, the subject is invaded by a hallucinatory access – therefore by a process according to the model of "perceptual identity" (Freud 1938) – a terror activated by a post-traumatic context, which threatens its entire psychic organization with collapse. The act is committed to "localize" in the current perception the hallucination of the early traumatic experience, and thus curb the hallucinatory return of it. Mr. Edrosa's clinical thesis on serial criminals – again the result of long-term clinical explorations carried out in prison – confirms the relevance of this hypothesis. The murderous act is committed in an attempt to stop the internal invasion linked to the return of subjective experiences of violence in which the subject was subjected to the terror of dying. The terror of dying – without actual death – pushed the subject to withdraw from the lived experience which was thus "spit out" according to Freud's expression, but which, having not been able to be integrated into the psyche, returns on the only mode of "identity of perception" therefore in a hallucinatory mode.

The subject's only resource is to return to another, a similar person, a "double," the murderous violence to which he had been subjected. In the article "The Fear of Breakdown," Winnicott mentioned one of his patients, who committed suicide, who requested him to understand why she was going to commit suicide. He understood 20 years later that she was waiting for him to be able to tell her that it was to bring up to date the experience that she had already died in early childhood. I would add that the reversal does not take place against another but against oneself, and undoubtedly in connection with the incorporation of an extreme situation resulting from the confrontation with an external object animated by a murderous movement. The terror thus provoked in her led to a withdrawal of her subjective presence and the impossibility of putting the terrifying situation into identifiable memory, and therefore of being able to even begin to integrate it. Bion's concept of "nameless terror" seems to me to describe this experience quite well.

These latest developments have taken us far from Freud's thinking and the metapsychology he constructed. I think that some of the proposals he makes about the end of his life, formulations which perhaps did not have the developments they deserved, can "dialogue" with them.

First, a remark on Freud's relationship to the "death drive." J. Derrida in "The Postcard" engages in a close reading, as philosophers know how to do, of "Beyond the Pleasure Principle" in which he highlights a real conflict of Freud who couldn't resolve to propose the concept of death drive as "sick at heart."

From 1920 until the last years of his life, traces of this conflict can still be found in his writings. It seems to me that Freud's position begins to shift in "Constructions in Analysis" (1937), when he proposes a fairly new interpretation of hallucination, in which he returns, it seems, to Moreau de Tour's hypothesis that hallucination is the return of a subject's previous experience, hallucination which comes "disguised in the perception." The opposition between hallucination and perception – the opposition at the origin of A. Green's conception of negative hallucination – to which he had previously adhered – gives way to the realization that the two processes can coincide. At the end of the article, Freud proposes to consider that what he had proposed for hysteria in 1895 – that the hysteric "suffers from reminiscences" – is in fact a general process of all forms of psychopathology, psychosis included, with only varying the form of the reminiscence and the age of the experience.

In one of the little notes he wrote during his final exile in London (1938–1939) – each note that would merit a colloquium to explore their full implications – he points out that the experiences that are most repeated are the "earliest experiences." The process of repetition was the cornerstone of Freud's metapsychological shift in 1920, when he noted that repetition occurs beyond the pleasure–displeasure principle. Freud proposes an "explanation" for the repetition of the earliest experiences, noting: (explanation: the weakness of synthesis capacity). He thus comes as close as possible to the idea that repetition is driven by a constraint to do the work of integration.

If we continue the logic of Freud's reasoning, then we arrive at the idea that experiences are repeated, which could not be integrated in the "archaic" era (before verbal language), and that the integrative function – the synthesis he evokes – of which the child is not yet capable alone, must be supported by the primary environment.

Before concluding, it remains for me to address an important point which concerns the central question of drive entanglement in the management of destructiveness. A moderate or severe trauma, early or later, compromises the possibility of instinctual entanglement to the extent that the processes of rejection of the experience take precedence: the psyche "spits," evacuates the experience which cannot be integrated, and entanglement cannot take place under good conditions when it can even begin.

Freud provides a metaphorical description of the process by which impulse entanglement takes place, i.e., how two such antagonistic impulse movements could "amalgamate" together, through what kind of experience such an encounter could even take place. How can the psyche simultaneously reject and integrate a subjective experience? In 1920, Freud pointed out that cellular grouping means that what is "waste" for one cellular group can be integrated by another. In 1925 (Problème économique du masochisme), he took up this hypothesis and made it more precise: what is displeasure for one psychic system (e.g. the Ego can be pleasure for another (e.g. the Superego). But he does not describe the process by which this is possible.

It was in Winnicott that I found a subjective experience and a process capable of making possible the possibility of thinking about the simultaneous presence of the two antagonistic impulse movements. Of course, Winnicott does not make the link with the question of drives entanglement, and it is necessary to identify how the experience he describes has this potentiality.

In the article he devotes to "The Use of an Object," Winnicott raises the question of the future of a process of destructive rage in young children. Destructive rage occurs when the infant is confronted with the failure of the "created-found" – and "found-created" – processes necessary for the experience of the illusion which conditions his integration of the experiences he is led to go through. The failure of the created-found – or found-created – process, that is to say, the failure of the integration of the experience, leads to an experience of helplessness and mobilizes an affect of rage in which he feels like he destroyed the world. The psyche therefore mobilizes an impulse reaction of rejection.

Winnicott then proposes the hypothesis that the outcome of this experience of destructiveness depends on the response of the environment to this affect of destructive rage. If the environment can "survive" this destructive rage Winnicott specifies, if it does not retaliate against the child or withdraw from the bond and the relationship, then it can take on an essential value in the construction of the psyche.

My clinical experience invited me to add two other conditions which appeared to me to be necessary. The human environment must "acknowledge receipt" of the impact of destructive rage – otherwise it risks being invalidated – and thus being at the origin of the evolution of the link and its relationship and must therefore also be sufficiently creative – this is what proves that it is "alive" and not destroyed.

Let us pursue Winnicott's hypothesis. The infant can then experience that the object has not been destroyed, that a limit is placed on his destructive rage, that the object escapes this, and that it can be conceived as other. Freud had proposed the hypothesis that "the object is born in hatred," Winnicott adds: "as long as it survives it."

It is on this background that the internal topic is constituted, through access to the difference between the experience – the fantasy – of destruction which belongs to the internal world, to subjectivity, and the effective destruction which belongs to the objective world. Destructiveness is not destruction, destruction – of the link, of the object – is the misfortune of destructiveness.

Winnicott further specifies that from the survival of the object, love is born – I would add the object is discovered as an other-subject, as another subject, and at the same time the infant can also be conceived as a subject. From the survival of the object arises the possibility of attacking, of rejecting the object, without serious damage to it, of attacking it in fantasy, in representation. Two antagonistic processes then co-exist; destructiveness and love are no longer exclusive of each other; they are intertwined. Ambivalence, the conflict of ambivalence, can then begin to be organized without dividing the two contradictory emotional movements.

I therefore propose the hypothesis that the experience of the "survival of the object" is undoubtedly one of the processes – perhaps the determining process? – of the constitution of the drive entanglement.

Furthermore, the model of object survival must be able to be extended beyond the early experiences described by Winnicott. It undoubtedly also applies in all emotional conflicts: love must survive hatred, but "hate" must also "survive love"; this is what will allow us to differentiate ourselves, to separate.

Perhaps also in the differentiation of the representation of the object and the reality of the object, therefore is the possibility "that we represent that we represent," in the meta-representation, etc. In short, it is one of the processes by which the psyche will be able to become more complex and build itself.

This proposition makes it possible to include psychic functioning in the movements which characterize biological functioning, it allows us to think how in psychic life the processes of transformation which characterize biological life also characterize the psyche. Transformation supposes both that the thing is like itself and at the same time that it finds a form compatible with the internal environment in which it must fit. We transform the air we breathe to supply us with oxygen, we transform what we eat into a form compatible with our digestion, etc., we must transform the subjective experiences with which life has confronted us into forms compatible with the laws of our processes of psychic integration.

As a conclusion

To conclude, I can summarize where I am in my reasoning concerning the sources of manifest forms of destructiveness.

*They must be thought of in connection with the traumatic failure of the primary drive entanglement processes which hinders the drive amalgamation – the synthesis – necessary for the primary psychic integration of lived subjective experiences.

They cause a psychological rejection of them. The traces of these experiences cannot therefore be integrated into "the course of psychic events" (Freud 1911); they then haunt the unconscious alcoves of the psyche in search of an inscription which would allow the transformation necessary for their subjective appropriation, and they are then subject to a "repetition constraint."

*One of the important sources of this failure refers to traumatic experiences linked to early narcissistic disappointments, which affect the "ego needs" (Winnicott), the psychological needs necessary for the psyche to be able to make the transformations essential to the integration of the experiences with which it is confronted. These then cause the development of "borderline functioning" and a "narcissistic" pathology, which threatens the feeling of identity.

*Another source of this even more pronounced failure, even more deleterious and with more deadly consequences, is determined by an affect of "terror" caused by the impact of experiences of threats or violence experienced in early childhood and inflicted by members of the early environment. Experiences of terror where the small child would expect, conversely, to receive the security necessary for his development. Instead of finding the support of an alpha function, to use Bion's formulation, he finds himself confronted with the omega function described by G. Williams, a deadly function if ever there was one. The primary environment may not simply be "not good enough" but frankly toxic or even potentially deadly. The forms of destructiveness then mobilized are more "extreme," more devastating, vengeful.

*Winnicott proposes in one of these end-of-life articles, – The 'use of the object' in "Play and Reality" – a hypothesis prior to any attempt at "care" or analysis of these extreme circumstances: the "survival of the object." According to Winnicott's hypothesis, the very young child, in his development process, goes through states of destructive rage which have an essential function to discover the object as a subject differentiated from him. This is provided that the object "survives" the attacks of destructive rage of the infant – in which it experiences the feeling that it destroys everything – that it exercises neither withdrawal nor reprisals. The "survival of the object" makes possible the organization of an internal topic, thanks to which the child can continue to destroy the object "fantastically" to the extent that this fantasy does not reach the reality of the object or become a differentiated "other-subject". This experience contributes in an essential way to the drive entanglement, it forms the matrix from which the psychic apparatus can be constructed and become more complex.

References

Anzieu, D. (1985). *The Skin Ego*. Translation N. Segal, Karnac, 2016.

Bergeret, J. (1984) *La violence fondamentale*, Dunod.

Freud, S. (1911). Formulations on the two principles of mental functioning. *The Standard Edition of the Complete Psychological Works of Sigmund Freud*, 12, 213–226.

Freud, S. (1915). Mourning and Melancholia. *The Standard Edition of the Complete Psychological Works of Sigmund Freud*, XIV (1914–1916).

Freud, S. (1917). Mourning and melancholia. *The Standard Edition, 14*(1914–1916), 237–258.

Freud, S. (1920). *Beyond the Pleasure Principle*. Paris: PUF.

Freud, S. (1925) Negation. *The Standard Edition of the Complete Psychological Works of Sigmund Freud*, 19, 233–240.

Freud, S. (1938). An outline of psycho-analysis. *The Standard Edition of the Complete Psychological Works of Sigmund Freud*, 23, 139–208.

Freud, S. (1939). *Construction in Analysis*. Paris: PUF.

Freud, S. (1989). *The Ego and the Id (1923)*. Paris: PUF.

Freud, S. (2003). *The Uncanny*. Paris: PUF.

Freud, S. (2015). The theme of the three caskets (1913). In *King Lear* (pp. 57–57). Routledge.

Freud, S. (2018). Formulations on the two principles of mental functioning. In *Unconscious Phantasy* (pp. 67–76). Routledge.

Gergely, G. (2004). The role of contingency detection in early affect–regulative interactions and in the development of different types of infant attachment. *Social Development, 13*(3), 468–478.

Green, A. (1993). *The Work of the Negative*. Free Association Books, 1999.

Hopkins, J. (1987). Failure of the holding relationship: Some effects of physical rejection on the child's attachment and on his inner experience. *Journal of Child Psychotherapy, 13*(1), 5–17.

Klein, M. (2013). *Envy and Gratitude: A Study of Unconscious Sources*. Routledge.

Laplanche, J. (1981). L'angoisse dans la topique. *Problématique. I. Paris, PUF.*

Ravit, M. et Roussillon, R. (2012). La scène du crime: cette autre image des confins de la subjectivité. *Revue française de psychanalyse*, 76(4), Paris, PUF.

Rochat, P. (2006). *Le monde des bébés*. O. Jacob, 313p.

Rosenfeld, H. A. (2018). *Psychotic States: A Psychoanalytic Approach*. Routledge.

Varela, F. J., Thompson, E., & Rosch, E. (2017). *The Embodied Mind, Revised Edition: Cognitive Science and Human Experience*. MIT press.

Williams, G. (2018). *Internal Landscapes and Foreign Bodies: Eating Disorders and Other Pathologies*. Routledge.

Winnicott, D. W. (1968). Playing: Its theoretical status in the clinical situation. *The International Journal of Psychoanalysis, 49*, 591–599.

Winnicott, D. W. (1980). Fear of breakdown: A clinical example. *The International Journal of Psychoanalysis, 61*, 351.

Winnicott, D. W. (1991). *Playing and Reality*. Psychology Press.

Chapter 4

Some notes on repetition, repetition compulsion and drive

Discussion of René Rousillon chapter

Howard B. Levine

1 The compulsion to repeat is not always or only best viewed as a daydreaming eroticism (Freud 1914), a self-soothing repetition (Freud 1920), or a
defense against unpleasurable and traumatic experience (Freud 1920). It
may, in addition, also be seen as an unconscious call for recognition by the
analyst – and even by the more reflective part of the patient's own mind – of
primary narcissistic, regulatory processing disturbances, and internal object
relational difficulties that need elucidation and address (Bion 1962; Levine
2023).
   The problems that these issues present may appear at the manifest level as:

- difficulties with impulse control, object constancy, basic trust, and security;
- feeling states of internal deadness, isolation, and autistic-like or schizoid
  withdrawal;
- incapacities in emotional elaboration and regulatory processing; or
- breakdowns in self-cohesion, stability and sense of self.

2 Consequently, the challenges presented by many of the patients that Christine Premmereur has reminded us of in the introduction of the book – blank
depressions, body/mind dissociations, somatic discharges, addictive solutions to extreme states of anxiety and neediness, etc.– should not always *only*
be seen as regressions, maladaptive reactions, signs of negativism, aggression, and attacks on the analyst or treatment. Embedded in many borderline and narcissistic personality disorders, impulse disorders, panic attacks,
addictions, perversions, psychosomatic discharges, and autistoid defenses
are unconscious appeals for emotional contact, connection, and intersubjective regulatory and developmental assistance needed for the stabilization and
maintenance of a sense of self.

3 A common feature often shared by these seemingly disparate, manifest diagnostic categories is an inability to mentalize, symbolize, and psychically link,
transform, and elaborate the powerful, potentially disruptive, uncontained psychic forces that Freud called the drives. Freud described the latter as originating in the body and producing a constant internal pressure: a demand upon

DOI: 10.4324/9781003647317-5

the mind for work. Bion (1962, 1965, 1970) added that we had to deal with analogous forces (beta elements) in need of containment and transformation that were an inevitable consequence of existing, being sensate, and 'being in the world'.

The very act of perception subjects us to an overwhelming influx of sensory data and stimulation that must be contained and transformed – i.e., assigned meaning, made sense of, given aim and object, and linked to ideational representations. Initially, the forces and pressures generated by the somatic and the perceptual are assumed to be devoid of ideational representation and specific object or aim. They constitute the category that I have written and spoken about as ideationally unrepresented psychic states (Levine 2012, 2022).

4   Note here that I am talking about matters that are very different from the organization or description of psychic functioning as described by Freud in his first topography. The symptomatic disturbances – ego splits and ego distortions – that they produce are 'beyond' or 'before' the consequences of neurotic conflict as described in classical formulations. As André Green (1975) emphasized in his 1974 London Congress paper, psychoanalytic theory needs to recognize this difference for effective management and treatment of borderline and other 'limit cases'.

Apropos the need for recognition in the clinical setting, I'm reminded of a comment that Donald Meltzer made to his supervisee, José Monteiro (Bion, 2024): "For a patient to discover that someone is interested in their mental life, in their emotional life, that is the real therapeutic factor." As we shall see, this interest may have to include the analyst's interest in the communication value of the patient's speech as *action* in addition to the lexical meaning of the words used.

5   In the period of the technique papers, Freud saw repetition as taking place in the service of the pleasure principle; i.e., seeking gratification of ideationally saturated, repressed, unconscious, unacceptable wishes, and desires. Then, in "Beyond the Pleasure Principle," Freud (1920) not only added the possibility that unconscious repetition could be a marker of self-punishment and unconscious guilt, but began to hypothesize the possibility of an inherent traumatolytic component to some unconscious, repetitive acts (Think here of the Fort-Da of the infant's spool game). Finally, in his paper on constructions, Freud (1937) recognized that some significant determinants of the patient's psychopathology would never appear or be indicated in the semantic meanings of the patient's verbal associations and that the curative work of analysis would require the analyst's offer of a never-before-thought *construction* – i.e., an intuitive conjecture – rather than an interpretive uncovering of an already formed but hidden (repressed) fantasy, memory, wish, or desire. This latter perspective came into bold focus in Winnicott's (1974) paper "Fear of Breakdown" and in Bion's (1962) description of unconscious communication at the level of the beta screen.

6   Here is how Bion (1962) described it:

> Thanks to the beta-screen the psychotic patient has a capacity for *evoking emotions* in the analyst; his associations are the elements of the beta-screen intended to evoke interpretations or other responses which are less related to his need for psycho-analytic interpretation than to *his need to produce an emotional involvement.*
>
> (p. 24, italics added)

Bion continues in a footnote (pp. 100–101) saying that the existence of the patient's 'choice' to evoke feelings in and produce an emotional involvement with the analyst suggests the presence of *intuition* in the patient and implies an unconscious purpose and intention controlled by the non-psychotic part of the personality. The 'purpose' referred to seems to be in the service of survival and primary narcissistic repair: a *need to make contact by evoking feelings and an emotional involvement with the object,* because

> the patient is starved of genuine therapeutic material, namely truth, and there-fore … his impulses that are directed to survival are overworked attempting to extract cure from therapeutically poor material.
>
> (Bion 1962, footnote 10.1.1., pp. 100–101)

And, perhaps, from an unreceptive, at that moment, countertransferentially limited or therapeutically misguided analyst?

7   This reading of Bion's (1962) original description of communication from the level of the beta screen has clinical implications that go beyond the more common assumption that these primitive forms of unconscious relating and communication are only or always defensive, evacuative, attacking, or avoidant. The more usual assumption made about such repetitive action is that they short-circuit the normative, elaborative thinking process of both patient and analyst and can lead to states of impulsive action or chronic somatic discharge. For example, Symington and Symington (1996) assert that

> The *beta screen* elicits feelings in the analyst rather than thinking which might eventuate in an interpretation, which in turn might get the patient in touch with the reality he hates and fears… It is as though the function of the *beta screen* is to stop the analyst from thinking and instead to act out.
>
> (p. 66)

While this is sometimes the case, it should not always be assumed to be the unconscious intent or desire of the patient. Stopping the analyst's thinking may also be the consequence of a very complex and often ambiguous situation. For example, described in terms of Ferro's (2002) Field Theory, unconsciously turning the analyst into an 'unthinking analyst' may represent the "casting" – i.e., unconscious introduction – of an unhelpful, unthinking object into the here-and-now of the emotional situation of the Field.

Recall that in Freud's technique papers, he said that in analysis we cannot slay the enemy by way of an effigy or in absentia. Thus, the temporary and unconscious recruitment of the analyst to the role of the obstructive and unhelpful object may prove necessary in order to actualize and eventually recognize and then analyze in the here-and-now of the present transference relationship the consequences of a past, not yet integrated, failure of provision (Winnicott 1974).

8   Increasingly, then, manifestations of the repetition compulsion may be wondered about as unconscious attempts to recruit intersubjective assistance in containment and psychic regulation of otherwise disorganizing and overwhelming psychic forces. It is in this sense that we are often faced with what Premmereur referred to as "Fragility when facing primitive anxieties, confusion between internal and external reality, and violence against the self can be interpreted as a search for an object…" In such instances, the object sought is not only an object of libidinal desire or "an object that could survive attacks," but an object that can help contain, make sense of, transform, regulate, and reduce the annihilation anxiety, chaos, pain, and dysregulation produced by the patient's own regulatory processing incapacities.

Bion (1958) described this in his paper "On Arrogance," when he recognized that his expectation and insistence that his psychotic patient communicate with him at a level of discourse that was beyond the patient's capacity was turning Bion in the patient's view into a projective identification refusing object and in essence driving the patient mad. Accepting the patient's mode of communication and trying to extract sense and meaning from the communicative *act* in addition to the lexical meaning of the words used would instead turn the analyst back into what Roussillon (2011) has described as a *symbolizing object*, an object sought out in relation to what Winnicott has called 'ego needs' rather than 'libidinal needs'.

9   If we consider Freud's (1923) second topography, his "Structural Theory," we can note along with André Green (2005) that the change in Freud's formulations from the Topographic to the Structural Theory involved a change from

> one model, at the centre of which one finds a form of thinking (desire, hope, wish), to another model based on the act (impulse as internal action, automatism, acting) … the analyst now not only has to deal with unconscious desire but with the drive itself, whose force (constant pressure) is undoubtedly its principal characteristic, capable of subverting both desire and thinking.
>
> (p. 47)

Although Freud did not elaborate upon the inherent connections between drive and object in 1923, a dyad that Green (2005) would later insist should not be considered separately, but should be seen as an *ensemble*,[1] Freud did imply that the ego functions that referred to in his second topography developed in the context of primary object interactions – "the ego is a precipitate of abandoned object relations." Eventually, the ego functions that begin in the crucible of early object relations, emerge and develop and become essential for homeostatic regulatory processes. Botella (2005) put it this way:

"…with the introduction of the second topography, the principal function of the psyche became one of achieving a "work of binding" (p. 201), which, in *Beyond the Pleasure Principle*, Freud described as one of the earliest and most significant functions of the mental apparatus.

And added:

Elaborating, binding, representing, in order to avoid disorganization and chaos, is presumed to be the primary objective of psychic life… [T]he transition from the first to the second topography implies that the psyche must from thereon be thought of more in terms of process than solely in terms of its representational contents and systems. Similarly, the concepts of ego, id and superego must be understood as referring to *processes* that are capable of permanent transformation, and must not be reduced to the ideas of circumscribed and fixed agencies.

(Botella 2005, p. 204, italics added)

Roussillon echoed this thought at the 2017 Montreal French Language conference when he said that what psychoanalysis needs is a metapsychology of process rather than a metapsychology of contents.

10   In viewing Freud's change from the first to the second topography, it is important to note that in the revised theory, there is an implied opposition between thinking and action, and a distinction between desire (wish) which is always ideationally represented – e.g., "I want this or that from you" – and drive force, which is purely energic, a force that must be contained, transformed, directed. This distinction may call into question our previous assumptions about the essential character of the untransformed drives, the locus of the origin of their aim and object, and the origins and limits of ideational representation in the psyche. Do we see the drives in their originary form as having intrinsic, pre-assigned ideationally represented aims and objects that are saturated in regard to meaning (love, hate, desire, sexual conquest, wish to destroy, etc.) or as being more purely energic phenomena that are not yet linked to ideational representations? Rather than talking about the id as a seething cauldron of wishes and desires, Freud's (1920, 1933) final formulations of drive theory make the more abstract and general assertion that there is nothing in the id that resembles what we call an idea in the ego; that eros *binds* and the death drive *unbinds*.

11   At this point, it is important to note the distinction made by Laplanche and Pontalis (1973) between drive and instinct and to notice that despite the misleading tradition begun by the Strachey translation, we should, in most instances, be properly referring to a death *drive* rather than a death *instinct*. An instinct

is a genetically determined, biological *fact* that is present in every biologically normal member of a species. Drive is a metapsychological hypothesis about a non-specific force with a variable aim and object.

The work of the cognitive psychologist Gyorgy Gergely (Gergely et al. 1995) shows us that the human infant has an *instinctive* curiosity about cause-and-effect relationships among temporally contiguous events and an *instinctive* desire to test out their own capacity for agency in causing effects that have attracted their attention (Think of engaging a previously unknown infant in a supermarket check-outline and starting to play a game of peek-a-boo). Roussillon helps clarify our thinking about drives when he says:

> we can only think of the drive in connection with the lived experience, and only as a reaction to it: the drive is not an "in itself" which would exist independently of the history of the subject and its psychological impact.

And could we provocatively add that the history of the subject, one's lived experience, almost always involves or implies an object with whom one is either in relation to or from whom a particular intersubjective and/or developmentally facilitating, homeostatic facilitating relationship is required?

12   When faced with the kind of extreme clinical situations referred to by Premmereur and described by Roussillon, it is commonplace for analysts to speak of "the destructive potential of the drives." But is it the drives themselves that are 'destructive' or does destruction follow from the force field produced by the absence or failure of certain kinds of needed environmental provision? Do we tend to reify the death drive as a 'thing' that causes consequences, when it is perhaps better thought of as a 'direction' of an internal psychic force field that follows from a developmental/relational situation or context? Is the reified death drive an unintentional over ascription of *content* and *motivation* – i.e., a mistaken or unhelpful hypothesizing of 'a thing that desires' – whereas the more useful alternative might be to see the death drive simply as a *force* that follows from untoward circumstances? This shift in understanding may be easier to achieve in French, where the word for drive is *pulsion,* a word that this carries with it the connotation of *pulse,* rather than the thing that causes the pulse. The latter, what causes the pulse, is often the result of a failure of environmental provision of a needed quality of developmentally or regulatory facilitating object relatedness...

13   In the example of the boy who broke things and was successfully treated by being 'wrapped,' Roussillon says: "terror ... was linked to experiences of an encounter with an external object and the behaviors and responses of this object." Roussillon's experience of the boy and the situation with his caretakers led him to come away with "the conviction that the 'destructiveness' embodied in and enacted by this boy needed therapeutically to be seen, understood, responded to and thereby linked to his feeling of being internally invaded by

a terror of bursting: he 'broke everything' to trying to escape the anxiety of being all broken himself."

I would add that perhaps the boy also broke everything as an unconscious way of signaling to his objects that the problem with which he needed inter-subjective assistance and could not manage on his own was the threat of 'everything is being or is about to be broken.' This threat is not one that the boy could *know* at a secondary process, 'speakable-about' level – put into words or reflect upon – but could only be signaled, not necessarily yet symbolized, by the action of breaking things.

Clearly, his breaking things evoked feelings in his objects. That is why he was hospitalized and sent to treatment. But should we not wonder if in this evocation, he was thereby unconsciously attempting to create a link or object tie, i.e., make emotional contact with an object, and unconsciously reassure himself of the connection by reifying, through the act of breaking things, the concrete manifest evidence of that link?

14 A concluding hypothesis: Certain early experiences that carry or are associated with an extreme threat to the psychological survival of the subject, leave non-ideationally represented traces that are unintegratable and persist as residues of force and pressure that continue to "haunt" the psyche in search of integration. The consequences of the failed regulatory processes that they produce or are associated with can appear as if something was attacking the psychic organization of one's self or one's objects, tending toward destruction of self or other, disrupting the capacity to think symbolically and elaboratively and eliciting maladaptive defenses.

These 'certain early experiences' are described by Winnicott as failures of environmental provision and by Bion as non-receptive, impenetrable, and projective identification refusing objects. The ensuing search for integration can entail either a tenacious, often hostile-dependent clinging to objects or a massive, compulsive preoccupation with attempts and actions aimed at self-holding or self-soothing. This is the realm of what I have called the ideationally unrepresented (Levine 2022), one expression of which can be the excessive, often chaotic or destructive forces (drives) in need of containment and transformation. But containment and transformation may not be possible, however, without the participation and inter-subjective help of a 'symbolizing object'.

As Roussillon, following Winnicott, notes, when transformation fails, it is often because the encounter with the object was disappointing; because the meeting of a fundamental psychic need was absent from this encounter, a fundamental need whose lack hinders the process of symbolization. He further reminds us that in the debate between Winnicott and Melanie Klein, Winnicott emphasizes that the originary sources of the various forms of destructive envy are not intelligible without reference to the primary narcissistic traumas that underlie them. Do we therefore need to revise our view of the drives, freeing them from any implication of their being thing-like entities and recasting them as Freud seemed to be doing in his last writings as energic forces in need and in search of containment, direction, transformation, and specification?

Note

1 See Loewald (1949) for a somewhat similar view.

References

Bion, W.R. (1958). On arrogance. *Int. J. Psychoanal. 39*: 144–146.

Bion, W.R. (1962). *Learning from Experience*. London: Heinemann.

Bion, W.R. (1965). *Transformations*. London: Heinemann.

Bion, W.R. (1970). *Attention and Interpretation*. New York: Basic Books.

Botella, C. (2005). Commentary on current psychoanalytic practice: psychic zones and the processes of unconscientization by Norbert Marucco. *In: Truth, Reality and the Psychoanalyst: Latin American Contributions to Psychoanalysis*. Lewkowicz, S. and Flechneer, S. eds. London: IPA, pp. 201–212.

Ferro, A. (2002). *In the Analyst's Consulting Room*. London: Routledge.

Freud, S. (1914). Remembering, repeating and working-through. *S.E. 12*: 145–156. London: Hogarth Press.

Freud, S. (1920). Beyond the pleasure principle. *S.E. 18*: 3–64.

Freud, S. (1923). *The ego and the id. S.E. 19*: 1–66.

Freud, S. (1933). New introductory lectures on psycho-analysis. *S.E. 21*: 1–182.

Freud, S. (1937). Constructions in analysis. *S.E. 23*: 255–270.

Gergely, G. et al (1995). Taking the intentional stance at 12 months of age. *Cognition 56*: 165–193.

Green, A. (1975). The analyst, symbolization and absence in the analytic setting (on changes in analytic practice and analytic experience)—In memory of D.W. Winnicott. *Int. J. Psychoanal. 56*: 1–22.

Green, A. (2005). *Key Ideas for a Contemporary Psychoanalysis. Misrecognition and Recognition of the Unconscious*. Translated by A. Weller. London: Routledge.

Laplanche, J. and Pontalis, J.B. (1973). *The Language of Psychoanalysis*. New York: Norton.

Levine, H.B. (2012). The colourless canvas: Representation, therapeutic action and the creation of mind. *Int. J. Psychoanal. 93*: 607–629.

Levine, H.B. (2022). *Affect, Representation and Language. Between the Silence and the Cry*. London: Routledge/IPA.

Levine, H.B. (2023). To feel in my flesh: Receptivity, resonance, representation and the beta screen. *Psychoanal. Quart. 92*: 641–664.

Loewald, H. (1949). Ego and reality. In: Loewald, H. ed. *Papers on Psycho-Analysis*. New Haven and London: Yale University Press, 1980, pp. 3–20.

Roussillon, R. (2011). *Primitive Agonies and Symbolization*. London: Karnac.

Symington, J. and Symington, N. (1996). *The clinical Thinking of Wilfred Bion*. London: Routledge.

Winnicott, D.W. (1974). Fear of breakdown. *IRPA 1*: 103–107.

Chapter 5

Repetition compulsion, from infancy to adulthood

A cross-reading of the articles by C. Anzieu-Premmereur and R. Roussillon

Germain Dillenseger

This chapter reviews the two articles published in this book by Christine Anzieu-Premmereur and René Roussillon, both of which propose a model of the early psychic processes that accompany the transition from the psychic apparatus of the *infans* – a very young child with no language, in a situation of total, real, and psychic dependence on his caregivers – to that of a subject capable of experiencing, even in the absence of the object, his own existence and that of the object, and thus of symbolizing, thinking and, therefore, existing.

Both authors agree that it is the experiences of this early period of development that will later become the object of repetition compulsion.

C. Anzieu-Premmereur reminds us that repetition compulsion is a "mental pressure forcing the subject to act or think, under the domination of unconscious impulses," which also plays a role in "defense against unpleasant and traumatic experiences." The two authors propose to distinguish two types of repetition compulsion.

The first, in line with the pleasure principle, would be at the service of binding, subjectivization, creativity, and openness to the world. All play in children, all transference from patient to analyst, is in fact based on a phenomenon of repetition (Anzieu-Premmereur, 2025).

The second, beyond the pleasure principle, painful or mortifying, would be on the side of unbinding, de-symbolization, self-enclosure, and destructiveness.

Which early relational contexts, which processes, will orient toward one or the other pole of psychic functioning?

On the one hand, on the "good enough" side, we find a context of reciprocity, of good affective harmony. The mother's behavior is part of a rhythm, an alternation of presence and absence, sufficiently regular and predictable, in the image of what seems to have been sought in the "Eat, Sleep and Console" approach (Young et al., 2023) cited by C. Anzieu-Premmereur. The mother acts as a mirror, sending back to the baby a representation of her own affective states, with slight variations; in other words, sending back the *same,* rather than the *identical* (De M'Uzan, 2017). Following in Bion's footsteps, as R. Roussillon suggests, the mother performs an alpha function, detoxifying the Beta elements projected by the *infans.*

DOI: 10.4324/9781003647317-6

In this configuration, the *infans* can seize situations in which his mother is absent, to develop auto-erotic activities, which at once still tell something of the bond to the object, and at the same time are an opportunity to experience sensations and emotions in relation to his own body, in the image of those babies observed by Willy Hoffer (1949), playing with their hands after breast-feeding. These are the beginnings of infantile sexuality. A transitional space develops. A sense of internal security is being built up. The *infans* can detach himself from his mother, because he is in the process or cathecting an internal mother (Anzieu-Premmereur, 2025). Experiences can be welcomed and passively received on the one hand, and at the same time, be partially rejected. The *infans* integrates these experiences into his psyche, managing to "digest" them, because he has been able, at his own pace, both to partially spit them out and, on the other hand, to eat them, to make them his own. There is *collage* with perception and *take-off* through the activity of representation (Roussillon, 2025). Here, repetition serves symbolization and subjectivization.

In less favorable or even traumatic relational situations, the *infans*, unable to psychically detach himself from the object, remains entirely dependent on it (Anzieu-Premmereur, 2025; Roussillon, 2025). Faced with the absence of the real object, he has to look for an object substitute – a concrete object or a repetitive, sometimes self-aggressive gesture – over which to exert control, repeated over and over again in identical fashion, in order to distance himself from the anguish and ensure, as best he can, a continued sense of existence. This is the clinical field that ranges from children "addicted" to their pacifiers, to self-rocking and self-mutilation, as well as a wide variety of addictions, be it to products, inflatable dolls, or screens. Instead of finding a way out of primary dependence, the subject has created a *neo-need* (Braunschweig-Damay and Fain, 1975), in a relationship with a *fetishized transitional object*, which rather than opening him up to the world, locks him in on himself (Anzieu-Premmereur, 2025). Here, it is something of the environment's response to the needs of the infans' ego that is missing from the encounter. This is the "primary narcissistic disappointment" (Roussillon, 2025). The subject remains in a "logic of the whole" wherein identity of perception remains necessary to obtain satisfaction. Access to symbolization, and therefore to thought, is impeded. This can give rise to melancholy, a mode of psychic functioning in which the subject experiences himself as a negative whole, like Richard III's "poop daemon," and paradoxical functioning, which reproduces the primary situation in the transferential relationship by turning it inside out, as in the case of R. Roussilon's adult patient in treatment, unable to receive anything good from her analyst, "for lack of having been able to receive it at the right time, from the right person and in the right way" (Roussillon, 2025).

In other cases, the *infans* is confronted with experiences of threat, violence, and/or toxic projections from their environment. Instead of an alpha function, the environment operates as an omega function (Williams, 2018), projecting onto the *infans* the bizarre Beta elements that it himself has been unable to integrate. Integration capacities are exceeded to the point where the *infans* cannot appropriate any representation of the experience. Only the affect, an affect of terror, persists, confronting the *infans* with the threat of annihilation, of psychic death (Roussillon, 2025). R. Roussilon suggests that, in this configuration, these threatening early experiences, which cannot be integrated and rejected, continue to haunt the psyche. This situation favors destructiveness, and a constraint of repetition that repeats the initial situation of primary violence in the present, as in the case of this young boy in the hospital, whose destructiveness provoked rejection from all the care teams he met. In other cases, R. Roussillon hypothesizes that, confronted with a post-traumatic affect of terror, the subject may be invaded by a hallucinatory access, on the model of the identity of perception, which would threaten his psychic integrity and to which he would respond by the murderous act, as if to localize in the present perception, the hallucination of the early traumatic experience that threatens him (Roussillon, 2025).

A clinical vignette: Mr. A

Mr. A initially comes to see me in a context of very pervasive anxiety, with the fear that disasters may affect some relatives. He describes a stable relationship with his wife, a woman who is present and faithful, but with whom he never seems to find the emotional sharing he is looking for. This relationship seems to repeat a feature of his relationship with his mother, a woman he describes as very anxious, always worrying about him, but with whom real emotional sharing seems impossible. When he is about to see the mother again, Mr. A has high hopes of having an emotional exchange with her, but at the moment of their reunion, overcome by a feeling of unease, he finally gives up on his project, and each time leaves disappointed that the genuine encounter he was expecting did not take place.

Previously, Mr. A had met several therapists, who had disappointed him in turn, and whom he had ended up leaving. Mr. A's consultations with me soon revealed a massive and ambivalent transferential cathexis, punctuated by repeated threats to stop everything, with Mr. A regularly and paradoxically reproaching me for not being there for him when he really needed it, i.e. between our appointments. After a long period of preliminary work, based on the interpretation of the transference and resistance to its symbolic attacks, he was finally able to accept a weekly face-to-face analytic framework.

During the course of his treatment, he mentioned eating disorders that had begun in adulthood. Although aware of his thinness, Mr. A restricts his eating and makes himself vomit, always in secret from his relatives. It is as if the prospect of satiety reminded him of an insurmountable anguish, a threat of psychic death, and that the only way to feel fully alive and safe from danger was by actively keeping a feeling of hunger. Mr. A had to be separated from his mother at birth, and hospitalized to deal with somatic problems including eating disorders, regurgitation, and poor weight gain, which continued to worry his mother throughout his first year of life. Subsequently, and right up to the present day, Mr. A describes an ambivalent relationship with his mother, marked by the fear–desire to worry her, notably through various bodily symptoms.

This clinical vignette seems to me to illustrate the way in which repetition compulsion can be clinically encountered and deployed, in different ways, with our patients. Here, a primary situation marked by experiences of discontinuity and early inadequacy of the environment may have contributed to the emergence of an experience of *primary narcissistic disappointment* in Mr. A as a baby. The scenario of an impossible affective encounter between a sick infant and his early environment seems to have been repeated in Mr. A's later relationship with his mother, but also in his relationship with his wife, as well as in his transferential relationships with his various therapists, including myself. Could Mr. A's eating disorders, which appeared in adulthood but bear the print of symptoms present in early childhood, be understood as an attempt to find, in the repeated mastery of the oral sphere, a substitute for an unreachable primary object relationship, and a continued sense of existence?

The two articles by Christine Anzieu-Premmereur and René Roussillon, exploring the different possible futures of repetition compulsion in children, adolescents, and adults, revive the interest of this central psychoanalytical notion in contemporary clinical approaches.

Bibliography

Anzieu-Premmereur, C. (2025), "Baby and Compulsion", The Body and Compulsion from Infancy to Young Adulthood, To be published in 2026, Routledge, London, UK.

Anzieu-Premmereur, C., Cornillot, M. (2003), Pratiques psychanalytiques avec les bébés, Paris, Dunod.

Braunschweig-Damay D., Fain, M. (1975), La nuit, le jour: essai psychanalytique sur le fonctionnement mental, Paris, 302p.

De M'Uzan, M. (2017), "Le même et l'identique", Cliniques, 13(1): 24–38.

Hoffer, W. (1949), "Mouth, Hand and Ego-integration", Psychoanalytic Study of the Child, 3: 49–56.

Roussillon, R. (2025), "Destructiveness, Melancholy and the Death Drive", To be published in 2026, Routledge, London, UK.

Williams, G. (2018), Internal Landscapes and Foreign Bodies: Eating Disorders and Other Pathologies, Routledge, London, UK.

Young, L.W. et al. (2023, June 22), "Eat, Sleep, Console Approach of Usual Car for Neonatal Opioid Withdrawal", The New England Journal of Medicine, 388(25): 2326–2337.

Part 2

Introduction

Facing the pain: from substance abuse to human dependence

Mary T. Brady and Ann Martini

Substance abuse is a frequent issue in the treatment of adolescents and young adults. The task of differentiating normal experimentation from abuse can be particularly challenging for analysts working with this age group. This section will consider the multiple functions of compulsive and addictive use of substances for adolescents and young adults.

We chose this topic within the larger realm of compulsive body/mind conditions, as we consider substance abuse or addiction to be under-discussed in psychoanalysis. We wonder why this is so? The treatment of substance addiction can include the difficult management of altered states – for instance, if a patient comes to sessions under the influence of drugs or alcohol. Not unlike patients with anorexia, who can suffer brain impairment that can affect their cognition when significantly undernourished, patients addicted to substances may present with little capacity for reflection. These altered states and other issues in patients with substance abuse and addiction can at times require a team approach to treatment, which can be a significant undertaking for a clinician. Yet, while these issues are relevant for both substance addictions and eating disorders, the analytic attention in the literature to eating disorders is much more robust than is its focus on substance abuse disorders. We wonder whether societal stigma related to substance addiction can infiltrate our analytic thinking. We also wonder whether the need for the patient to treat the analyst as a substance instead of as human can be very hard for us to tolerate. We hope to redress the limited analytic discourse on substance dependence in some measure here, as we find that for all of us as analysts treating adolescents and young adults, we are frequently faced with patients in various stages of the substance abuse, dependence, addiction continuum, and need to be equipped to meet it thoughtfully. To this end, clinical material will be presented in the next three chapters from the analyses of an adolescent boy, an older adolescent girl and a late adolescent/young adult female with significant addiction issues. Chapter 9 will be a discussion commenting on the prior three chapters.

Substance abuse and addiction will be viewed from various perspectives in the chapters ahead: as an effort to numb oneself and simultaneously to 'speak' symptomatically of problems that the patient cannot yet name, as an identification with an ill or dead object, and as an effort to defend against psychotic anxieties and terrible

DOI: 10.4324/9781003647317-7

experiences of non-existence. Addiction can represent failures of caregiving that result in difficulties in self-esteem, self-reliance, and self-protection. It can act as self-medication, as a pathological retreat from the external world and as an effort to soothe distressing affects. Substance abuse, if severe enough, can contribute to arrests in development that can yield a young adult unequipped for life. The contribution of contemporary neuropsychoanalysis will be discussed in Chapter 8, for instance in terms of alteration of primary emotional systems.

Aspects of containment by the analyst that contribute to the patient's capacity to think about their self-destructiveness will be discussed, as will be the need for confrontation and the meanings of ancillary care when an adolescent's substance abuse becomes life-threatening. It can be a perilous journey from substance addiction to tolerating human dependence.

Chapter 6

Substance abuse in an adolescent boy

Waking the object

Mary T. Brady

In this chapter, I suggest that escalating substance abuse, particularly in adolescence, can reflect an effort to rouse or awaken an ill or dead object. I will describe a crisis in the analysis of an adolescent boy that had the effect of rousing me into action. Likewise, his parents were forced awake into being parents and into some contact with their son. I will also relate how my deepening understanding of object relations theory aided my thinking about this boy, whom I finished working with several years ago.

My understanding of the relationship between symptoms and unconscious object relations is influenced by Herbert Rosenfeld (1960/1966). He suggests that in some individuals, substance abuse can reflect an unconscious relationship to a psychically ill or dead object. Rosenfeld discusses drug addiction in relation to mania, depression, and splitting of the ego. Here, I will focus on the relation of drug addiction to depression, as this issue was particularly relevant for my patient. Herbert Rosenfeld (1960/1966) suggests:

> (T)he essential factor of the relation of drug addiction to depression is the identification with an ill or dead object. The drug in such cases stands for such an object and the drugging implies a very concrete incorporation of this object. The pharmacotoxic effect is used to reinforce the reality both of the introjection of the object and of the identification with it.[1]

> (p. 131)

Deadening oneself with substances may reflect an unconscious identification with, and relationship to, an ill or dead object. Thus, a drug could unconsciously represent an ill or dead object, leading to an endless, repetitive need for it, as the substance/object is not alive or satisfying. The drug/dead object is also repetitively imbibed because giving it up would unconsciously represent separation from an object in danger of dying. The relationship to the drug can be an effort to stay in contact with an ill or dead object and thus represents an involvement or even concern with the object. Self-stimulation by some drug addicts may also represent a frantic effort to punctuate a deadened state. David Rosenfeld (2006) describes a

DOI: 10.4324/9781003647317-8

severely ill patient who identified with a dead object and used drugs to feel a thrill, to feel "alive for a short while" (p. 79).

Substance abuse in some adolescents may involve an identification with a dead object, but also an attempt to wake ill or dead objects.[2] This view grew out of my experience with my patient. Once he woke me and others through a crisis related to his substance abuse, the hold of his addiction loosened. My view here is akin to Winnicott's (1958) conceptualization of the anti-social tendencies in adolescence. Winnicott sees the antisocial tendency as "characterized by an *element in it which compels the environment to be important.* The patient, through unconscious drives, compels someone to attend to management" (p. 309). He adds that "understanding that the antisocial act is an expression of hope is vital in the treatment of children ... the treatment of the antisocial tendency is not psycho-analysis but management, a going to meet and match the moment of hope" (p. 309). Repetitive or escalating substance abuse in adolescence can be a demand for those around them to wake up and engage by "going to meet."

In some cases, the analyst of an adolescent needs to understand the deadness (the depressed mother who neglects her child emotionally can be experienced as dead) expressed in the drug abuse, as well as to take action. In the work I will describe below, I set limits, involved the parents, and referred for ancillary care. While I had been interpreting my patient's substance abuse for some time, I think that for this patient thought without action seemed like inactive deadness. Particularly with adolescents, who so often engage us by action, our thoughts can seem bereft without action, just as our actions can seem bereft without thought.

Firm responses on the part of the analyst to escalating adolescent substance abuse are environmental provision, but they can also enliven the adolescent's unconscious object relations. That is, setting a truly necessary limit (particularly if the parent is not doing so) can contribute to the adolescent's experience of a live and durable object. In this way, an analyst is stepping into a void created by a dead/ill/neglectful object.

Negotiating healthy or experimental drug and alcohol use is part of most adolescents' experiences. Experimentation with drugs and alcohol is often part of teens getting to know themselves, as they "try on" different experiences and see how they fit. They often see substance use as a rite of passage announcing their newfound freedom. Differentiating experimentation from substance use that veers into dependence, addiction, and/or serious danger, however, is a particularly slippery slope for analyst and adolescent to negotiate.

Substance abuse in adolescence (conducted under parents' noses) can have a more communicative quality than it does in adulthood, when it can represent an established symptomatic equilibrium. Substance abuse is also a way for adolescents to get to know their objects as they are changing, and we are challenged to change with them —are we afraid to see, overly protective, unengaged, depressively unavailable, etc.

Identification with a dead object implies that thinking itself is deadened. A subtext of this chapter is the question: What interpretive and non-interpretive modes allow an adolescent to stop deadening himself to what he cannot yet think?

Bion's (1962) concept of containment suggests some of the conditions under which thinking, learning, and introjection take place. Alvarez (1992) notes, however, that the metaphoric images of containment are concave, such as a "lap-like mind" (p. 77). She contends that while containment sometimes needs to be soothing, it sometimes also needs to be firm. The "maternal object needs also to be seen as *pulling the child, drawing the child, attracting the child or interesting the child*" (her italics, p. 77).[3] In the clinical material, I will discuss the movement from concave containment (understanding and absorbing emotion) to firm and strong containment. Earlier developmental tasks involving separation, autonomy, and identity are recapitulated during adolescence, requiring new forms of containment. Adolescent crises cry out for firm containment, which sometimes allow new experiences and thoughts to emerge.

There are many "unthinkable" or "not yet thinkable" thoughts in adolescence. At the most basic level, physiological changes are not yet represented in the mind. Altering their bodily experience with substances may have special meanings for adolescents, as hormonal substances radically alter their bodies. The effort to take over the body with substances may at times be an "unthought" response to feeling subject to uncontrollable changes.

While an adolescent can communicate his problems verbally at times, he can also communicate urgently through his substance abuse. Adolescents frequently distance themselves from concern about their substance abuse and project anxiety into parents and analysts. Such provocation of parents and analysts can, for some adolescents, also be an effort to awaken an ill or dead object.

Ill or dead aspects of parents may not yet be thinkable for some adolescents. Adolescents have to negotiate profound shifts as separation and individuation require them to see themselves and their parents differently. Clarification can occur in an adolescent's mind as he compares the difference between his analyst's and his parents' responses to his substance abuse. This may allow him to think about the problems in his objects instead of endlessly enacting deadened states. Paradoxically, an action by the analyst (confrontation and referral for substance abuse treatment) can sometimes allow a patient to begin to think. A notion of action and verbalization as always being opposites is simplistic. Sometimes an action is the way toward thought — for instance, an adolescent's substance abuse could be a communication about an unthought deadness in the parent. Sometimes an action on the analyst's part might be felt as more of a direct communication than an interpretation might. For example, if we interpret and an adolescent continues to hurt himself, he could feel that we don't really mean to protect him, or that we are not really present. At times, action might go hand in hand with thought. It might be possible to foster a conversation during a tumultuous interaction that links the patient's action and his inner life with the analyst's inner life. Some adolescents have had little experience of action and thinking being linked — that we might do or not do something because of a consideration of our own or others' feelings.

Ideally, confrontation does not just aim at stopping a destructive behavior, but also recognizes that the behavior is a communication conveyed in a bodily manner. In adolescence, the process toward symbolization requires that the meanings underlying a symptom emotionally register in the minds of adults. Sometimes complex meaning may be conveyed in a confrontation. If an adolescent sees an analyst as solely trying to control him, he is not likely to feel understood. A severe bodily symptom can be comprehended as an effort to rouse the object, but the adolescent also has to be helped to survive it.

Acting out and focusing on the external world are characteristic of adolescence, "just as playing is of childhood, or communication through language of adulthood" (Flechner, 2005, p. 1395). Flechner asserts that "(C)onsecutive disappointments owing to deep feelings of loss and isolation experienced precociously, identification difficulties, the poverty of the symbolizing process" lead the adolescent toward acting out and away from "mental elaboration" (p. 1395). I agree, and add that adolescent acting out calls for an adult response that at times needs to be in action form in order to create the conditions for thought.[4] As Flechner describes it, self-destructiveness can represent hate "toward the maternal figure — even though at the manifest level the adolescent is the one who suffers the aggression (generally at a bodily level)" (p. 1395).

In adolescent treatment, action, instead of symbolically expressed thought, often conveys the meaning. It is as if by acting out adolescents feel that it is not sufficient to say something abstractly — and of course there is great variation in this capacity amongst adolescents and at different times in the same adolescent. They want to *make an impact*. "The whole process of experiencing feelings, processing them and working through them is frequently replaced by an enactment" (Anderson, 2000, p. 11). Most adolescents project unprocessed experiences. "But in those at risk it is usually more extreme, and is associated with issues of death, destructiveness and damage" (p. 12).

The frequency of physical symptoms in adolescence — such as substance abuse — also signals a request to the object to wake up to the physical experience of his body. Adolescent substance abuse can convey that one is no longer in a child's body with child problems, but in an adult's body with adult problems. There is a special intensity to adolescent bodily communications when there is a developmental last chance for parents to respond before their children become adults. Thus, the effort to wake the object might be seen as characteristic of the adolescent process — "wake up to my changing body and my changing mind before it is too late." Unfortunately, for more troubled adolescents with objects experienced as ill or dead, the effort to wake the object may take on dangerous proportions.

Neil

Introduction

'Neil' is a tall, handsome boy, who looks older than his actual age. His physical appearance is that of a cool teenager. He began therapy at eleven, overwrought concerning his parents' painful marital separation a few months earlier.

Neil has one sibling — a sister two years older. Neil's mother suffered postpartum depression after his birth, likely related to her own mother's suicide when she was a small child. His care was largely delegated to nannies. His early memories are of his mother being in bed. Neil's family is quite affluent. His father is an accomplished artist whose life is a whirl of social and artistic occasions. Neil's mother sees her ex-husband as an ever-absent parent and herself much more present for the children. Neil's father attributes their split to her depression.

Neil's mother acknowledges long-standing depression, but feels that it improved in the latter years of the marriage. Both parents acknowledge contention related to his father's bohemian lifestyle and that Neil had begged them to stop fighting. They had agreed to work on the marriage and his father had expressed a willingness to be a "family man." However, soon after this resolution, the father left the marriage, preferring his unconventional lifestyle and leaving his mother feeling betrayed and full of rage. The children live primarily with the mother, but have regular visits with the father.

I will comment briefly on the early phase of the treatment, in order to focus on the period of Neil's substance abuse.

Early treatment

Neil wept bitterly during his first session and described his experience of his parents' break-up, as "like the sun hit the earth, and that I wanted to die." He said that if he found a gun on the ground he would shoot himself. Neil was interested in rap, gangs, and violence. His sense of the world seemed post-apocalyptic. There had been a catastrophe, and all that was left were the ruins. He told me about the lyrics of a rap song that referred to despair and suicide and added that he would bring it for me to hear.

Neil's pain at his relationships with both parents was palpable. He felt that taking care of the house and the children were too much for his mother. He also talked about how his dad flirted with everyone, and contemptuously called him a "pimp." Neil began to appear less depressed as our work proceeded. We gradually increased from two to four meetings a week.

Neil's grades improved and he continued to seem less depressed. He then began to express an interest in marijuana. In the beginning of 8th grade, Neil also began to be interested in the girl he would be involved with for the next two years. I was impressed by his growing ability to talk directly about his feelings.

Period of escalating substance use

Neil began to experiment with marijuana and alcohol when he was thirteen. He joked that I might be a *Stasi* spy. I said that I thought behind his jokes he was worried about the privacy of what he told me, as some of his thoughts were now harder to tell me. He responded by telling me a joke about sex. At times he exerted pressure on his parents to cut back his treatment. His father was willing to agree, but Neil could see that his mother was doing the harder thing by trying to hold firm. I worked with his mother to try to help her to keep the analysis steady, as I thought Neil was struggling with too little parental discipline and limits. Now, I am aware that my thinking at the time, taken from notes I kept, was an accurate enough description — "too little parental discipline and limits" — but not dynamic enough. I realize that, through the action of trying to get his parents to cut back the treatment, Neil was trying to see if anyone was awake. In this case, his mother was not solely deadened, but trying to be awake.

Neil's next older sister also was interested in drugs. Neil seemed to be following in her substance abuse footsteps, and spoke often of friends using drugs. At the same time, he seemed worried about his sister's drug use. One day he brought in his bong for me to see, and was disappointed in my reaction. I asked how I could be enthusiastic about something that could hurt him. I said that when he reassured himself that a lot of other people used pot, it relieved his own guilt and anxiety about it. I said that I thought he was trying to draw me into his marijuana use, as if there was nothing to question about it. Though angry at times when I looked into his drug use, a close feeling between us continued.

Neil's sister's drug use continued to escalate. Neil's father took Neil and his sister for a vacation to an artists' colony where drug use was very apparent and idealized. Shortly afterward, Neil had a dream in which his father said it was okay to drive a car off a cliff. I thought this dream represented feelings about his father's permissiveness, as well as a reckless part of Neil.

Neil told me of opening his mother's drawer and seeing an array of sedatives. His reaction was that "nothing will change with her, and she can't face life without medications." I thought that he was recognizing his identification with his mother's depressive deadness and his need to stay close to her through depression and dependence on substances. Separating from his mother was particularly fraught for Neil both because of her hopeless depression and because of his father's mistreatment of her. Neil's relationships with me and with his girlfriend seemed to represent some capacity to reach toward relatively live objects.

Neil was disappointed with both his mother and his father, and was consolidating a group of friends in high school who used drugs. His choice of a group of older drug-using friends seemed to be a repetition of a parental denial of harm. I spoke with him about turning to marijuana when he didn't feel close to his mother or father. He decided to take a break from marijuana and stayed off it for a month, although he did drink during this time. I continued to have concerns about the level of parental involvement and supervision at home, which I took up with his parents.

One week Neil had asked to reschedule a session from earlier in the week until Friday. When Friday came, he cancelled the session to party with his friends. I felt that he'd manipulated me to put his partying before the analysis in a somewhat duplicitous way. When I saw him, I said that he expected me to be straight with him, and that I expected him to be straight with me. He said that he hadn't expected me to be so mad about it, echoing a sense that limits and rules often weren't held to at home. He seemed to have expected an apathetic, dead disinterest to what he was putting in my face. He has not subsequently repeated this slipperiness around his handling of sessions.

Neil (now 14) told me, "I dreamt that I was with my friends and saw some crack-heads and was repulsed by them, but then I became one of them."[5] I commented that he might start out thinking something dangerous wouldn't hook him, but then it could begin to seem normal. He told me that he had come high to a session the day before as he'd been off from school, and that I hadn't noticed. In the transference, he experienced me as dead and oblivious. I said that he might feel like putting something over on me, but in doing so he would begin to take me less seriously. I told him that I did see his marijuana use as a problem, that he was using it way too much (daily, substantial use at this point). He decided to take another month break from marijuana, and also to be on the swim team the next season. Over the next months, he seemed to be moving away from marijuana.

In this period, Neil did not get high when he spent time with me or with his girlfriend. It seemed that when he felt he could be with someone awake to him he didn't want to be high. He experienced his mother as unavailable due to her depressive preoccupation. At times, he would begin to reflect on the history of substance abuse in his family (siblings of both parents were alcoholic), but then cut this thinking off. I pointed out the way he limited his own freedom of thought.

After two years of being intensely close to Neil, his girlfriend told him she wanted to break up with him. She gave no real reason, just that she wanted to be independent. He had felt her drawing away from him in the weeks before and had said to me that he'd "fall apart" if she broke up with him. I said "you worry you wouldn't care about yourself at all if Kate doesn't continue to love you." He replied, "Honestly, I think I'd be like my mother, I'd be wrecked." We spoke of the "fault-line" he felt inside of potential depression, if someone he needed separated from him. He said, "I do feel like my mother in that way, but I guess I understand more about myself. And I would be able to talk about it with you." Commenting on Neil's feeling unlovable in the face of the break-up was a way of talking about a danger of deadness. When he loses his girlfriend, he feels left with a dead internal object. At this point, his internalization of new and enlivening object ties with me and his girlfriend were not strong enough to free him from an identification with a dead object and a feeling that his object is dead and so there is no possibility of love.

Neil's marijuana use increased following the break-up. At times he sounded like an addict defending his choice, but at other times he seemed to be coming toward me and grappling with things I'd said to him about his dependence on the drug. He felt torn between his/my concern about his drug use and his peers' reactions when he stepped back, as depicted in the following exchange:

P: I have one friend who does *llelo* [Spanish slang for cocaine] who's twitching and another who's done so much E [Ecstasy] he can't even feel it anymore. With pot I feel like I can control it so that it won't hurt me. My friend was hecka mad at me that I didn't go to the party. I'm going to stop smoking cigarettes for swimming. It won't be like seeing babies crawling on the ceiling.

A: No, but it will be hard.

P: We respect it when someone's taking a break from pot, but we also tweak the person – like blow smoke in their face.

A: You wouldn't want someone to get hurt, like when your sister got in the accident, but it also sounds like you and others feel anxious when someone is trying to change because it brings in that there are risks involved. It may be hard for you to wish that your friends might really support you in feeling less dependent on drugs.

Neil was worn out by his struggle and by the background feeling of a dead and deadening object. He seemed to identify with a mother who felt beaten by life. Although Neil wasn't getting high before the sessions, he was in an ongoing dulled state. He often talked about being "washed," or worn out, after getting high the night before. I commented to Neil about how much more numb he seemed than in the past. Neil flared: "It seems like you don't accept me as I am like when using drugs. You just want me to be that other Neil, but I'm not, I'm older and smoke pot and that's the Neil you're going to get." I replied, "I don't think about it that way. You and the drugs are two different things in my mind. Are you saying you see yourself as the same? My feelings about you are what make me concerned about the drugs." Neil responded that he was feeling really rejected by his ex-girlfriend. The drugs served as a way of blunting his pain of rejection.

Neil told me his mother seemed "sad all the time, she's the saddest looking person." I acknowledged that his mother's day-to-day sadness could be more deadening than a crisis like the divorce. I added that he was sometimes afraid he wouldn't be able to handle his own sadness. He said, "When I used to come home from a vacation with my father my mom would be like — 'oh, hello,' but Kate would be so happy to see me." I said, "You feel your mother has been beaten by life, and doesn't have room to enjoy you." I said that his feeling he couldn't make it without marijuana was like his mother feeling beaten by life. I suggested he could feel sad for her, but not have to accept that state for himself. He acknowledged that it felt harder to think about stopping his marijuana use for a month now than it had in the past. I said it was good to notice that he was getting more dependent on marijuana. He said, "Fuck," with humor — acknowledging the truth in what I was saying, but that marijuana also felt like a friend to him.

In a recent session Neil told me that his ex-girlfriend had "hooked up with another guy."

P: I started shaking and I couldn't stop. I was awake for three hours, I almost called you but it was two in the morning. I wasn't sure if I'd get you.

A: It seems like your body was telling you something with the shaking, that was hard to find words for.

P: I don't know, the strange thing was I didn't cry.

A: It makes me think of when someone's in shock, or so cold that they start to shake.

P: I guess I felt betrayed. I'm going to stop talking to her; it's too fucking pain-
      ful. It's probably related to — I didn't stick to my break [from drugs and
      alcohol] this weekend. [He tells me of the various social occasions he felt
      obliged to get high for.]
A: So you're telling me all the social reasons for getting stoned, but you started
      by linking it with the break-up.
P: I've never had anything like this happen to me before. When my parents
      broke up, I was so young and so burdened. Drugs weren't in the picture then.
A: It sounds like you feel if they had been, they might have gotten the better of
      you.
P: (Nods).
A: What did go into your thinking about calling me or not on Friday night?
P: I know it doesn't make sense but I guess it felt like if you didn't pick up the
      phone like you didn't care either.

I interpreted that if he couldn't reach me, he could feel I was not alive to him or
he to me. He responded, "Maybe it was the alcohol, but the first weekend after my
girlfriend broke up with me, I felt like there was no point in living." Neil's marijuana and alcohol use expressed hopelessness in reaching a live and loving object,
and was also an effort to hide his feelings from himself and others.

At times Neil seemed to want to draw me into his drug use, as if I approved of it.
David Rosenfeld (2006) describes that drug abusers "erect a world of their own and
want the analyst to believe them" (p. 80). Neil treated comments on my part that
addressed the destructiveness of his drug use as if I was just a downer. He denied
his own concern about the consequences of his substance abuse and projected it
into me where it could be ridiculed. Neil seemed to be putting me in the position
of standing by as his drug use continued. My efforts to control him were also problematic as he could then evade me and externalize any concern for his drug use.
Neil alluded to "trying nitrous" and selling marijuana. I was carrying a constant
feeling of concern for him. I think at this point he was not willing or able to carry
much of this concern within himself, but he was certainly able to evoke it in me.
I am conceiving of Neil's escalating substance abuse as a communicative projective identification here. That is, he needed me to experience severe anxiety in order
to begin to make aspects of himself known. I see Neil's ability to evoke concern
in me as some capacity in him to wake the object. On the other hand, I was often
made into a useless, dead object.

Neil spoke increasingly about his mother "giving up on him" and "not wanting
to know" about his substance use. I responded to him by saying,

At times you feel I express concern about your substance use, but you might
not listen to what draws you so much about marijuana. You might feel I am not
really listening to you about that. I would want you to know I am concerned
about it, but it might be harder to give something up without our taking seriously
why it's so important to you.

Next is part of an hour conveying Neil's sense of abandonment in the face of the break-up with his girlfriend, which had links to his underlying depression and despair.

Neil comes on time, wearing a shirt with punk rock band on it, which says in small letters "die hippies." He looks unhappy. He tells me about seeing Kate with another boy and feeling depressed.

P: Can I use the couch?

A: Sure.

P: I want to be done with it, it's been a month and I still feel the same way. I tried smoking a lot of pot and that didn't help, I tried ignoring her and that didn't help.

A: I know you feel that way in part, but I think you also know you have to go into the feeling.

P: It's just that I've been here before, feeling sad.

A: And there's more of it.

P: (Crying) I feel really hopeless. She was the thing that made me most happy, and now she's gone, and not just gone, but she doesn't love me anymore.

A: I was thinking about how the last time you used the couch was when you wanted to tell me about where you were with Kate physically, and all the good and excited feelings about your physical relationship. It must feel like you had the rug under you, and then had it pulled out.

P: Pretty much. I honestly feel she was the best thing that ever happened to me. That she made me feel hope about a lot of things, and we know how I can not feel hopeful about people. But now it feels like the hope is gone.

A: That is part of what makes it feel so hard. This break-up does remind me of how you felt when your parents broke up. You did feel really devastated by that, but then you did also begin to feel better.

P: I just want it to be over with.

A: I can understand that, but I think it was a good decision to use the couch, that it had to do with knowing you have to go into it.

P: (Crying) When my parents broke up, it took a year. Why does this always happen to me. I feel like it's my fate for someone not to love me and stay with me. It feels like everyone.

A: I can see why it would feel like bad luck, when you did let yourself love so much. It's bad enough to get broken up with, but even harder to feel like there's no chance for you in life, and as if there will never be anyone that stands by you.

P: It's how I feel right now, really hopeless. People used to say I was the best boyfriend.

A: And now it feels not only have you lost Kate, but almost like you've lost your own sense that it's a capacity inside of yourself to have real intimacy in relationships. We've got to stop, but you know I'm here.

P: Yeah, bye.

[I feel so sad for him and feel pained to end the hour. I feel acutely aware that his mother is in Europe and that he is going home to the household help. The sad feeling stays with me throughout the evening.]

My sadness for Neil had an "urgent" quality (see Alvarez, 1992) to do with carrying a live part for him that he could not steadily carry for himself. His loving and being loved by his girlfriend had enlivened his sense of possibility in life and now he had lost hold of it.[6] My urgent concern for him reflected his ability to engage me, as well as my feeling of risk that his despair and deadness could win out.

Neil's substance use and selling drugs escalated in the following months. His attitude toward me in the hours was "don't tell me what to do." He saw my concern about his substance use as my own narcissistic wish to control him. I told him that I thought he had been bargaining with himself about his drug use and that it was time for him to stop using drugs. I said that even so I wasn't sure he could stop. Meanwhile, Neil's sister overdosed on hydrocodone and could have died.

Neil stopped using marijuana and told me about strange experiences when he withdrew from the drug. He said he was hearing angry voices, imagining angry images and that hearing himself breathe was disturbing. Anxiety and anger broke through without the constant use of marijuana.[7] He came in and told me he had smoked hashish. There was a constant back and forth with addictive substances.

Crossing a line

Neil came into a session and told me he had gotten high on Saturday night, after trying to stop smoking pot. He asserted that it was different than before, as he would just smoke occasionally now. Then he told me "Last night [Sunday] was sketchy. I had nine or ten beers and a fifth of gin. I passed out and vomited while I was passed out. I woke up and had to clean myself up." At this point I felt Neil had crossed a line. He could have choked on his vomit when he was passed out and died. Neil told me of passing out and vomiting without a level of concern that might provide some indication that he could protect himself from further incidences. Additionally, his own efforts to moderate his substance abuse regularly slipped away.[8] I told Neil that he was endangering his life and that he was going to need to be in a substance abuse treatment program. I offered to break the news to his parents with him because I knew it would be difficult for him and for his parents to acknowledge his putting his life at risk. I described telling his parents as part of coming to grips with his own inability to stop endangering himself with drugs. I told him that, if he couldn't tell his parents, I would do it for him, but that it would be better if he could.

At this point, I had to live with the anxiety that Neil's anger at me for this confrontation would be the end of our work together. Neil's response was to bargain that he didn't want to be sent away for drug treatment. This response reflected some acknowledgement that he needed more help and his fear of the internal and external separations further treatment would require. Neil agreed to a meeting with his parents, which I arranged. Father initially tried to evade the meeting over an insignificant scheduling conflict, conveying his panic at having to face family problems. During the meeting, Neil told his parents about his substance abuse. He also told them that he and his sister could "fly a Boeing 747" through their lack of parental communication. In fact, his parents had not spoken to each other directly for some years before this meeting. I told his parents that Neil needed additional substance abuse treatment and that a residential or intensive outpatient program was necessary.

During this period, I researched both outpatient and residential programs. Because of Neil's strong preference "not to be sent away," I recommended an intensive outpatient program that would require group and family therapy. It also required randomized urine testing. The program staff was hesitant to allow a patient to continue with a therapist outside of the program, but they ultimately agreed that he stay in analysis while in the program.

I scheduled one further family meeting to finalize Neil's entry into the substance abuse treatment program. His parents seemed to be hesitating out of fear. Neil's mother expressed a feeling that "we're not a family." Neil told her, "that's not good enough." She replied that "I did try" and that it was father's fault as "he left." Neil replied that that was "five years ago, everybody gets their heart broken — get over it." Neil brought up her "sniping" about his father and said that he and his sister "don't have parents." I queried that neither parent seemed to express anxiety or concern about their son passing out and vomiting in his sleep. I told his mother that while I knew she had tried, that she had to give serious thought to functioning together as parents on Neil's behalf. I told Neil's father that he needed to be much more involved with his son and that he seemed to often just respond to me with "lip service." At the end of the session, Neil asked if we could meet again. I said to his parents "as awkward as it is for us to meet together that it is important to Neil." His parents' passivity in stepping forward to meet his problems was very clear to Neil in this meeting. He became increasingly able to see his parents as having real limitations as well as assets. His bringing his parents together through a crisis seemed to wake his parents up somewhat to functioning as parents and to simultaneously wake him up to what they could and couldn't be for him as parents.

I will leave my narrative of Neil's treatment here. He did complete the substance abuse treatment program and both of his parents participated in it with him, even if with somewhat partial efforts. As the program included family treatment, I did not meet with Neil and his parents together again. However, I thought that Neil had brought his parents together and constructed a more alive and usable set of parents through this crisis. He continued in analysis with me for another year after this period. I have heard from him periodically since, and he is progressing well.

Discussion

Neil's marijuana and alcohol dependence involved an identification with a "grey" and deadened maternal object, who herself sedated her emotions. Green (1983) describes that the child's experience of the "dead mother" "takes place in the presence of the object, which is itself absorbed by a bereavement" (p. 149). Neil's mother suffered a post-partum depression likely linked to her own mother's suicide by overdose when she was a child. Her husband's abandonment of her seemed to compound and entrench her feeling of bereavement and narcissistic injury. Neil's mother exemplified Green's description of a mother whose "sorrow and lessening of interest in her infant are in the foreground" (p. 149). Neil's self-sedation also seemed like an effort to numb his feelings of sadness, anger and sensitivity.

Green's (1983) work is well known for relating the experience of a "dead mother" to depression in a child.[9] The absence of the mother's love is experienced as the loss of meaning in life. Green says, "(T)he dead mother ... is a mother who remains alive but who is, so to speak, psychically dead in the eyes of the young child" (p. 142). Green viewed that a patient with a "dead mother" could experience the passivity of classical analysis as a repetition of deadness. Instead, he advocated: "By using the setting as a transitional space, [the work] makes an ever-living object of the analyst, who is interested, awakened by the analysand, giving proof of his vitality by the associative links he communicates to him" (p. 163).

Neil's substance abuse also expressed an identification with an over-permissive paternal object. Kohon (1999), commenting on Green, describes that:

...often a distant mother is accompanied by an absent father (who refuses, or does not know how to respond to the child): the infant cannot turn to anybody, and is caught in "a unique movement with two aspects" following the decathexis of the maternal object, the child unconsciously identifies with the mother.

(p. 3)

In the transference-countertransference, this took the shape of Neil's expectation of an oblivious deadness on my part to his self-destructive substance abuse and my corresponding feeling of impotence. Neil's escalating substance abuse was an unconscious effort to wake up his objects and force us to change, particularly in the crisis related above. My experience was of having to grow to grapple with Neil's drug abuse. I had to question some of my own assumptions about analysis, such as a presumption that drug treatment would not be needed in an actively engaged analysis. Likewise, Neil's parents had to at least minimally deal with each other and cooperate with me and with Neil's drug treatment. The fact that Neil was able to remain clean and sober in the year ahead seems an indication that he felt his underlying identification with a dead object was altered. He could face life awake if he had awake objects.

My confrontation also allowed Neil to "make a thought thinkable" (Alvarez, 1992) to compare my attitude with his and his parents' attitudes[10] toward his substance abuse and make differentiations. Neil became more able to think about and curb his own over-permissiveness. His growing perspective on his parents reflected his mind coming to life and was more than just externalization of blame.

Retrospectively, I thought that several factors eventually helped Neil to stop abusing drugs and alcohol. First, interpretive work allowed Neil some window into the functioning of his mind and his relationships that permitted him to think and talk with me. Second, a boundary seemed to wake Neil up from his withdrawal into substance abuse. Crashing up against a limit with an analyst or parent often seems necessary to meet the numbing and deadening effects of substance abuse. Third, entrance into a substance abuse treatment program entailed a semi-public acknowledgement of a problem — important because of the secrecy and denial in this family. His parents' oblivion to his troubles made Neil feel he had dead and useless objects. He had little sense that an emotional problem could be understood and met. Undoubtedly, elements of the program itself were also helpful.[11] Finally, the crisis required Neil's parents to look at his pain and make some contribution to the solution. For instance, his father stopped drinking himself to support his son's sobriety.

My own experience of this crisis was of being forced to grow. I felt deeply for this boy and was frightened and challenged by his problems. My feeling of urgency and alarm for Neil reflected his unconscious communication that valuable parts of him were in peril. Prior to this case, I might have felt it as something of a failure for an analysis to require substance abuse treatment. This case made clear to me how much the analyst of an adolescent has to be able to go where the adolescent needs her to go. My patient needed me to be able to question preconceived ideas to accompany him. While this patient struggled with a particularly "dead object," I believe that adolescents can often throw down the gauntlet of self-destructiveness to see if their objects are alive and awake and ready to accompany them through arduous changes.

In addition to the non-interpretive interventions required in this case, such as limit setting, this case also raises issues in terms of an analytic understanding of collaborative care. At times patients can feel rejected when a referral for additional care is made, as if we are unwilling to know a part of them, or are abandoning them. I did not think that was the case with Neil. He suffered from a lack of coopera-tive parenting in which differences are put aside on a child's behalf. Both parents loved him (in a rather ineffectual manner), but had not been able to work together for him. Seeing adults cooperate on his behalf helped Neil to internalize a feel-ing of usable and alive love that can sustain difficulties. While Herbert Rosenfeld (1960/1966) and Green (1983) discuss deadness in terms of a primary object, I am extending this conceptualization to that of a "dead parental couple." Neil had no current evidence of a couple that loved him enough to bear the difficulties of col-laborating. The lived experience of bringing his parents together to function as parents for him could allow some revision of internal object representations. A deadened couple, previously seeming incapable of awakening on behalf of their children could be aroused somewhat.

While not ideal, Neil's parents' response did allow some experience of a coop-erating parental couple, making them more real parents to Neil. In addition to his experience of a "dead mother," Neil's neglect of the safety of his own mind and body communicated the neglectful containment shared by his parents. His parents were in denial of the harm inflicted on their son by their refusal to function together as parents, unconsciously isolating Neil with a sense of neglect. Neil's ability to move away from his substance abuse was facilitated by a beginning experience of a live object in the transference-countertransference, a limit-setting parental couple that could function somewhat on his behalf, and some sense of the larger community (as represented by the drug treatment program) having some help to offer him. In this case, I believe that interpretation alone without confrontation, involvement of the parents, and ancillary care would have been insufficient and been experienced by Neil as my not really being alive and awake. This work also helped me to register more deeply the unconscious object relations involved in symptoms and the way an "awake" object needs to be internalized for an adolescent to begin to face life with less overwhelming need for his symptoms.

Notes

1 Dodes (2003) contends that there can be a variety of motivations for addiction including self-medication, affect regulation, object substitution, etc. It is beyond the scope of this chapter to consider the multiple determinants of addiction, which include genetic, neurological, gender, social and cultural contributions. Rather, I am trying to explicate the complex familial relations and internalizations of these relations, which can be addressed in the psychoanalytic setting. Dodes adds that "(P)atients with addictions run the gamut of mental health and their analyzability depends upon their overall level of psychological function, not their addiction" (p. 123).

2 Sabshin (1995), working from an ego-psychological model (not utilizing concepts such as "unconscious object relations" or "projective identification") could be seen as describing a dead, absent or neglectful object when she says:

> (M)any contemporary psychoanalytic workers view addictive behavior not primarily as a self-destructive impulse, but as a deficit of adequate internalization of parental figures with subsequent impairment of the capacity for self-protection… (A) considerable body of research literature describes a frequent association of personality disorders and depression with drug addiction.
>
> (p. 7)

3 Herbert Rosenfeld (1960/1966) comments that treating the drug addicted is particularly difficult because the analyst:

> …is confronted with the combination of a mental state and the intoxication and confusion caused by drugs. As a severely intoxicated patient is not accessible to analysis, an attempt has to be made from the beginning of the treatment, or when the drug addiction is diagnosed while the patient is under analysis, to get the severe drugging under control, and the patient has to accept either private nursing or residence in a nursing home or hospital. If the patient accepts the condition of control of the drugging, analysis can proceed… The control cannot be too severe and absolute because this would amount virtually to imprisonment of the patient, a situation which he would experience as a punishment and not as help in his attempt to give up the drugs.
>
> (p. 128)

4 Director (2002), from a relational perspective, suggests that the chronic alcohol or drug user with his action orientation, particularly requires an active approach in treatment to feel meaningfully engaged, and even "gripped" by the analyst (p. 555).

5 Yorke (2003) describes that in addiction, the need for the addictive substance is a major preoccupation:

> …the addict is prepared to do almost *anything,* including steal and lie, to satisfy his/ her craving. There are, necessarily limitations on the lengths to which any given person is prepared to go to achieve this end, but those limits may become increasingly elastic as addiction takes greater hold and internal resistances loosen.
>
> (p.44)

My patient's dream seemed to represent his own unconscious concern about his increasing addiction.

6 Klein's (1935) concept of the importance of reparative processes in relation to depression is useful here. She regards reparation as a normal mechanism of overcoming depressive anxieties. Depression results when reparative mechanisms are interfered with, such as here by the break-up. Klein sees "the dread of harbouring dying and dead objects, especially the parents inside, and an identification of the ego with objects" (p. 26) in children and adults suffering from depression. Neil's experience of loving and being loved by his girlfriend reassured him of his capacity for loving and being loved. When this love was disturbed, he was returned to despair and fear that he could not enliven his object. Klein sees the sense of despair in depression as related to the feeling of failure in an individual to secure his good internalized object.

7 Neil clearly met the diagnostic criteria for Cannabis Use Disorder in the DSM-5 (2013). New to DSM-5 is the recognition that:

> …abrupt cessation of daily or near-daily cannabis use often results in the onset of cannabis withdrawal syndrome. Common symptoms of withdrawal include irritability, anger or aggression, anxiety, depressed mood, restlessness, sleep difficulty, and decreased appetite or weight loss.
>
> (p. 511)

8 Anderson (2000) describes the capacity of a patient to care for and help himself as crucial in an assessment of self-harm.

9 Green attended seminars with Herbert Rosenfeld and was influenced by his work (Kohon, 1999).

10 Part of the difficulty of the work with Neil was that he had internalized his parents' tendency to evade difficulties. Unconsciously dominated modes of relating are active in families as well as in individuals. In analytic work with parents, unconscious issues are addressed both by interpretation as well as by actions, such as my referral for substance abuse treatment. I have discussed Bionian conceptuatalizations of the family group when children are in psychotherapy or psychoanalysis elsewhere (Brady, 2011). I would consider this family as dominated by an unconscious group process of flight from anxiety.

11 The program had professionally trained staff and also utilized an A.A./twelve step model for groups. In her psychoanalytic studies of addictive behaviors, Sabshin (1995) comments:

> …although AA promotes the disease model, its methods actually address psychological needs and facilitate personality change. Abstinence is achieved in the context of a concerned and caring community of fellow-sufferers. This experience with caring figures can be internalized; in a similar manner self-concern, self-control, and self-esteem can be internalized from a psychotherapist.
>
> (p. 6)

She sees AA as helping the alcohol abuser with impulse control and affect management, which benefit can be extended by therapeutic efforts to facilitate insight. Others, such as Dodes (2002, 2003) are critical of the AA model for a variety of reasons, including "unintentionally demeaning alcoholics by setting them apart as if they were different from people with other emotional symptomatology" (2003, p. 128).

References

Alvarez, A. (1992). Making the thought thinkable: perspectives on introjection and projection. In: *Live Company: Psychoanalytic Psychotherapy with Autistic, Borderline, Deprived and Abused Children.* New York: Routledge, pp. 77–91.

Anderson, R. (2000). Assessing the risk of self-harm in adolescents: a psychoanalytical perspective. *Psychoanalytic Psychotherapy,* 14, pp. 9–21.

Bion, W. (1962). *Learning from Experience.* New York: Basic Books.

Brady, M.T. (2011). The individual in the group: An application of Bion's group theory to parent work in child analysis and child psychotherapy. *Contemporary Psychoanalysis,* 47, pp. 420–437.

Director, L. (2002). The value of relational psychoanalysis in the treatment of chronic drug and alcohol use. *Psychoanalytic Dialogues,* 12, pp. 551–579.

Dodes, L. (2002). *The Heart of Addiction.* New York: Harper Collins.

Dodes, L. (2003). Addiction and psychoanalysis. *Canadian Journal of Psychoanalysis,* 11, pp. 123–134.

Flechner, S. (2005). On aggressiveness and violence in adolescence. *International Journal of Psychoanalysis,* 86, pp. 1391–1403.

Green, A. (1983). The dead mother. In: *On Private Madness.* London: Hogarth Press, pp.142–173.

Klein, M. (1935). A contribution to the psychogenesis of manic-depressive states. *International Journal of Psychoanalysis,* 16, pp. 145–174.

Kohon, G. (1999). Introduction. In: *The Dead Mother – The Work of Andre Green.* New York: The New Library of Psychoanalysis, Routledge, pp. 1–9.

Rosenfeld, D. (2006). Drug abuse, regression, and primitive object relations. In: *The Soul, the Mind, and the Psychoanalyst: The Creation of the Psychoanalytic Setting in Patients with Psychotic Aspects.* London: Karnac, pp. 77–116.

Rosenfeld, H. (1966). On drug addiction. In: *Psychotic States: A Psycho-Analytical Approach.* New York: International Universities Press, Inc., pp. 128–143. (Original work published 1960)

Sabshin, E. (1995). Psychoanalytic studies of addictive behavior: a review. In: S. Dowling (Ed.), *The Psychology and Treatment of Addictive Behavior.* American Psychoanalytic Association Monograph 8. Madison, CT: International Universities Press, pp. 3–15.

Winnicott, D.W. (1958). The anti-social tendency. In: *Through Paediatrics to Psychoanalysis.* London: Tavistock, pp. 306–315.

Yorke, C. (2003). Commentary on "Understanding addictive vulnerability." *Neuropsychoanalysis,* 5, pp. 42–53.

Chapter 7

Substance use as part of a pathological organization

Disturbing the persecutor/protector of an adolescent girl

Kristin Fiorella

Gone child

I began seeing 'Margaret' when she was 16. When I met with her mother, Nari, prior to meeting Margaret, Nari struggled to describe why Margaret was requesting therapy. Hovering over this consultation was the significant trauma this family had endured, although Nari insisted that that had nothing to do with Margaret's request. Both Nari and Yohan, Margaret's father, were second-generation Korean Americans. Yohan had been a successful businessman who had died of a heart attack when Margaret was nine. Nari's therapist told me Yohan was demanding and cruel with all of the children.

Margaret had been diagnosed with an auditory processing disorder as a child. This disorder was presumed to be purely neurological in origin and yet, for some unknown reason, according to Nari, it was suddenly causing Margaret emotional distress and shame. One last thing: Nari described Margaret as the quietest of her four children. The other three, she said, struggled significantly. One was severely depressed and had taken a leave from school. Another was about to be released from a residential treatment program for an eating disorder. Margaret was "basically fine," Nari said. She has friends but no close friends. I felt unsettled by the thinness of Nari's description of Margaret and also by how mystified Nari seemed by the disturbance of her other children.

Not long after, Margaret came to see me. At the appointed hour, I found her alone in the waiting room outside my office, looking at the ground. When I said her name, Margaret looked up slowly, as if I might have been addressing some other Margaret nearby. She stood and walked cautiously to my office. Margaret then sat down and looked in my direction, as if waiting for me to begin. Margaret seemed to have no idea why she was in my office or what we might speak about. I shared with her my limited understanding of what brought her in, and I asked questions to draw her out. Margaret answered but never elaborated. I had a sense of a profound inner blankness and absence, as if Margaret had given up on relationships.

Our second session unfolded in a similar fashion, and I began to wonder if some disturbance in Margaret's life had broken down her defensive organization, prompting her to seek help. Perhaps distress about her auditory processing disorder

DOI: 10.4324/9781003647317-9

had just been a frame that Margaret used to communicate her need for help. Whatever this disturbance had been, however, Margaret appeared to have dissociated both from it and the subsequent breakdown and now to be using treatment, unconsciously, as a means of reestablishing her pre-existing dissociative organization. I felt I was in danger of colluding with this dissociative falseness in my effort to structure and drive our communication.

Toward the end of our third hour, as Margaret sat quietly, I said, "I don't think you're here."

To my surprise, she looked at me with presence and nodded: *Yes. I am not here.*

In our fourth hour, Margaret began to describe an experience of what she called "blanking out." Margaret blamed this on her auditory processing disorder and said that she increasingly experienced it with everyone in her life. I felt, but did not say, that her auditory processing disorder was, at best, peripheral to whatever was going on. I wondered if, in an encapsulated part of her, she was what Paul Williams (2022) refers to as a "Gone child … unable to know anything, … learn or change." Such children may learn something from experience, Williams writes, "but if the learning apparatus is stillborn, adaptation is the sole option, there being no one available to learn anything."

I began to sense in Margaret a kind of tenuous false self that allowed her to move through home and school without attracting attention. Her diagnosis of an auditory processing disorder helped obscure her profound dissociation and supported her masquerade as a functioning person who participated in life. My recognition of this seemed to stimulate, in Margaret, a very weak object-seeking dimension of her mind. She began to reach towards me and even report on the events of her day – a TV show, an interaction in a class, a friend that she wasn't sure if she liked. Each of these topics engaged Margaret only briefly before she lost animation again. I felt as though Margaret were throwing out fragments of her day to see if one might find a life between us. As each failed to do so, she slid back into a haze. I tried describing to Margaret what I sensed of this, but my description also felt lifeless.

Gradually, Margaret began to describe how isolated she felt. In speaking to others, Margaret said, she mimicked what she believed to be thoughtful comments but could never tell if she got it right. Margaret felt bored by her relationships and disliked her friends. I suggested that her boredom made sense: these relationships were more like imitations of relationships. Margaret seemed mildly interested in this idea. In our next hour together, Margaret said she had thought about it and decided she did not want to "really be" in any of her relationships.

"It's more trouble than it's worth," Margaret said.

"I think something troubling has happened to you," I replied. "If you were really *in* relationships, something bad could happen again."

Margaret looked at me and nodded slightly.

I said that she seemed more open with me.

Margaret agreed and said that she was surprised by how much she told me.

Sharing her experience went very much against the grain, for her, I said.

She agreed. It made her very anxious, she said, and sometimes she dreaded coming to see me.

After an hour in which she made meaningful contact with me, Margaret showed up for the next session withdrawn and dissociated, often claiming not even to remember the prior hour. Although I was still quite in the dark about much of what she was experiencing, I began to suspect that she had what Rosenfeld, in 1971, described as a pathological organization–a tightly knit structure of psychic defense meant to keep one safe from overwhelming feelings that arise in contact with others. In Margaret's case, some dimension of her mind experienced the possibility of connection with me as deeply threatening. The role of the pathological organization, then, would be to obliterate any bond between us that began to form and return Margaret to the safety of an anesthetized state. I also wondered about Margaret's drug use. Her relationships felt so thin that I felt it likely that drugs were part of what held them together. I did not ask at this point in the treatment, as I did not feel that she would feel ready to tell me, and I did not want to put her in a position where she would need to lie.

Sadistic annihilation and a thing-like pact

Several months into our work together, Margaret began talking about her father's cruelty. During her childhood, she said, he was obsessed with cleanliness and routinely conveyed disgust with Margaret for her dirtiness, which she took to signify his global rejection of her. When he was upset with Margaret, he filled the bathtub with water, put her inside, turned off the lights, and shut the door. Margaret said that her father did not lock the bathroom door, but he didn't need to. She didn't experience herself as someone who could open the door. Margaret always just sat in the dark water, she said, until her mother appeared and turned on the lights and told her to get out.

Margaret's father, it seemed to me, had evacuated some unbearable feeling of contamination into Margaret while her mother offered neither protection nor containment. The bathtub memories seemed to me a site of annihilation, as Margaret described the shattering of her self, and I felt this experience of terrifying fragmentation had made her vulnerable to the pseudo-structure of a pathological organization. She surrendered to her father's sadism, incorporating it as a powerful, omniscient internal presence. At this point in the treatment, I still had only a vague picture of Margaret's pathological organization, but I felt increasingly confident that she experienced this sadistic internalized figure as a protector. In this way, she had become a nonhuman thing in a relatively stable system.

Margaret also began to reveal experiences of depersonalization that felt more disturbed. She spoke of feeling that the world was a "simulation chamber" in which everyone was unaware that it was all artificially manufactured and made to look real. This putative insight gave Margaret an almost religious feeling of superiority: the world was false but Margaret had transcended that falseness by retreating into a private realm with her cynical protector.

During hours in which Margaret was emotionally connected to herself and to me, we spoke of her sense of the world as simulation in terms of two related dimensions.

First, whenever Margaret felt something with me, she quickly felt deeply threatened and dissociated. This kept her radically detached from other people and also from any embodied connection to herself, thereby leaving her vulnerable to depersonalization. Margaret also mimicked–simulated–whatever she thought might pass as a "normal response" to interactions. In this very straightforward sense, then, her life *was* a simulation chamber–protecting her from anxiety and pain by allowing her to function only as a hollow actor.

The second dimension of Margaret's simulation chamber had to do with suspicious circumstances surrounding her father's death. She had reason to wonder if he had taken his own life and thought her mother and siblings wondered too, although they had never spoken about it. They all pretended to believe that Margaret's father died of natural causes–yet another simulation. After talking about this with me, Margaret decided to ask her mother, who claimed to have been curious about the possibility of suicide and to have ordered an autopsy only to have it identify the cause of death as, again, heart attack. For Margaret, this shut a door. I was not convinced but did not say so. I said, "Regardless, you and your mother both felt that your father was someone who *could have* committed suicide." This idea helped Margaret continue to think about her father's suicidality and self-destructive behavior.

Five months into treatment, Margaret and I stopped for a few weeks so that she could travel with family. When Margaret returned, she said that she had been depressed while away. This was unusual for Margaret–reporting directly on a feeling state–and I read it as a sign of our deepening connection with me, albeit amidst her enduring dissociative emptiness. Margaret then told me that she felt strongly that her mother could not tolerate having another kid who was struggling. One of her brothers was still seriously depressed. Her sister used drugs and had severe anorexia and a violent temper.

Having raised her sister's drug use, I asked Margaret about her own. It turned out that she had started using marijuana a few years earlier and now found herself turning to it more and more frequently. As we explored her increased use, it was clear that as she had become more aware of her internal world, she was increasing her marijuana use. I took that as a sign that she felt overwhelmed by what was emerging, and I wondered if she needed more from me. I suggested that we add a fourth hour. She agreed.

Our sessions still oscillated between those marked by painful emotional connection and those in which Margaret seemed once again vacant. The more we spoke of her drug use, the more I suspected that it had become an operant element within her pathological organization. The dissociative states brought on by marijuana supported Margaret's thing-like tie with the cruel internal protector who demanded allegiance to the idea of the world as fabricated. In return for this dissociated, drug-induced allegiance, Margaret was kept safe from the disintegrating anxiety that characterized her childhood. Drug use also permitted Margaret to remain complicit in her family's unknowingness about the death of Margaret's father. Even then, I suspected that drug use had also been critical to the stability of Margaret's deadening organization, although I did not appreciate just how dangerous it might be to undermine that stability.

Pathological organizations

When I first started working with Margaret, I thought of her as mostly just dissociated, if profoundly so. Over time, though, I began to think in terms of two related theoretical constructs. The first of these, Rosenfeld's notion of the pathological organization (1971), is an omnipotent part of the self that threatens and controls a saner, more object-seeking part. Precursors to this idea include Fairbairn's internal saboteur and Bion's differentiation between nonpsychotic states of mind and psychotic ones that attack links with others in order to avoid pain (Williams 2014). In pathological organizations, a destructive, seemingly all-knowing aspect of the self fights to prevent dependence on other people. Rosenfeld refers to this as a kind of "mafia" organization and reports that violent criminal gangs often appear in the dreams of patients with such internal structures. This internal mafia draws the patient's weak ego into a kind of protection racket, a dream of being cut off from all pain and anxiety in exchange for giving up on growth and human connection.

The second theoretical construct that helped my thinking about Margaret was Steiner's idea of psychotic psychic retreat. In his *Psychic Retreats* (1993), Steiner described these states as manifestations of underlying pathological organization. Psychotic psychic retreats, in Steiner's account, arise as a kind of refuge or pseudo-structure for a mind chaotically fragmented by trauma and provide a relatively stable refuge from reality.

As Margaret's delusional world provided a much-needed sense of order, her psychotic retreat, in my estimation, incorporated aspects of her family's obscuration of multiple traumas. It also amplified that obscuration to psychotic dimensions, transmuting it into the very fabric of reality. Margaret's was no longer a world in which caretakers told lies; it was a simulation chamber in which everyone's thoughts were programmed by some unknown force. With the accompaniment of her internal figure, Margaret could feel that she had transcended her need for that false world and all its simulated human inhabitants. Margaret's psychotic world was not so successful that she wasn't still vulnerable to feelings of depersonalization, but at least she was less terrorized by the risk of outright disintegration.

Viewed through this lens, Margaret's drug use was integral to the economy of her psychic retreat, supporting the mandate of Margaret's internal figure that she remain a thing-like entity. I suspected that the sadism of her pathological organization had been soothed by her use of substances, but I did not anticipate the violence of what would emerge if she stopped using drugs entirely.

Margaret told me that she had been using Xanax purchased on the black market. I told Margaret that street Xanax can be laced with other, dangerous drugs and asked her if she would consider quitting its use and seeing a psychiatrist. Margaret agreed and a psychiatrist quickly prescribed Lamictal. He told Margaret that she would need to stop using not only Xanax but also marijuana, as the latter could increase the side effects of Lamictal. Margaret obliged and rapidly decompensated.

In many fairy tales and folklore, a once-benevolent figure turns diabolical. In Rapunzel, for example, an enchantress hides the princess in a tower. Only when the prince enters and the space becomes triangular–rather than dyadic–does the enchantress suddenly become a raging witch. Something similar occurred to Margaret's psychotic internal figure. While still using drugs, she experienced that figure as protective. Without drugs, this internal object's mandate was threatened and it became significantly more sadistic and hateful, telling Margaret that the world was murderous and everyone would be better off if she were to take her own life.

Steiner (1987) also described patients oscillating, just like Margaret, between pathological organization and paranoid/schizoid and depressive anxieties. While using drugs, Margaret would often move within a session from the safety of her pathological organization into depressive guilt about her hatred of her parents and her imminent destruction of herself. Then, between sessions, she would move into a paranoid/schizoid position where I was experienced as an extreme threat, and she returned to her pathological organization, in which she remained during the next hour. In the subsequent hour, she would re-emerge and find a depressive position from which she could describe what had happened after our prior contact with her pain. Once Margaret quit using drugs, her oscillations between depressive and paranoid/ schizoid positions and her pathological organization were rapid and extreme, fluctuating minute-by-minute within a session.

Paul Williams writes of the need for the analyst to find a triangular space within the pathological organization (2004, 2014). Through tracking and interpreting the nature of the pathological organization, its demands and its threats. In this way, the analyst works to break the patient's fusion with her pathological organization and strengthen her ego. But Williams also warns of the inherent danger: relinquishment of a pathological organization for a dependent relationship with a fallible human analyst can resurface the anxiety of fragmentation and annihilation. In the face of this catastrophe, according to Williams, there is sometimes a period of psychosis as the patient untangles from identification with the pathological object. For Margaret, I have come to believe, psychosis was a critical part of her pathological organization from the beginning. As she began to experience triangulation and as she stopped her substance use, her psychosis became more openly hateful and terrorizing.

Killing her mother/me/herself

In the absence of marijuana and recreational Xanax, Margaret's sense of herself as a nonhuman thing in an unreal world began to express itself in full-blown delusions. A voice told her that others should not be trusted and were mere simulations anyway. She felt that people were possessed. If someone seemed kind, there was doubtless a more violent person hidden inside. Perhaps this more violent person would kill her.

K: I imagine you feel this with me too.
M: Yes. I do … Are you mad?
K: I'm not. But that might not feel believable … I think you're worried that I could hurt you, kill you.
M: I'm told not to trust you.

I felt, in Margaret, a negotiation between her desire for me to know what was happening inside and her anxiety about the threat I posed to her pathological organization and the concomitant hateful attacks she faced from the internal figure at the center of it for any emotional links she forged with me. I felt guilty for having not anticipated the degree to which drug use stabilized Margaret's psychotic world. During this period, I was in frequent communication with Margaret's mother, Nari, and also with Margaret's psychiatrist who added an antipsychotic. Then, as we were assessing if she needed to be hospitalized, I got a voicemail from Nari saying that Margaret had made a suicide attempt and was in the hospital.

When I spoke to Nari, she said that Margaret consumed a bottle of Advil and told her sister but instructed her sister not to tell anyone else. Margaret's sister had disobeyed that order and told Nari who took Margaret to the hospital and called me. It was clear that Margaret needed a longer hospital stay so that she could be stabilized, and we could create a plan. We got her into a residential psychiatric ward, and I spoke with Margaret by telephone several times during her weeks in that facility. Margaret was afraid that I would be angry with her because of her attempted suicide. She said she had only done it–taken the Advil–because the internal voice told her she needed to die. Margaret said that unfamiliar memories were now surfacing, too. She wanted me to know about these memories, but felt unready to tell me. Upon her release, Margaret took a leave from school. She joined an intensive outpatient program for early psychosis, submitted to drug-use monitoring, and resumed treatment with me.

Over the next several months, as we got back to meeting four times a week, I was surprised to find Margaret periodically engaged and thoughtful. She was genuinely frightened by her self-destructiveness but sometimes shifted into an excited identification with it. During periods of lucidity, Margaret wanted to know how it was possible to hate her father so much while simultaneously missing him. In some moments, exploring this seemed generative for Margaret. At other times, Margaret's bond to her father seemed utterly incomprehensible to her. Margaret could not understand it in any straightforward way. She needed me to know and resonate with this. The extreme trauma she had suffered as a result of her father's cruelty was simply unassimilable by its very nature, as it involved death of Margaret's self that had never been experienced and therefore continuously reappeared. As it did, both the rupture in Margaret's being and the ungraspable nature of that rupture were repeated. Equally unassimilable, for Margaret, was the very fact of father's death. As I have mentioned earlier, she had legitimate reasons to suspect that he had taken his own life–perhaps by consuming something that triggered a fatal heart attack. At times, Margaret felt as if a lie hung over the entire family, disturbing her siblings as well.

The pain and anxiety of bearing the incomprehensible dimensions of her trauma often drove Margaret back into the relative certainty of her old pathological organization–retreating into angry silence and telling me, with contempt, "I'm fine. I don't even know why I'm here. I might not come back." In the next hour, Margaret invariably failed to remember why she had been angry and worried that I might retaliate. Margaret was sometimes aware that she did need others, including me, and she found this unbearable. As Rosenfeld puts it, a person with a pathological organization, when exposed to the degree of their dependence on others, will often prefer to die and thereby disappear into the safety of oblivion (1971).

Margaret had already conveyed her longing to die in her suicide attempt and she often reminded me that this desire for death was still present. She sometimes taunted me with the possibility that she might try again.

"Poor you, you can't help me," she said.

At other times, Margaret said with despair that her voice insisted everyone would be better off if Margaret were dead. Nari knew that Margaret was too suicidal to be left alone and this, too, created turbulence. Margaret felt increasingly rageful at her mother's neglect but also anxious that her mother might fall apart. Margaret seemed to believe that her own suicide could convey this fury to her mother without burdening Margaret herself with guilt for Nari's unraveling. In the midst of this, the two of them were constantly together, and Margaret was not allowed to shut her bedroom door.

Over time, Margaret became furious with me for having disrupted her anesthetized state and thereby awakened her pain. She felt that I had ripped away the only protection she had and was either too weak or too hateful to help any further. At other moments, Margaret worried that I would get fed up and abandon her. She oscillated quickly between three transferences–seeing me as, alternately, a weak and neglectful mother, a hateful mother, and a potentially loving mother.

In one hour, Margaret wept as she described feeling that, as a child, she had not even existed. Only moments later, Margaret said, "This is pointless. I don't want to come tomorrow. I hate coming here. I hate you."

K: You were feeling so much pain just now. You are frightened and hate me–

M: Yes, I hate you. You like watching this happen. And then I'll go home and you'll…

K: I won't be there. You feel I'm opening you to all this pain and leaving you alone with it.

M: It's ok. I can always kill myself.

K: You were just telling me you already died. We're trying to help you find a way to live.

M: What if I don't want to? You want me to live because you'd feel bad if I die.
K: I would be very sad if you died.

I made that last comment out of desperation and immediately worried that it would provoke Margaret's sadism. To my surprise, she softened and seemed touched. We were quiet for a while. In the following hour, Margaret sat for the first twenty minutes in an angry, paranoid silence. I told her that I wondered if she was being punished for her previous openness. I offered drawing materials, as she sometimes she liked to make sketches during tense hours. She took them and drew what looked to me like a tight muscle. I felt Margaret relax, so I began to relax as well.

K   I think the voice is here… telling you not to talk to me.
       She nods. Several minutes pass.
M: I don't know what's happening.
K: Are you unsafe?
       She nods.
K: It's so confusing. You don't know if talking with me could help or make things worse.
       She nods again
K: Did you start feeling scared on your way here?
M: No, at school. It started at school.
K: Did something happen?
M: I can't tell you.
K: I see.
M: I don't want to listen to it. (She cries. We're quiet for a bit).
K: You want to be able to tell me what's happening. But the voice is telling you not to. When you're open with me, painful, scary feelings come up.
M: And you're not there.
K: You know you can call or text me.
M: I don't want to.
K: You want me to be there and I'm not. It feels like I opened something painful and then you're on your own… The voice tells you not to trust me.
M: It's right. It's part of me.
       (I'm surprised by this and it seems progressive that she owns this voice as part of herself.)
K: You're right. It's part of you. I don't think it's all of you.
       She nudges her drawing toward me to show me.

Return to substances

It soon became apparent that Margaret had started using marijuana and Xanax again. Now, though, her drug use seemed less about compliance with her internal other and more about communicating with external others–namely, her mother and myself. Margaret clearly wanted to terrorize us both, and prove that we could not stop her from harming herself. In a way, this struck me as a positive change. Margaret now lived in a world inhabited by objects towards whom she could express rage. Yet, I feared this situation was untenable. Margaret began to report risky behavior, sometimes provocatively. She reported unsafe sex and driving while high to a bridge to sit on its edge. I worried that she would again attempt suicide, and perhaps die that way.

I met with Nari several times and tried to awaken her to the danger in which I felt Margaret to be. I urged Nari to move Margaret to a higher level of care. Nari seemed in an overwhelmed stupor and somehow dimly convinced that I would keep Margaret safe because Margaret was attached to me. Only when I made it clear several times that I could not keep Margaret safe did Nari agree to find another residential setting for Margaret.

As Nari searched for an appropriate facility, Margaret made it clear that she did not want this. She was doing fine, she said, and needed neither her mother or myself. At other times, Margaret said that she did not want to stop seeing me and felt that I was abandoning her. She had a point. I did not feel that I had a choice but, at some level, I was abandoning her.

During this period, I had dreams of despair over leaving Margaret in this way. We spoke about how difficult it was for Margaret as she became more aware of her rage, to be at home with her mother. She wanted to convey this to her mother but worried that it would cause her mother to collapse. So, instead, Margaret conveyed her rage through increasingly self-destructive behavior–as if still maintaining a murderous pact with her father. In still other moments, Margaret spoke as if leaving home might allow her to have a future.

Enacted abandonment

Margaret was ultimately transferred to a residential treatment facility. I helped with the transition and collaborated with Margaret's new treatment team. As we said good-bye, Margaret expressed what felt like genuine gratitude toward me, but I also felt she was anxious that I was getting rid of her, and she wanted to prop me up. She had frequently expressed that I had opened her to excruciating realities that I could not protect her from. This termination seemed to reinforce that, and I felt guilty that we would enact yet another abandonment. I was also relieved that Margaret would no longer be in her home and would be kept safe, at least for a while.

When she first got to the treatment facility, Margaret became paranoid, refused to eat, and complained that the staff were trying to poison her. After several weeks, though, Margaret settled in. She stayed in that facility for a year. Upon her release, Margaret wanted to restart treatment with me. At the time, I was only one month from maternity leave, which I dreaded telling her. So, I found a colleague to work with Margaret.

I stayed in communication with this therapist, and she conveyed that Margaret still could not allow herself to feel angry with me. Margaret needed to hold onto me as an idealized object, it seemed, and perhaps also to protect me from her rage. Margaret later returned to residential treatment and stayed another couple of months. She has since been out for several years. She wrote to me recently, saying that she had finished her first year of college, and expressing hope for the future. She wanted me to know, now, about the memories that she had been unable to share during treatment. Unsurprisingly, these involved sexual abuse by her father. She wrote, "I worked really hard to get to a place where I am not as ashamed of what happened to me. I am really grateful that I was able to get help."

Final comments

I had not anticipated that the character of Margaret's pathological organization would shift so dramatically without her substance use. When it did, Margaret's overwhelmed mother was not in a position to manage what unfolded. There was truth in Margaret's accusation that I had exposed her to pain that we could not contain, and she could not work this through with me. She preserved me as a good object but was not able to move to object usage (Winnicott, 1969). Her emails to me remain grateful, but it is hard to know if I am still a fragile object who cannot receive her rage. When Margaret asked to come back, I had refused her because of my real baby. To my knowledge, the pain and abandonment of that reality have yet to consciously emerge for Margaret.

References

Rosenfeld, Herbert. (1971). A Clinical Approach to the Psychoanalytic Theory of the Life and Death Instincts: An Investigation into the Aggressive Aspects of Narcissism. *International Journal of Psychoanalysis* 52: 169–178.

Steiner, John. (1987). The Interplay between Pathological Organizations and the Paranoid-Schizoid and Depressive Positions. *International Journal of Psychoanalysis* 68: 69–80.

Steiner, John. (1993). *Psychic Retreats*. London and New York: Routledge.

Williams, Paul. (2004). Incorporation of an Invasive Object. *International Journal of Psychoanalysis* 85: 1333–1348.

Williams, Paul. (2014). Orientations of Psychotic Activity in Defensive Pathological Organizations. *International Journal of Psychoanalysis* 95: 423–440.

Williams, Paul. (2022). *The Authority of Tenderness: Dignity and the True Self in Psychoanalysis*. London and New York: Routledge.

Winnicott, Donald W. (1969) The Use of an Object. *International Journal of Psychoanalysis* 50: 711–716.

Chapter 8

A shelter of numbness

Claudia Spadazzi

Over the last 20 years, the psychic structure of patients (Wu et al., 2023; Moreno et al., 2020) has seen some changes and, consequently, intervention techniques. Among other changes, psychoanalysts' attitudes towards addictions have also shifted quite radically. On the one hand, patients with various forms of dependency are being welcomed into therapy – and psychoanalysis offers different points of view on this theme. On the other hand, today's modern life presents a varied scenario of dependencies, from traditional drugs to new substances. Finally, Western society faces increasing behavioural or "sine substantia" dependencies, such as Internet (gaming and social media) addiction, Internet pornography addiction, shopping addiction and online gambling addiction.

I will discuss my work with Angelica from a double perspective, neuroscientific and psychoanalytic, or, more briefly, neuropsychoanalytic, focusing on the first two years of treatment. Angelica's psychological development was impaired, partly due to her cannabinoid dependence. The evolution of Angelica's capacity for symbolization, her capacity to use my mind as well as her own in the treatment, and the intensification of the transference–countertransference happened in conjunction with her gradual weaning off dependence on cannabinoids.

When we first met, Angelica was a 20-year-old young woman who seemed like a girl. She was unable to express herself regarding her affects, as well as events, dates, memories or projects. She would make no effort to communicate – to the point that, in the beginning, I wondered whether, alongside the obvious psychic withdrawal, there could have been a slight cognitive disorder. I was dubious as to the advisability of starting psychotherapy with this young woman who seemed like a girl on the verge of adolescence. A slender creature who would climb the stairs to my practice with such light elusiveness and appear on the doorstep as a frail young twig.

From the very beginning of her therapy, Angelica started to reveal a suffering she seemed unaware of and a distress that would be conveyed through her withheld giggles, fragmented sentences, choices of often approximate – sometimes missing – vocabulary … as if she was incapable of putting together a complete sentence. Every expression was either confused, unexpressed, incomplete, truncated and constantly interrupted by interjections, mumbles and giggles.

DOI: 10.4324/9781003647317-10

A gesture which was characteristic from the very beginning – and which she continued to perform until we, eventually, gave it an interpretation – consisted in holding her head with both hands, as if simulating madness or trying to contain within her skull something which was attempting to escape.

The first two years of Angelica's therapy were face to face. From the beginning, I considered visual mirroring as fundamental: as if the analyst's gaze could give greater sturdiness to this young patient's fragile Self. Angelica oscillated between surprisingly deep insights and a superficial disregard towards herself and the surrounding world. When we started to work together, her process of becoming-a-subject was at stake, the laborious appropriation of one's own psychic functioning as described by Cahn (1996).

Angelica also suffered from a compensated form of eating disorder. She restricted her eating and came to sessions, after a 40-minute walk, fasting or with a very low calorie intake. She found it normal to wake in early afternoon and have dinner as her first and only meal. She was very thin, and it was clear that she had an altered representation of her body. Body representation is the result of the combination of interoceptive and exteroceptive bodily processes, which interact with each other to modulate body experience (Zamariola et al., 2017). Body Image is a complex concept which was firstly highlighted in 1934 by Schilder, a trained psychoanalyst and psychiatrist who described it as a function of the brain which allows a person's inside view. According to this author, body image is the representation of our own body we form in our mind. Schilder was a forerunner of intersubjectivity and clarified how Body Image construction is influenced by several factors. Since then, the multifaceted concept of Body Image has been enriched by many contributions, both philosophical and neurological (Dennet, 1991; Gallagher, 2005; de Vignemont, 2018; Merleau-Ponty, 1964; Tsakiris, 2010).

Intersubjective processes, unconscious dynamics, personal experiences, traumas and cultural and social environment, all contribute to create one's own Body Image (Gallagher, 2021). "Body image is in fact a complex construct that includes thoughts, feelings, evaluations and behaviors related to one's body. It refers to a conscious and explicit visual representation of the way our body appears as seen from the outside" (Sattin et al., 2023). The brain area more involved in the representation of one's own Body Image is the insula, an area whose neural circuits are strictly linked with emotions. As often happens in eating disorders, Angelica spoke of her body as a third object. According to some recent research, in eating disorders the sense of embodiment is lowered while agency is increased in terms of food control (Ben David & Ataria, 2021). Food avoidance helps attenuate emotional dysregulation, and avoidance mechanisms involve specific dopaminergic receptors of the nucleus accumbens. But Angelica seemed to enjoy food, she only restricted her number of meals and quantity of calories, in order to try to become thinner and thinner. Her constant worry about her weight and a general displeasure about her appearance was in contrast with her real prettiness.

Angelica struggled with eye contact, which she tried to avoid by covering part of her face with her long curly hair. I did not interpret her need to hide her face, waiting patiently for an internal movement that would signify that this need was starting to be overcome. In the second year of psychotherapy, "How do I look?" were the first doubtful words she said, entering my office with a lovely ponytail. The 'ponytail session' was a big step, and it inaugurated a long period of considerations about her appearance and trying hairstyles and dresses. Angelica was struggling to find a satisfying image of herself to exhibit in the first phase of some social exchange. She was trying to create a novel representation of her Self, a novel identity to test her interaction with possible social interlocutors.

Although she denied it in the beginning, the theme of addiction emerged as soon as an initial trust was established. Massive, daily use of cannabinoids and occasional use of cocaine went together with a series of behavioural alterations. Angelica's sleep–wake rhythm was severely altered: she never fell asleep before 5:00–6:00 a.m. and woke up around 2:00–3:00 p.m. Night hours were spent in her room, listening to music, watching TV and so on. She had withdrawn from any kind of social interaction except with one (girl) friend; the discontinuation of all studies, sports or play activities went together with the loss of any plans for her future. On the weekends, Angelica would spend evenings consuming excessive amounts of alcohol with her only friend, often finding herself in situations that were out of her control, and sometimes dangerous.

The lack of self-care is common in addictive patients. I worried about her during the weekends, not only for her abuse of alcohol and/or substances, but also for possible sexually risky behaviours and wandering about the town in an altered state of consciousness, in the middle of the night, or even at dawn. Regarding cannabinoids, Angelica denied being an addict, and, on the contrary, speculated as to its benefits: in her view, it resulted in increased lucidity, faster thinking, greater insight, more intense perceptions and feelings of well-being.

A: You see, being stoned is so pleasant, you just feel like you don't need anything else.
An: I see your point. But which kind of world do you live in when you are stoned? Maybe it is not so real…
A: It's not like that! It is a real world, actually it's better! One gets ideas you wouldn't get without hashish and you feel alert, things are more likeable, and you understand yourself much better…

At the time of the above interchange, Angelica lived a limited life generally confined to her very messy bedroom, where open drawers, shelves and cupboards were strewn with stuffed animals and stationery items – as if she were still in middle school. Angelica's room seemed to me the representation of her state of mind, a "psychic retreat" (Steiner, 1993), the symbolic "retreat to a refuge where the patient can feel relatively free from anxieties but where development was minimal" (p. 14).

Angelica asked for help because her withdrawn condition had worsened during her first year of university. She spent this year abroad, all alone, becoming heavily involved in substance abuse and starting to live a reclusive life in her apartment. Since then and during the first two years of psychotherapy, Angelica's withdrawal had been an element of isolation and loss of social contacts. It is necessary to take into consideration the impact of this isolation on Angelica's mind, in the age of the transition from adolescence to young adulthood.

Corona virus pandemic forced Angelica to return home, with just her mother (her sister lived in another city and at the time her mother was single). The Corona precautionary measures forced mother and daughter into a hitherto unthought-of and unthinkable rapprochement.

Angelica's mother is an actress. Her daughter described her as extremely beautiful, cold and distant and their relationship as always being detached. But during this period of proximity – due to Corona restrictions – Angelica suddenly confessed to her mother about the sexual abuse she had suffered from the age of 12 to 16. Being so close to her mother was a new experience for Angelica, and she probably felt "seen" for the first time. Mother had been in psychotherapy in the last few years and apparently was more in contact with her inner world, so that made Angelica feel safe enough to recall her traumatic experience. The abuser was a relative close to the family. The confusion of tongues between tenderness and passion pushed Angelica, in her pubertal age, in a state of confusion where she was not able to distinguish her perceptions and her feelings. Keeping in mind Ferenczi's words, we know how dissociation is the main consequence of experiences of abuse, and how much the identification with the aggressor contributes to the dissociation. From a neurological point of view, Schore (2009) suggests how the symptomatology of dissociation reflects a structural impairment of a right brain regulatory system and its accompanying deficiencies of affect regulation.

Angelica was sexually touched in a gentle and ambiguous way; she recalls feeling confused and distant at the same time and also feeling embarrassed and ashamed. She strongly tried to be elsewhere with her mind. Dissociation is a protective defence, as Bromberg writes:

> It is a defence against trauma, which, unlike defences against internal conflict, does not simply deny the self access to potentially threatening feelings, thoughts, and memories; it effectively obliterates, at least temporarily, the *existence* of that self to whom the trauma could occur, and it is in that sense like a 'quasi-death'. The rebuilding of linkages, the re-entry into life, involves pain not unlike that of mourning. The return to life means the recognition and facing of death; not simply the death of one's early objects as real people, but the death of those aspects of self with which those objects have been united. At the point the patient begins to abandon the instant and absolute 'truth' of dissociative reality in favour of internal conflict and human relatedness, the patient discovers that there is no path without pain.
>
> (1993, p. 154)

As a neglected child, Angelica was probably also flattered by the attention of an adult and desperately looking for a "privileged" relationship. The disproportion between the abuser's libido and the child's is one of most traumatic elements of sexual abuse. A sense of guilt and shame are also heavily involved, which derive partly from the abuser's, through an identification process, and partly from the perception of the child's own arousal. Angelica had never told anyone about having been abused. The retelling of the trauma to her mother brought about a breakthrough, and she herself called me to ask for an appointment.

Her parents have been separated since Angelica was eight years old. Both the separation and the divorce were extremely contentious. The father, a successful and powerful man, a film producer, has always been perceived by Angelica as judgmental, dismissive and incapable of emotional control. As a child, Angelica lacked self-confidence, feared him and would not dare to express her opinion in front of him. As a teenager, she started to experience feelings of oppositional anger. At the age of 17, during a weekend at her father's country house, a violent argument broke out between them. Very shaken, Angelica left the house, severing all relationships with him. When Angelica started therapy, she had not seen or heard from her father in four years.

During her second year of psychotherapy Angelica said:

A: I know that sooner or later I'll have to see my father again ... but I'm scared, it's too much, the idea of seeing him ... also, he would ask me what I'm up to, what I'm studying ... I can't tell him I stay in my room all day ... he would judge me too severely...

An: You have suffered a great deal, Angelica, ever since your childhood, and that's why you stay locked up in your room...

A: Yes, now I understand my own past much more clearly, but really I can't see him, it's impossible...

An: Do you think your father is in any way responsible for your present situation?

A: As a child, I wasn't allowed to decide anything in my life ... everything was already decided and planned by my parents, without taking my wishes or needs into consideration... My father insulted me all the time, he showed no respect, and he lost his temper very often ... until that last terrible scene, when I left his home forever. I was a few minutes late for lunch. He had guests. He came into my bathroom, shouting, while I was having a quick shower ... I felt ashamed and furious ... I know I should see him, but I really can't face it.

The father's narcissistic personality has prevented his emotional investment with Angelica and caused her deep feelings of worthlessness and anger.

Seesawing between her very formal good manners and her naive and fragmented communications, Angelica started to find words to describe her inner world, wherein her main affects were shame and anger.

After a few months of psychotherapy, I was surprised by Angelica's ability to express her feelings, which improved rapidly. She never missed a session and respected the setting with extreme precision. For the first two years, sessions were necessarily scheduled in the late afternoon. A cautious anticipation to the early afternoon and, finally, a shift to morning sessions were not only the result of the transference relationship intensification but also the progressive recovery of a normal sleep–wake rhythm.

In the month before our first summer vacation, Angelica felt anxious and nervous. We spoke about the period when she had lived very close to her mother, during the Corona virus, and she experienced, for the first time, a strong anxiety when her mother went to work and she remained alone at home. She recalled that she was surprised to fear that her mother could die in a car accident. Angelica linked the separation from her analyst to that period and felt relieved. But she asked to remain in contact over phone from time to time during my summer vacation, and so we did. Due to her early childhood experiences, Angelica was not able to tolerate an intimate relationship, but in the meantime was frightened by separation, which she perceived as a threatening abandonment.

According to Angelica's memories, it was clear that she was a neglected child from an emotional point of view, in contrast with her educational opportunities and affluent lifestyle. She remembered feeling lonely and abandoned in a limousine with a driver, often moved from one place to another like an object. I think Angelica felt how deeply I understood this feeling. There were no other family members involved in her infancy. But luckily, an affectionate caregiver was in charge to raise her for as long as she could remember. Meals, holidays and afternoons were spent with the caregiver until the age of ten. Since the beginning of the treatment, the quality of this close relationship with her caregiver seemed important to me for its function as an attachment figure and for the development of the transference.

Some research demonstrates that addicted individuals remember their dreams with difficulty, due to reduced REM brain activity. During the first two years of psychotherapy, probably due to the substance abuse, Angelica was unable to recall her dreams, beyond some rare, confused and generally very distressing images. One day, shortly before leaving on a family trip to Latin America, Angelica recalled a short but structured dream. This was the first trip she was planning, after some years of withdrawal. She was very ambivalent at the idea of leaving, and I myself had some worries about this important step.

A: I dreamt that I was preparing my luggage for the trip, in my room. On my bed, on the chairs, everywhere, there were lots of light, coloured, feminine dresses … dozens and dozens of them … I felt so happy and ready for this trip.

An: A short interesting dream, with many new things…

A: My first trip after so many years! Lovely dresses and colours, but generally speaking … how do I look?

An: You look like a girl who enjoys travelling and beautifully coloured dresses

I felt Angelica was relieved by this dream and I too felt the same relief: as if a light had appeared, the scene of her dreams and her unconscious was opening to more colourful libidinal images. It seemed to me that this was one of those "turning over a page" dreams, but in a way different than what Quinodoz (2002) describes, that is, the paradoxical dream which indicates a progression even if accompanied by anxiety and fear. I think this dream shows how "the manifest content of a dream can be a very useful indicator of the present therapeutic process, especially when it is accompanied by a widening of the affective spectrum and the appearance of positive affects" (Castellet et al., 2023, p. 7).

Ramachandran (2011), one of the most influential neurologists of this century, proposed a complex neuroscientific understanding of the Self. According to this author, the seven main characteristics of the Self are continuity, embodiment, coherence of Self, ownership or sense of agency, free will, social embedding and Self-awareness. Ramachandran writes:

> These seven aspects, like table legs, work together to hold up what we call the self. However, as you can already see, they are vulnerable to illusions, delusions, and disorders. The table of the self can continue to stand without one these legs, but if too many are lost then its stability becomes severely compromised.
>
> (2011, p. 201)

Considering some of the aspects of the Self described by this author, we can hypothesize that Angelica's traumatic childhood is one of the main factors of the impairment of those essential Self fundaments, increased by the abuse of cannabinoids. With some similarity to Winnicott's theory, Ramachandran first describes "continuity" as "a sense of unbroken thread running through the whole fabric of our experience with the accompanying feeling of past, present and future" (2004, pp. 96–98). Since the beginning of her treatment, Angelica's confusion regarding her past, the uncertainty of her present and the disinterest about her future made clear that the thread of continuity was severely frayed and with some breakage points. Since we first met, the patient seemed surprised and somehow pleased at the importance that the analyst attributed to our common work of restoration of continuity. I often had the impression of putting together pieces of a puzzle, where some were missing, at least for the moment. Secondly, Ramachandran describes "unity or coherence of Self": "in spite of the diversity of sensory experiences, memories, beliefs and thoughts, we each experience ourselves as one person, as a unity" (2004, pp. 96–98).

At the beginning of her treatment, I had the feeling that Angelica was on the edge of fragmentation, and her weakened coherence of Self was perceived partly with suffering, partly as being disoriented. The numbness, to which the title of this clinical case refers, was due to the dissociation she used as a defence mechanism, in a quite massive way. Third, "embodiment or ownership" can be understood from several perspectives. According to Ramachandran's point of view, embodiment is the "sense of being firmly anchored to our bodies" (2004, pp. 96–98). The body has a double inscription in the brain: a cortical inscription like an external object and a subcortical inscription as an internal body (Solms & Panksepp, 2021). Angelica did not feel "firmly anchored" to her slender body, on the contrary, she gave the impression of a feeling of detachment, sometimes as if her thin body was not really belonging to her.

Finally, as for "ownership or agency", Ramachandran's definition is "being in charge of our own action and destinies" (2004, pp. 96–98). Angelica could not feel in charge of her action, and even less of her destiny, as she was passively going with the flow. Passive immobility with a tendency to risky behaviours and self-harming conducts were underlying this flow. Angelica's Self-frailty determined the characteristics described and led her to suffering, low self-esteem, and basic emotional dysregulation. Within this frame, the use of substances was an illusory solution.

In his Self-Medication Hypothesis, Khantzian (1997) explains how addiction is a form of self-healing, when the individual is not able to tolerate his/her pain and rely on an external resource to mentally survive. He says: "Regulating emotions, self-esteem, relationships, and self-care are among the main functions upon which our survival depends. In my experience, individuals self-medicate the distress and pain associated with their self-regulation difficulties" (Khantzian, 2012, p. 275).

Substances and addictive behaviours can have different functions. In this clinical case, substance addiction seems to be able to create a numbing effect that will protect and isolate the patient from reality and succeeds in soothing the pain of a neglected and abused child. The framework is one of abandonment loneliness and massive absence of parental investment. This absence failed to supply psychic nourishment, capable of fostering development and growth. Moreover, I would like to point out how the shelter protected Angelica from her sexual drive. This protection kept her in a regressive position where she could avoid the guilt and shame caused by the sexual abuse suffered during puberty. The substance created a shelter of numbness, in which Angelica felt safe and protected. "Comfortably numb", as in the Pink Floyd song: "The child is grown, the dream has gone, and I have become comfortably numb…"

In my clinical experience, the neuro psychoanalytic perspective of addiction is extremely useful to understand the dynamics which underpin the need of a substance, as well as the compulsion in behavioural addiction. According to Panksepp (1998, 2005, 2007), Panksepp et al. (2012), the primary emotional systems involved in addictions are the SEEKING/REWARD system and the PANIC/GRIEF system. When the PANIC/GRIEF system is chronically activated, the attempt to self-heal through substances (Khantzian, 2012) is common, especially among adolescents.

Substances interact with receptors through neurotransmitters, offering a feeling of well-being which is brought on by the consumption of the substance. In the meantime, the substances also determine a progressive decrease of the SEEKING system activity. The dopaminergic SEEKING/REWARD system is altered by all kinds of substances, such as drugs, opioids, alcohol and psychostimulants. This alteration triggers a progressive reduction of all appetite for affects unrelated to each specific substance. Neural and behavioural alterations underpin the transition from acute consequences of substance assumption to a condition of chronic addiction. The SEEKING system de-activation leads to a progressive withdrawal from the external world, including the loss of interest in object relations, as clearly happened in this patient's case.

The outline of the balance between SEEKING/REWARD system and GRIEF/PAIN system has been extremely useful in Angelica's treatment.

I also took the opportunity to explain to the patient how her indifference towards life and the progressive loss of desire she experienced was linked to the consumption of substances. Moreover, this indifference and this loss contributed to her withdrawal from relationships and from interaction with the outer world. Eventually, we managed to clarify the need to work in analysis in absence of the numbness created by her being continuously under the effect of cannabinoids. This was the start of her gradual weaning off dependency on cannabinoids which led to a complete de-addiction and to a slow rehabilitation in terms not only of social and affective relationships, but also of important personal achievements.

According to affective neuroscience, the PLEASURE system is not involved in addiction, while eso and endocannabinoids are involved in the suppression of neurotransmission and excitability, which is essential in controlling pathological states of excitotoxicity, such as chronic pain (Araùjo, 2023). While esocannabinoids are introduced in the body through the drug, the endocannabinoid system (ECS) is a neuro modulator involved in many bodily functions. New research is focusing its interaction with endorphins and other endogenous opioids. Alongside their effects on oncologic pain, as well as inflammatory diseases, we understand how cannabinoids, like opiates, can reduce mental pain and function as self-medication.

During Angelica's treatment, the transference relationship has grown in parallel to the de-addiction from drug abuse. According to Zusman (2021), the development of the relationship with the analyst is able to foster a condition of dependency and reduce the process of de-humanization due to isolation and numbing. Addictions mask the pain of a life devoid of human connection. He points out how the two axes dependency/independency are related and how addicted patients need to shift to dependency in the transference relationship.

> Since objects of addiction operate according to the magical thought process particular to infancy, there is no clear distinction between animate and inanimate objects. As a result, drugs or addictive behaviour seductively appear in place of genuine connections with other people.
>
> (Zusman, 2021)

The complexity of this clinical case, in which substance addiction (cannabinoids, cocaine and alcohol) were overlapped by an eating disorder, dysmorphia, early relational trauma and sexual abuse during puberty, seemed to portend a lengthy treatment with an uncertain outcome. Nevertheless, the patient was amazingly involved in the treatment. She reached unhoped goals in the following years, notwithstanding some inevitable back and forth.

I would like to conclude by highlighting how the development of the analytic relationship and the de-addiction process worked synergistically towards the resumption and expansion of Angelica's psychic development, subsequently leading this young patient to progressive and unexpected life experiences.

Bibliography

Araùjo, M. (2023) The cannabinoids mechanism of action: an overview. *Brazilian Journal of Pain.* https://doi.org/10.5935/2595-0118.20230028-en

Ben David, A., Ataria, Y. (2021) The body image–body schema/ownership–agency model for pathologies: four case studies. In Y. Ataria, S. Tanaka, & S. Gallagher (Eds.), *Body Schema and Body Image: New Directions* (pp. 328–332). Oxford: OUP.

Bromberg, P.M. (1993) Shadow and substance: a relational perspective on clinical process. *Psychoanalytic Psychology, 10*(2): 147–168. https://doi.org/10.1037/h0079464

Cahn, R. (1996) *The adolescent in psychoanalysis-The adventure of subjectivation* [The adolescent in Psychoanalysis: the adventure of becoming-a-subject]. Paris: Presse Universitaire de France.

Castellet, F., Spadazzi, C., Spagnolo, R. (2023) A neuropsychodynamic view of dreaming *Neuropsychoanalysis, 25*(1): 1–10. https://doi.org/10.1080/15294145.2023.2197002

Dennet, D. (1991) *Consciousness Explained.* Boston, MA: Penguin.

de Vignemont, F. (2018) *Mind the Body.* Oxford: OUP.

Ferenczi, S. (1949) Confusion of tongues between the adult and the child. *The International Journal of Psychoanalysis, 30,* 225–230.

Gallagher, S. (2005) *How the Body Shapes the Mind.* Oxford: Clarendon Press.

Gallagher, S. (2021) Reimagining the body image. In Y. Ataria, S. Tanaka, & S. Gallagher (Eds.), *Body Schema and Body Image: New Directions* (pp. 85–98). Oxford: OUP.

Khantzian, J.E. (1997) The self-medication hypothesis of substance use disorders: a reconsideration and recent applications. *Harvard Review of Psychiatry, 4*(5): 231–244. https://doi.org/10.3109/10673229709030550

Khantzian, J.E. (2012) Reflections on addictive disorders: a psychodynamic perspective. *National Library of Medicine, 21*(3): 274–279

Merleau-Ponty, M. (1964) *The Primacy of Perception* (J. Edie, Ed.). Evanston, IL: Northwestern University Press.

Moreno, C., et al. (2020) How mental health care should change as a consequence of the COVID-19 pandemic. *The Lancet Psychiatry, 7*(9): 813–824.

Quinodoz, J.M. (2002) *Dreams That Turn Over a Page: Paradoxical Dreams in Psychoanalysis.* London: The New Library in Psychoanalysis.

Panksepp, J. (1998) *Affective Neuroscience: The Foundations of Human and Animal Emotions.* New York: Oxford University Press.

Panksepp, J. (2005) Affective consciousness: core emotional feelings in animals and humans. *Consciousness and Cognition, 14,* 30–80. https://doi.org/10.1016/j.concog.2004.10.004

Panksepp, J. (2007) Emotional feelings originate below the neocortex: toward a neurobiology of the soul. *Behavioral and Brain Sciences, 30,* 101–103. https://doi.org/10.1017/S0140525X07001094

Panksepp, J., Biven, L. (2012) The archaeology of mind: neuroevolutionary origins of human emotions. In *The Norton Series on Interpersonal Neurobiology* (1st ed., pp. 95–144; pp. 311–350). New York: Norton.

Quinodoz, J.M. (2002) *Dreams That Turn Over a Page: Paradoxical Dreams in Psychoanalysis.* London: The New Library in Psychoanalysis.

Ramachandran, V.S. (2004) *A Brief Tour of Human Consciousness.* New York: Plume Editor.

Ramachandran, V.S. (2011) *The Tell-tale Brain.* New York: Norton.

Sattin, D., et al. (2023) An overview of the body schema and body image: theoretical models, methodological settings and pitfalls for rehabilitation of persons with neurological disorders. *Brain Science, 13*(10), 1410. https://doi.org/10.3390/brainsci13101410

Schilder, P. (1935) *The Image and the Appearance of the Human Body*. New York: International Universities Press.

Schore, A.N. (2009) Attachment trauma and the developing right brain: origins of pathological dissociation. In P.F. Dell & J.A. O'Neil (Eds.), *Dissociation and the Dissociative Disorders: DSM-V and beyond* (pp. 107–141). London: Routledge/Taylor & Francis Group.

Solms, M., Panksepp, J. (2021) The 'id' knows more than the 'ego' admits. *Brain Science*, 2, 147–175.

Steiner, J. (1993) *Psychic Retreats: Pathological Organisations in Psychotic, Neurotic and Borderline Patients*. London: Routledge.

Tsakiris, M. (2010) My body in the brain: a neurocognitive model of body ownership. *Neuropsychologia*, 48, 703–712.

Wu, Y., Wang, L., Menjung, T., Huiru, C., Yuan, H., Mingquan, H., Xingqui, C., Kai, W., Chunnyan, Z. (2023, November 7) Changing trends in the global burden of mental disorders from 1990 to 2019 and predicted levels in 25 years. *Epidemiology and Psychiatric Sciences*, 32, e63. https://doi.org/10.1017/S2045796023000756

Zamariola, G., Cardini., F, Mian, E., Serino, A., Tsakiris, M. (2017, February 14) Can you feel the body that you see? On the relationship between interoceptive accuracy and body image. *Body Image*, 20, 130–136. https://doi.org/10.1016/j.bodyim.2017.01.005

Zellner, M.R., Watt, D.F., Solms M., Panksepp, J. (2011) Affective neuroscientific and neuropsychoanalytic approaches to two intractable psychiatric problems: why depression feels so bad and what addicts really want. *Neuroscience & Biobehavioral Reviews*. https://doi.org/10.1016/j.neubiorev.2011.01.003

Zusman, J. (2021) Between dependency and addiction. The Psychoanalytic Study of the Child, 74(1), 280–293. https://doi.org/10.1080/00797308.2020.1859304

Chapter 9

Discussion on addiction in adolescence through three clinical cases

José Alberto Zusman

The texts under consideration provide detailed case studies of three adolescents struggling with substance abuse as a means of coping with profound emotional and familial issues. According to Sierra: "the use of drugs in adolescence is closely connected with failed attempts to deal with intense sexual and aggressive feelings" (Sierra, 2013, p. 69). Despite the different circumstances and individual characteristics of Angelica (Claudia Spadazzi's chapter), Margaret (Kristin Fiorella's chapter), and Neil (Mary Brady's chapter), several similarities and some differences can be drawn from their experiences and therapeutic journeys. The first thing the three cases show us is that every addiction comes with a story of some kind of failure in human connection. Addiction is merely an end product that exposes in several ways a deep fracture in human development. We all depend on the good object we internalize to feel alive, human, and properly nourished by our self-esteem. If we don't find, in the beginning of our lives, a good enough environment (Winnicott) that works as an adequate container (Bion) for our aggressive and loving impulses, we hardly manage to go beyond the process of hominization to reach the humanization process. The abstract-symbolization path to acquiring the valuable components of our civilizing processes requires both a good enough environment and adequate containment. Self-care and compassion rely heavily on these.

Although without unanimity, for Dodes (2019), addictions are subsets of compulsive disorders. He posits that true addiction is rooted in a psychological problem and psychoanalysts are the best professionals to treat addicts (p. 20). The three difficult cases, beautifully discussed in the preceding three chapters, show that his thought deserves to be taken into consideration, especially with regard to the advantage psychoanalysts have, compared to other health professionals, in reaching the deepest layers of the addict personality. Psychoanalysts are also uniquely suited to be able to understand and make use of the unconscious transference/countertransference when faced with the difficulties of an enacted communication without words.

All three cases refer to adolescents who resort to drugs to cope with the neglect, abuse, or absence of their parents. Overwhelming feelings of narcissistic rage, depression, and unbearable helplessness, and the consequent use of denial, dissociation, and displacement were some of the difficulties and the defenses they

DOI: 10.4324/9781003647317-11

had to deal with the difficulty of their terribly painful daily life. It is important to have in mind that addiction always carries a story more enacted than described by words. It may take a long time until interpretation finds its fit. Clarification and confrontation may have to come much earlier and for a long period. It is important to have in mind the necessity to build a concept first to be able to recognize and make use of its presence later. During this phase, when stories are communicated without words, sensations take precedence over feelings. The sensations I refer to are to be understood as physical sensations or immediate experiences, like tension or anxiety that arise before the analytic pair can understand the emotions expressed through words. The therapist must rely heavily on their skills, manage emotional discomfort, and tap into unconscious forms of communication. This approach helps make human interaction viable.

In my own work shown (Zusman, 2022), I commonly say that all humans are born dependent, dependency being a trait of our altricial species. All of us occasionally recur to an addictive object in moments of deep emotional distress. Independence is a reaction formation that hides our natural state of dependency. In that way we try to keep hidden from ourselves and others what we understand as our vulnerable core. But, different from normal people, addicts live imprisoned in the world of addictive objects and our job consists in establishing a human connection to help them emerge from there. For that we may have to bear with our addict patients the pain and difficulties they need to share with a non-judgmental human being so that they feel supported enough to follow the difficult paths of humanization.

My view (Zusman, 2012) is that addicts are imprisoned in what I call the 'axis of addiction' and the therapist has to help them migrate to the 'axis of dependency'. In normal human development we all move continuously from one axis to another in a free and loose way according to the internal and external circumstances we are faced with. The addiction axis is related to human survival while the dependency axis is related to human development (Zusman, 2012). In other words, if our psychoanalytic work goes well, we may say that where the drug is working as an ego function, an analyst will be – at least until the formerly addicted person becomes able to rely on his/her own ego function to make good and healthy choices for life.

Since the 30's psychoanalysis has been slow to broaden its scope to include the research and treatment of the internal mechanisms of addiction. According to Yalisove:

> Glover (1932) and Radó (1933) noted that: affect tolerance problems are common in addicts, Knight (1937) and Simmel (1939), working at the Psychoanalytic Sanatorium at the Menninger Clinic, offered a modification treatment based on a warm, trusting relationship with the patient.
>
> (Yalisove, 1997, p. 116)

Although still undervalued, psychoanalytic tools are gradually seen by many as fundamental for understanding the deepest layers of the addict's mind and for assessing their intricate internal world. The understanding of object relations and attachment dynamics are essential. Through concepts like object constancy and therapeutic alliance, psychoanalysts may increasingly play a greater role in entering this difficult field.

Melanie Klein introduced the concept of a bad object, split off from the good object in order to protect it. The "bad object," while normal in early development, can lead to pathological internal object relations if unmodified. A continued over-reliance on splitting could leave an individual prone to turning to addiction to escape states of destructiveness or fear of destructiveness. Andre Green introduced the concept of the "dead mother," who while alive is experienced as dead, as she is sunk in depression and mourning. Mothers experienced as 'bad' or 'dead' leave an emotional void that disrupts the development of live, human relationships. Either unconscious object relationship may function as a gateway to the world of addiction. In this sense, the roots of addiction are to be found in early life. Addiction is an end product of a heterogeneous condition marked by severe deficits in early object relations and/or overwhelming conflicts due to the internalization of early bad experiences. Johnson suggests that situation is due to a defensive pattern of denial and affirms: "if there is no denial there is no addiction" (1999, p. 797).

All three adolescents in the prior chapters show some sort of unbearable emotional distress. Firstly, all of them had very difficult relationships with their parents, and feeling very lonely after all their attempts to deal with their desperate life situation, they ended up using substances to handle their emotional pain, trauma and neglect, indicating a common coping mechanism. It's not uncommon that people in that position, where humans systematically failed to support them, establish a defensive distance from their human condition as Margaret and Angelica did or fall into a severe depressed condition as Neil did. Angelica turned to cannabinoids, occasionally using cocaine; Margaret extensively used marijuana and Xanax; and Neil heavily relied on marijuana and alcohol, with occasional experimentation with other substances. Interesting to register is that sometimes substances may keep psychotic disintegration at bay and sometimes they do the exact opposite.

Secondly, significant family dysfunction is evident in all cases, contributing to the adolescents' struggles. Angelica's relationship with her parents was marked by a distant and cold mother and an abusive, judgmental and narcissistic father. Margaret's family dynamics were equally troubled, with an abusive cruel father who died prematurely, a passive mother, and siblings with severe mental health issues. Neil's difficulties stemmed from his parents' contentious divorce, his mother's depression, and his father's frequent absence. In all cases the patients had no one who really cared for them and in the absence of reliable human bond, the seduction of substances gained great relevance.

Another similarity found in all cases lies in the severe emotional isolation described. They all struggled with expressing or processing their feelings. Angelica exhibited social withdrawal and had significant difficulty communicating her emotions. Margaret dealt with profound dissociation and emotional numbness, feeling disconnected from her experiences and surroundings. Neil faced emotional instability and had trouble managing his feelings of loss and abandonment, which got worse when he lost his girlfriend with whom he had established an addicted relationship. That will be described below where I'll refer to behavioral addiction.

In terms of therapeutic challenges, each case demonstrated how substance use complicated the therapeutic process. For Angelica, therapy focused on the gradual reduction of substance dependence and improvement in self-expression. Margaret's therapy aimed to understand and address her dissociation and substance dependence, often complicated by her profound sense of being nonhuman. Neil's therapy was concerned with addressing his emotional abandonment and the dangers of his escalating substance abuse. It's important to have in mind that no addiction begins with the use of substances, but the introduction of substances into the scene worsens the addict's difficulties and puts the life of the addict at greater risk. Khantzian (1985), through his Self-Medication Hypothesis (SMH), explains the misunderstanding that made people think addicts seek pleasure instead of seeking human contact and comfort. Substances work as a temporary relief.

The three patients also had in common a story of serious neglect, a severe lack of a secure attachment, and a feeling of emptiness due to the emotional distancing from parents. Patients like that commonly may see themselves as nonhumans and consequently learn to rely more on nonhuman objects than to trust other human beings. People have failed them and caused overwhelming emotional pain. Once the human resources of the addict have been shattered, they have no other option but to turn to drugs as a self-healing process. They feel as if they are part of a nonhuman world where things are friendly, close, and under control as an unconscious defense strategy. They create a kind of an internal parallel world where they feel protected, well put by Steiner with his concept of psychic retreat. According to Steiner: "…They seem to be experienced spatially as places of safety in which the patient can seek refuge from reality and hence from anxiety and guilt" (1996, p. 1075).

Part of the difficulty in treating addicted patients, as I described elsewhere (Zusman, 2012), comes from the fact that it is painful for the patient to be treated as a human being as it is for the therapist to be treated as a nonhuman object or objectified. According to Volkan: "As the therapist takes over the role of the good external object, he or she may begin to feel treated like a drug" (Volkan, 1994, p. 119). Following the same line of thought D. Rosenfeld says that: "…the therapist's most difficult task regarding his countertransference is to stop feeling like, and being, the drug or inanimate object, since this is the role these patients continuously force on him" (Rosenfeld, 1992, p. 209). On the other hand, that pain is the very sign of the formation of a new bond of trust between two people who intend to walk together and explore the amazing human possibilities in life (Zusman and Khantzian, 2022, pp. 125–140).

Despite these similarities present in all three adolescents in question, there are also some differences among the cases. There are no equal addicts, as there are no equal people in general. Every person has his own singularities and stories, and that is no different with addicts. The nature of substance use varied significantly. Each uses the substance of their choice but with the same purpose of achieving a feeling of an internal temporary integration. I say integration because they are all so heavily broken inside that to feel whole, even for a short period of time, is a relief no matter the dire consequences of that choice. Angelica was primarily hooked on cannabinoids, while Margaret was involved in extensive use of marijuana and Xanax. Neil's substance abuse primarily involved heavy use of marijuana and alcohol, with occasional experimentation with other substances. Here it is necessary to add that it is very common that addicts may change the substance of choice over time just as they can also use a combination of them during the same period. They can even change from substance addiction to behavioral addiction.

The primary psychological and emotional issues also differed. Angelica's main issues included social withdrawal, dependence on cannabinoids, and a history of sexual abuse as a child. Margaret's therapy revealed severe dissociation, emotional numbness, and trauma from her father's cruel behavior and sexual abuse. Neil's therapy focused on his emotional instability following his parents' divorce and subsequent substance abuse escalation as his identification with his depressed mother became more visible after the breakup of his relationship with his girlfriend.

Family dynamics further distinguished the cases. Angelica contended with a cold and distant mother and an abusive father, leading to a strained and emotionally barren home environment. Margaret faced the loss of her abusive father, her mother's passive acceptance of abuse, and siblings who also struggled with severe mental health issues. Neil grappled with the aftermath of his parents' divorce, his mother's pervasive depression, and his father's absence due to his bohemian life, which left him feeling unsupported and abandoned.

The developmental impacts on each adolescent also showed some distinction. Angelica struggled primarily with social interactions and self-expression, often feeling emotionally stunted. Margaret, the most mentally disturbed of the group, experienced profound states of dissociation, feeling disconnected from herself and viewing the world as a make-believe experience and herself as a nonhuman entity. Neil, identified with his depressed mother, had difficulty managing emotional losses and dealing with the neglect and permissiveness of his parents.

The therapeutic focus in each case varied accordingly. Angelica's therapy emphasized reducing substance dependence and improving her emotional expression, helping her navigate her complex emotions and social interactions. Margaret's therapy aimed to address her severe dissociation, understand the role of substance use in her life, and process the trauma of her father's abuse. Neil's therapy involved confronting his substance abuse, addressing his emotional abandonment, and ensuring his safety through structured interventions offering the limits he needed to make sure people cared about him.

Finally, the outcomes of each case highlighted the challenges and progress in therapy. Although all patients showed some progress each one had a path to be built. Angelica showed improvement in self-expression and a reduction in substance use over four years of therapy, indicating a gradual but positive change. Margaret's experience was more tumultuous, with severe psychotic symptoms emerging when she stopped using drugs (having to cope with the pathological organization that took her by storm after the death of her cruel father), leading to hospitalizations and a complex therapeutic process. Neil participated in a substance abuse treatment program and showed improvement in handling his emotional issues, but his journey involved ongoing struggles with substance use and emotional stability.

In conclusion, while Angelica, Margaret, and Neil's cases share the common thread of using substances to cope with severe emotional and familial issues, the specifics of their substance use, family dynamics, primary psychological issues, and therapeutic approaches reveal significant differences. These cases collectively underscore the intricate interplay between substance abuse, emotional pain, and family dysfunction, highlighting the complexities and challenges involved in treating adolescents with such backgrounds.

Last but not least is the co-occurrence of behavioral addiction, which is so clear in Neil's case, as shown by the addictive relationship he developed with his girlfriend and the devastating consequences he had to face when she broke up with him. Nevertheless, in all cases, the feeling of not being sufficiently loved was present and that hurt caused a destructive reaction. According to Wumser: "there is no sharp line between substance addictions and addictive behavior in general except for the contingencies of the physical aspects induced by specific drugs" (Volkan, 1994, p. XVI).

I would like to add something regarding the treatment of addictive states. For that I'll begin by citing Sierra once more who wrote: "While is true that the number of confirmed addicts asking for psychoanalytic treatment is small, it is also true that, regretfully the number of psychoanalysts and psychotherapists prepared to accept them for treatment is even smaller" (Weegman and Cohen, 2002, p. 142/p.143). What Sierra points out deserves some reflection. When treating addicted patients, we may have to deal with our most primitive countertransference. It is possible that defensively we might treat those patients in a rude and aggressive way or be led to believe that there is no chance for their improvement. Being taken over by these unwanted reactions or thoughts, we can unconsciously find the perfect excuses to justify our distancing from those who desperately need our help. Perhaps it would be fairer to say that it is easy to move away from the discomfort that addict patients impose on us through their unconscious communication (projection) and on the other hand, have in mind that without our psychoanalytic understanding they won't have much chance to change to alter the pattern that has accompanied them since the start. In all three cases, the psychoanalysts spoke openly about their difficulties and each time their dedicated persistence resulted in an improvement for the critically ill patients who were able to become humanized and move on with their lives. The bond they made with their analysts gave them the ability to feel gratitude and to acquire hope about the life they still had ahead of them. According to Khantzian quoted in Phylip Flores: "The worst fate is not to suffer, but to suffer alone" (Flores, 2012, p. xv).

It is becoming increasingly clear that psychoanalysis plays an important role in the treatment of patients struggling with addiction. Although this approach is still questioned by many, including some psychoanalysts themselves, psychoanalytic tools have proven to be highly effective in understanding the deeper layers of the addiction experience. These tools are gradually making their mark in the field of addictions, overcoming various barriers, including those set up by psychoanalysts themselves.

Despite facing numerous challenges, serious clinical work, as exemplified in the preceding chapters, has demonstrated that psychoanalysis can be consistently effective for those who do not shy away from addressing these conditions. According to Aksar and Savelle- Rocklin (2019, p. 152): "unmasking defensive operations ... reconstructing the traumatic origins of anguish and navigating between holding character resistances and interpreting their gradually emerging transference-based aims constitute the essential ingredients of the deeper work such patients need."

In conclusion, the psychoanalysis in the preceding three chapters showed profound concern for their patients struggling with addiction. As Dr. Brady aptly noted in her chapter, this concern motivated her to take action, whenever words were no longer enough for communication, fostering the best possible therapeutic relationship. Each patient found in their treatment the emotional support needed to confront their emotional issues, enabling them to develop abstract thinking and creativity as they moved towards humanization. In doing so they discovered a sense of recognition and gratitude for the help they received. While some of the patients' challenges remained, they were significantly lessened, representing a form of development that had previously been unattainable. Ultimately, each individual transformed their childhood emotional imprisonment into a path of freedom needed to build a hopeful and meaningful life.

References

Dodes, L. (2019), Chapter 1 in Beyond the Primal Addiction. Savelle-Rocklin, N. and Akhtar, S. (Editors). Routledge: London and New York.

Flores, P. J. (2012) Forward in Addiction as an Attachment Disorder. Jason Aronson: New York.

Johnson, B. (1999) Three Perspectives on Addiction. Journal of the American Psychoanalytic Association, 47: 791–815.

Khantzian, E. J. (1985) The Self Medication Hypothesis of Addictive Disorders. American Journal of Psychiatry 142: 1259–1264.

Rosenfeld, D. A. (1992) The Psychotic: Aspects of the Personality. London: Karnak Books.

Savelle-Rocklin, N. and Akhar, S. (2019) *Beyond the Primal Addiction: Food, Sex, Gambling, Internet, Shopping, and Work*. Routledge/Taylor & Francis Group. New York.

Sierra, L. R. S. (2013) A Neglected Field in Addictive States of Mind. (Tavistock Clinic Series. Bower, M. Karnak. London

Steiner, J. (1996) The Aim of Psychoanalysis in Theory and in Practice. International Journal of Psychoanalysis, 77: 1073–1083.

Weegman, M. and Cohen, R. (2022) The Psychodynamics of Addiction. London: Whurr Publishers Ltd, London and Philadelph (USA)

Wumser in Volkan, K. (1996) Dancing among the Maenads. New York: Peter Lang Publishing.

Yalisove, L. D. (1997) Essential Papers on Addiction. New York and London: New York University Press.

Zusman, J. A. (2012) Between Dependency and Addiction. The Psychoanalytic Study of the Child, 74(1): 280–293. Routledge.

Zusman, J. A. and Khantzian, E. J. (2022) How a Lack of Human Connection May Lead to Dehumanization and Addiction. In Applying Psychoanalysis in Medical Care. Harvey Schwartz (Ed.). London and New York: Routledge.

Part 3

Introduction

Self-harming, a challenge for both patients and psychoanalysts

Christine Franckx

This section focuses on the psychic pain and suffering as expressed through compulsive self-harming behavior. The authors bring vivid clinical examples covering a wide age range of patients, from tiny premature babies in a neonatology ward to independent young adults seeking psychoanalytic treatment. These serious and often life-threatening clinical situations are difficult to treat as patients with self-aggressive symptomatology and/or eating disorders desperately cling to their symptoms. They need this pathological compulsive shield to hide an inner vulnerability behind a hard, impenetrable structure that attempts to make them unreachable. Self-harming behavior has a paradoxical unconscious significance as on the one hand it serves a defense against psychic breakdown, and therefore cannot be let go off easily, but on the other hand the violence of the symptomatology continues the impact of destructiveness. The patient is trying to find relief by way of this compulsive activity, which has a self-soothing quality. However, this works only for a short while and the self-harming needs to be repeated over and over again to keep the self-protective system active. On a more profound level of psychoanalytic understanding, this behavior is also a frantic attempt to bring the internal parents of early relationships back to life, or to make sure they have survived unconscious compulsive attacks. In this way, the patient is caught up in an ongoing cycle of self-destructiveness.

Freud (1915) described how the progressive transformation of the non-organized physiological state at the beginning of extra-uterine life into drives that are directed toward objects is essentially dependent on the participation of a third party. But post-Freudian authors (Meltzer, Tustin, Bick, Haag, Houzel, Golse, and others), also pointed out the important role of the innate capacity of the infant to look for help to integrate sensory experiences (Squires, 2022). Newborns have a rudimentary system at their disposal to regulate bodily and external tension, as is shown in the Neonatal Behavioral Assessment Scale, developed by Berry Brazelton (1978).

Esther Bick (1968) wrote:

> In its most primitive form the parts of the personality are felt to have no binding force amongst themselves and must therefore be held together in a way that is experienced by them passively, by the skin functioning as a boundary. But this

DOI: 10.4324/9781003647317-12

internal function of containing the parts is dependent initially on the introjection of an external object, capable of fulfilling this function.

If the primary human need to find containment of the destructive force of the drives and turned for help to primary object relationships, then failure of this process will be registered in the personality as a lifelong threat of disorganization of the intra-psychic world. Because the infant, who did not experience good enough parental holding to calm its physiological excitation, will not be able to integrate sufficiently a capacity for self-containment and cannot create strong emotional intrapsychic links with its bodily experiences. It is the libidinal co-excitation of the primary environment, who assist 'at the right temperature' the infantile immature and weak system for digestion of the raw sensory elements (beta-elements) it experiences, with the infant's availability and reaching out for the primary object that will create the links needed for the construction of a safe internal world.

The baby's body is the site where the sensory perceptions from within and from outside have their impact and leave memory traces; it is the primary meeting place of the baby with the external world. The fate of autoerotism as a communication between body and mind is defined by these very early processes. If all goes well enough, autoerotism can open the body to a psychic area of phantasy, dreams, thoughts, and intersubjectivity; but if the links between internal and external worlds were not sufficiently bonded the human infant, child, adolescent or adult enters into an infernal cycle of repetition compulsion and can develop serious men-tal suffering.

Therefore, the theatre of destructiveness in self-harming behavior presents later in life is the body, as the frozen emotions of early infancy never became sufficiently mentalized, and the connection between body and mind could not be mediated in the primary object relationship. Maiello (2000) makes a conceptual distinction between the furious attack of frustrating internal objects and the passive breakdown of the human disposition for creating emotional links. The violence of self-harming behavior can in some cases be understood in both ways, as a way to resuscitate the internal parental object destroyed in phantasy by envious attacks, as well as the, what Maiello calls 'frozen', violence that no longer seems to address an internal object.

From the above, it is obvious that psychoanalytic treatment of these clinical situations is very challenging because of the complex task of understanding as and strengthening the fragile links between body and mind to help the patient in creat-ing meaningful links between the body and phantasy life, while keeping all the time the vital role of the defensive system in mind.

In this section, the chapter written by Monica Cardenal demonstrates the role of infant observation according to Esther Bick to show the profound impact of early trauma on the baby's bodily behavior, when an internal container object is deficient. She describes "the muscle tension and self-harming that make the chil-dren feel they exist in a very particular way, and are also in a particular form of relationship with the love objects, tinged with sensoriality." The pathological infant cases show "a certain way of 'existing' in the world for the early Self, where body tension and self-harming are a 'hard' way of integrating and holding oneself up. This is a mental state, very far removed from the internalization of the 'softness of the mother's body.'" Cardenal shares in a highly sensitive way how the complexity of very early mental stages can be apprehended in babies who are at psychological and physical risk. The different vignettes show the baby's desperate attempts to hold on to life itself.

The chapter by Jeanne Magagna pictures a moving account of the difficult psychoanalytic work with anorectic patients, who are "omnipotently trying to control their bodies when there is a profound loss of security derived from an intimate relationship with containing good internalized parents." The case of 14-year-old Maria illustrates the attacks on the internal mother object, the absence of thinking and nothing but "denial, obsessional control, intellectualization in which the vulnerable self is split off and not easily accessible." Magagna stresses the need for psychotherapists working with anorectic patients to be able to rely on a sufficiently solid internal container themselves because of the complexity of their task in "encountering a very primitive infantile part of the anorectic young person who is forming a bond with the therapist."

Humberto Lorenzo Persano discusses self-harming behavior in adolescents as described in different classical psychoanalytic writings, and goes on to insist on the societal pressures that impact today's youngsters. He relates the incidence of self-harm to the experience of time, and connects it further to contemporary societal dynamics: "The loss of slower, contemplative, and introspective time—essential for emotional processing and identity formation—has created a vacuum in which impulsive actions, such as restrictive eating and self-harm, offer an illusion of control and immediacy." In another chapter, Persano gives a profound description of the role of social media in the identification process of adolescents

> who feel isolated or misunderstood and engage with self-harming content to form connections with others who appear to share their pain. This identification process fosters a sense of community but simultaneously reinforces masochistic tendencies and externalizes internal conflicts through harmful acts.

In his contribution from a French psychoanalytic perspective, Panos Aloupis, French psychosomatician, clarifies the different psychic levels of self-harm, both as a conscious self-aggressive behavior and as the expression of a complex unconscious phenomenon, but always the result of early trauma. He states that "each case shows how displeasure becomes unbearable, and how aggression against the body appears to be the only way to escape a murderous object." Psychomotricity as the seat of autoerotism is conceptualized as the capacity of the infant to start intricating the drives, therefore relying on help by the primary object. Aloupis reminds the readers of the work done by Denise Braunschweig and Michel Fain (1975) who made a useful clinical differentiation between the calming and the satisfying mother to understand the impact of the real mother's holding style on the infant's mental development. The latter takes shared pleasure in her baby and makes herself available for libidinal co-excitation, an unconscious process, that

> results in the psychic acceptance of the object and the investment of passivity facing the active mother-object. In this way, the absence, estrangement and aggression of the primary object can be psychically transformed to become the subject of dream work and of masochistic elaboration, in which the two drives, life and death, remain intertwined.

In contrast, the calming mother does not help her infant discover a space for the interplay of life and death drives; the latter is left unbound and is "more at the service of exhausting internal and external destructiveness than for transformation of excitement and tolerance of the cataclysm of life." The baby cannot allow the experience of passivity, which is experienced as deadening, only rigid control by the musculature can offer a subjective feeling of being in control.

In the last chapter, written by Anouk Meurrens, we meet two young women in psychoanalytic treatment who share the characteristics of an internal hyperstructure of control, which has in both cases a paradoxical meaning of survival and self-destruction. "It is almost like an imaginary friend, accompanying them everywhere. It stood between them and the world, providing security and a barrier, but it also made things possible, by preventing catastrophic anxiety."

The patients describe feeling a hard, bony structure for holding onto in an attempt to create a distance between their inner world and the outside environment. It is a protective inner shield of "cracked concrete, rotten wood. It's a kind of hollow hyper-skeleton, both rigid and fragile... Although they recognize the rigidity of this mechanism, they do not see it as solid. And yet it contains and prevents all the fluid movements of the body and, of course, all the impulsive life.

Sexual impulses are crushed by tons of reinforced concrete, and aggressive impulses that are turned against their own bodies." In this description of her female, intellectually high-functioning patients, the author demonstrates how the deficiency of an inner containing object not only creates the need for a quasi-inorganic object as a desperate resort for holding the self together but also how all aspects of adult libidinal life are touched by the basic fault.

In conclusion, the reader will discover in this section an in-depth presentation of self-harm behavior over a wide age range in the different contributions of experienced psychoanalysts. Our hypothesis is that this psychopathological profile is always a result of an early trauma that has left the infant with a basic deficient capacity for self-containment due to the impossibility of creating strong enough internal emotional linking of the bodily excitation. The clinical material is convincing of the seriousness of this clinical condition as well as the need for a professional treatment offer that can be challenging for the psychoanalyst's own containing availability.

References

Bick, E. 1968. The Experience of the Skin in Early Object-Relations. *Int J Psychoanal*. 49: 484–486.

Braunschweig, D. & Fain, M. 1975. *La nuit, le jour. Essai psychanalytique sur le fonctionnement mental*. PUF, le fil rouge.

Brazelton, T.B. 1978. The Brazelton Neonatal Behavior Assessment Scale: introduction. *Monogr Soc Res Child Dev*. 43: 5–6.

Freud, S. 1915. Instincts and their Vicissitudes. *SE*. 14: 104–140.

Maiello, S. 2000. Broken Links: Attacks or Breakdown? *J Child Psychother*. 26(1): 5–24.

Squires, C. 2022. La capacité contenante et l'espace de rêverie du psychanalyste. *Corps Psychisme*. N° 80–81: 15–28.

Chapter 10

Self-harming in early life and the difficulty in living for some infants

Mónica Cardenal

Introduction

In this chapter, which follows the conference on the same topic organized in September 2024 by the IPA Committee on Child and Adolescent Psychoanalysis (COCAP), the author wants to discuss the psychoanalytic work with children and adolescents who demonstrate psychopathological tendencies that are difficult to understand and to address. She would like to share observation material of babies who are at psychological and physical risk, and bring the reader closer to the origin of very complex early mental stages and to the vicissitudes of the primary ties. It is hoped that the observation of these processes will help professionals of early childhood to broaden their comprehension of the emotional life of a young child and, consequently, of psychopathology when it presents itself in such a cruel and deadly way.

How can self-harming in a baby be defined? The mind of a baby does not have the same level of maturity as that of a child of schoolgoing age or of an adolescent, and its experience with the world is being built. Babies depend absolutely on their primary objects to survive.

Self-harming in an infant does not appear in the same way nor does it have the same conditions as can be observed in an adolescent or adult case. The tendency to self harm or allow oneself to die is very unnatural and evokes a wide variety of phantasies, anxieties, and defenses, which all need to be understood. The author will show what the internal scenario is like for a baby that is harming itself. It is such a complex situation that even specialized professionals often cannot bear to even face that possibility.

Theoretical and clinical contributions

Serge Lebovici described cases of infant anorexia for the first time in the 70s. The author had the opportunity to become acquainted with his work and that of René Diatkine at the Binet Center in the late 80s. They worked on the early bonding between mother and baby. Jeanne Magagna, a specialist on this topic, has a chapter in this book.

DOI: 10.4324/9781003647317-13

The Spitz studies and the Robertson films at Tavistock during the Second World War and post-war times show infants who, when separated from their parents, become depressed to the point of letting themselves die. Spitz discovered the dramatic death by marasmus.

It is the early relationship that is at risk. We can state that the beauty of the world has disappeared for these children, and it cannot be apprehended. The kind of beauty the author refers to is what Donald Meltzer (1988) described when he linked it to the presence of the mother at the beginning of life, to her face and interiority, and the conflict this generates. Meg Harris (APdeBA Conference, 2022) highlights a very interesting point when referring to the aesthetic conflict described by Meltzer and its link with psychopathology:

> This means that instead of the death instinct, the negative anti-life position (which is neither a force nor an instinct) can be seen in terms of withdrawal from the aesthetic conflict. According to Meltzer, this covers all types of psychopathology, from the sensitivity of autism to the tyrannical projections of the claustrum.

The author has seen young children with autism, some of them not even two years old, trying to go through walls as if these did not exist, banging their heads against a hard surface, and biting their hands or lips compulsively until they were bleeding. Also, children living on the streets are in extremely vulnerable conditions, introducing small objects or trash into body orifices such as ears or nostrils. In both types of psychopathological situations, the children compulsively eat any type of non-food object, developing what is known as pica disorder, in which serious damage can be caused inside the body apart from the visible external lesions.

As Esther Bick (1968) described, second skin phenomena emerge when the mind remains without an internal container object capable of sustaining and unifying the Self. Due to different circumstances, internal or external, such container objects cannot be internalized and can be destroyed or fragmented, leaving the Self without integration and support. This is experienced concretely at body level; somatic symptoms, self-harming, false independence and reckless and impulsive behavior predominate. In this type of psychic functioning, a narcissistic organization is obvious and affects the contact of the Self with the beauty of the world, love relationships and life in general (Cardenal, 2022).

Stephen Briggs (1998) carried out an interesting investigation about eating disorders in babies and their relationship with impoverishment of symbolic development. He defined three types of links, based on Bion's container-contained idea (1967). One of his most valuable contributions may be the description of a very painful interaction for the baby, which he calls "proto-masochist," where the use of musculature as described by the author (2020?) predominates as a way of being and relating.

Briggs presents the case of baby Hester, who was weaned prematurely, initially feeding in a passive, indifferent way and often regurgitating. As she grew, her attitude became more aggressive with herself and with her mother, violently refusing food. This caused her to lose a lot of weight. Her mother called her a "smelly glutton cow."

Hester

Observation: six weeks old

Yvonne (mother) said that Hester still scratched herself and pointed at the marks on her forehead. She bent over as she pulled the baby towards her. Then she turned her body towards the child, hitting her in the eye and moved back saying "Oops, I pricked you in the eye."

Observation: three months old

Hester was on the floor, she lowered her legs and rolled over onto her back. She stretched out her arms and lifted her legs, touching the baby's activity gym. She grabbed the legs of the frame, lifted them over her face, licking one extreme … She then lifted it so that it slid out of her mouth and then seemed to squeeze it against her chin and neck. She lifted it again, took it in her mouth and licked it and then squeezed her neck again with it.

The author interprets that in the face of the premature loss of the breast, the child internalized a painful, cruel aspect of her mother, one of "abuse."

An interesting study carried out by Rosa Mascaro (*9th International Conference of Infant Observation According to the Method of Esther Bick, Senegal, 2012*) in the North of France in early 2000 shows babies with a body tension we had never observed before. Those babies had been separated from their addicted parents and raised in a specialized daycare for several months. The small group of babies aged three months to two years was cared for by a number of different nurses and expert professionals. The neck of one of the three-month-old girls was completely turned to one side so that a kinesiologist had to work delicately with her to correct that posture. It was shocking to see this baby's body tension, avoiding the human face. Another baby, a few months old, remained in a rigid permanent posture, arms and legs curled up; he was tensely curled into himself and spent several months in that position, which would seem impossible to maintain, if not for the enormous effort and muscle tension that he exerted.

Illustrations from Infant Observation according to Esther Bick

These theoretical and clinical references, which are the result of more recent conceptual psychoanalytic investigations, will serve to introduce the topic, which will be illustrated by observation material. The Infant Observation Seminar, according

to Esther Bick, the Tavistock model, has been taught at the Italian Hospital in Buenos Aires since the 1980s, thanks to Kamala Di Tella, Bick's direct disciple in
London. It has always been a central part of the training of child and adolescent
psychotherapists and psychiatrists. A brief clinical vignette about a young adult in
vulnerable conditions will be included, as this is an interesting way of understanding the infantile mental states described before.

All cases highlight the use of "musculature" (body tension) in relation to objects.
A certain way of "existing" in the world for the early Self, where body tension
and self-harming are a "hard" way of integrating and holding oneself up. This is
a mental state, very far removed from the internalization of the "softness" of the
mother's body. The author believes these children haven't been able to identify
internally with a container object, which, following Bick's ideas (1968), is a recep-
tive object in which the experience of being integrated and lodged in the mother's
mind has been possible. However, as mentioned, when in the face of a traumatic
situation, the internal container object which offers an experience of interiority to
digest emotions, thoughts, or dreams is destroyed or fragmented. In these emotional conditions, it is the muscle tension and self-harming that make the children
feel that they exist in a very particular way, and also in a particular form of relationship with the love objects, tinged with sensoriality.

"Baby"

A baby wants to disappear

Observation: seven days old

> I enter Neonatology and go to the cot where the baby is. I ask the nurse if they
> know anything about the mother, who has asked not to be shown the baby,
> not even at birth. A relative came to see the baby and left delicately prepared
> clothes. When the nurse leaves I remain by the cot. The baby is sleeping on
> his back, his arms are half bent beside his head with his hands making fists. In
> the first minutes of observation I see him suck with a faint smile on his lips.
> He moves his lower lips more. Then he starts to tremble at times as he sleeps,
> tightening his fists. After a while a doctor approaches and tells me that he sleeps
> all day, he hardly ever cries. I am shocked to see that the baby's body is very
> tense, too motionless (the observer later commented in the supervision group
> that "he seemed dead"). The baby continues in that position, trembles, sucks a
> little more, and continues sleeping.

Observation: 14 days old

> He is awake on his back, his arms outstretched and his eyes open. He is entirely
> covered by the blanket. He starts flexing and stretching his arms as he cries.
> He puts his arms together over his chest and calms down. He closes his eyes,

opens his mouth wide and cries. He now takes his hands to his face, clasps them and closes his eyes. He calms down. After a few minutes he cries again and the nurse comes over. She swaddles him in his blanket, arms inside. The baby calms down. The nurse says he likes being tightly wrapped. The baby is quiet for a while, then starts crying again. He starts flailing his arms and legs brusquely. The nurse comes back and gives him his pacifier, which he sucks emphatically and calms down. The nurse leaves and he starts crying again. He opens his mouth widely. The nurse comes back and puts the pacifier back in his mouth. He continues to cry. The nurse picks him up and says: "He likes to be held"… The nurse bottle-feeds him, Baby starts suckling energetically, swallowing loudly.

Observation: 17 days old

He is sleeping on his back with his arms extended at the sides. His neck is stretched and he is facing the ceiling, his face is entirely covered by his cap. A doctor approaches and asks me if I am the observer. I ask him why his face is covered with his cap, he looks at the baby and asks the nurses: "Is this a new procedure for sleeping?" He smiles and removes the cap from his face. Baby is asleep, but when the doctor removes the cap he opens his eyes and moves his head a little. I approach and say hello. He stares at me. The nurse approaches and I mention the incident with the cap, saying it might be too big for him. She agrees and looks for a smaller one among his clothes. She takes a light blue fleece cap and puts it on, saying: "this one is better." She leaves. He takes his hands towards his face. He starts to make noises as if about to cry. He clasps his hands over his chest and calms down. He opens his mouth and looks for the pacifier beside him. He tries to take it into his mouth but can't and starts crying. I put his pacifier in his mouth and he starts sucking energetically. He calms down and puts his hands close to his cheeks, his eyes start closing slowly. He drops the pacifier and he protests again. I put it back in his mouth. He calms down, closes his eyes and stops sucking. He starts sucking again for a few minutes and falls asleep with his hands clasped over his chest and his face to one side. He remains very still, he seems fast asleep. Suddenly, he starts moving his head and stretches his neck upwards and downwards, as if trying to 'get into something'. I notice that with that movement his cap slides down and starts to cover his forehead. He stays still and continues sleeping, he then starts moving his head and neck again, now the cap covers his eyes and reaches his nose. The nurse approaches and says: "is your cap over your face again?" She fixes it. Baby continues sleeping, on his back with his hands clasped over his chest and his face to one side.

This newborn baby did everything he could to "disappear," in spite of the care and affection he received, the body and mind of his mother were missing. It was shocking to see how he strained every muscle in his face and neck to cover his face with his cap. In spite of this, he fed and sucked intensely on his pacifier, maybe at times his mind could be "working," "thinking" about the object which he had known sensorially for nine months during pregnancy. It is merely a conjecture, but as time went by, he seemed less "deadly rigid and still" and more willing to suckle.

Roma

When the bottle nipples are destroyed, what is left for digesting?

Observation: one month and fifteen days old

> I see the mother and the baby in the living room on the couch. Roma is in her mother's arms having her bottle. She tells me the baby has been bottle fed since the first day, as she wouldn't attach to her breast properly. She says that they both cried when she had to breastfeed her, because her nipples hurt a lot. She then decided to put an end to the "struggle" one day when the baby vomited blood. She tells me about her frustration, since she had read a lot to prepare for breastfeeding and in the end everything went wrong. She was upset, since she could no longer "milk herself" eight times a day. In addition, the milk gave the baby reflux and she vomited it. Roma is lying over her mother's right arm, her gaze is fixed on the light coming through the window, her arms are flexed close to her face, her hands in fists and her legs relaxed. She sucks slowly and every now and then the nipple sinks inwards. The mother fixes this and offers it to her again, the baby continues to drink.

It was incredible to watch the baby indenting the nipple with the muscles in her mouth, making it impossible to feed. Very hostile emotions circulated between the baby and her mother. Severe destructive forces targeted the nipple—the 'breast'—hindering the baby's initial growth and later leading to the development of somatic intestinal symptoms. Roma had blood in her stools, being alternately constipated or with diarrhea. It is inevitable to refer to Bion, for Roma the relationship with her mother cannot be fantasized, "dreamed," just like the food cannot be well digested, on the contrary, it is vomited or evacuated painfully.

Observation: one month and twenty-one days old

"The mother brings the bottle and picks up the baby, who is crying. She tells her that 'she is going to eat now, she shouldn't make her feel that she is starving her.' She holds the baby against her body, holding her head with her arm, and offers her the bottle. Roma continues crying with the bottle in her mouth, the mother removes it and tells her that she does not seem to want to eat. She offers it again, this time Roma sucks hard. She stares at a point on the wall, her hands making fists. The mother comments that Roma is pulling hard, 'she thinks that I am going to take the bottle away from her.' She says she doesn't have any milk left, and that every time she offers her breast, Roma cries and rejects it. She adds that they are going to see the pediatrician the next day, and will tell her she is only bottle-feeding now, and that she is giving her less milk than what the pediatrician suggested 'so as not to fatten her,' or to prevent vomiting after feeding. 'Oh, well, love, when you are older you will tell your psychologist that your mother used to starve you.'"

Observation: two months old

> The mother settles the baby on her lap over a cushion covered by a sheet and says "I will make you too hot otherwise." She starts feeding her with the bottle, the baby's fists are tightly closed beside her face, the mother tells her "loosen your hands, love, you seem to fear I will take your food away, I won't do that." The mother often turns the bottle in the baby's mouth, "to avoid bubbles." The baby sucks from the tip of the nipple. When she finishes, the mother removes the bottle, Roma quickly takes one of her fists to her mouth. The mother removes it. She tells me she took her to the pediatrician because the baby had diarrhea and blood in her stools.

It is important to mention that as she grew, Roma broke all the bottle nipples because she indented them when sucking. Her body tone was tense during the first months of her life, for example, she liked to be held standing up even though she wasn't prepared for that. We consider that the presence of the observer was key to help digest the hostility between this mother and her baby. It was interesting to see how affectionate and grateful two-year-old Roma seemed toward the end of the observation (Cardenal, 2020).

Maria case: how to be outside oneself or intensely intruded in the object in order to avoid pain

In Brazil, we accompany and advise a large group of colleagues active in an action program with vulnerable populations, SOS BRAZIL. In this context, we supervised the case of a young woman, Maria, who had been abandoned by her mother at the age of one year. She had been raised together with five siblings by a demanding father and had been deprived of many things. She was a teenage mother and was used to moving and changing jobs. Her reason for consulting was her intense rage, especially toward her husband and at times toward her young children. In one of the episodes of intense hatred, she intentionally cut her arm until "her tendons and muscles" were visible; she commented that she had been doing that since she was very young.

We understand that she was like a "homeless child" who needed to see if her skin was hard enough to protect her. She was trying to know what kind of interior she had, and—we could add—what the interior of the object was like. We wondered what the girl phantasized about the interior of the maternal object and pondered whether she might be trying to know about this through the intense sadism when cutting herself.

This type of identification, very different from introjective processes, is called adhesive (Bick, 1968; Meltzer, 1975), in which the outer hardness is felt sensorially in the body or the skin, for example, and holds the Self in the face of the lack of a containing internal object. She was a "hard" young woman, demanding, violent at times and without showing any signs of tenderness.

Gianna Williams, who coordinated the supervision with the author, drew attention to the way Maria related to the object: maybe she cut herself as the only way of entering the "hard mother." In this patient's infantile phantasy, the only way to enter the mother was in this violent and intrusive way. Both types of identifications, adhesive and intrusive projective, can be present when the mind is very affected. In the world of internal relationships, different forms of being within the object can coexist, from the most moderate to the most extreme. This also has an effect on the external object relationships and the world in general.

Summary

This chapter discusses the complex mental states and the vicissitudes of the primary internal and external links in babies and young children who are at high psychological or vital risk. Self-harming in an infant does not present the same evidence that can be observed in an adolescent or an adult. We may state that for these children some of the beauty of the world disappears. They have to find a way to sustain and integrate the Self through repetition of self-harming behavior and they have not been able to construct or lean on an internal containing object, this is a possible vortex of comprehension of the predominant compulsion. They are infants who "exist" outside themselves, immersed in a world of sensations. Through the material we could discuss the early depressive aspects that can invade the Self. The chapter will explore, in this manner, Esther Bick's concepts related to the second skin and the different types of identification that are set in motion in these psychopathological processes. These mental states tinged with opposing emotions, both for the Self and for the object, have an enormous impact on the early object relationships. The symbolic capacity of the mind has become impoverished for these infants, just like their interaction with the world.

Bibliography

Bick E. (1968) The experience of the skin in early object relations. *International Journal of Psychoanalysis.* 49: 484–486.

Bion W. (1967) *Second Thoughts*. Karnac Books, UK.

Briggs S. (1998) The contribution of Infant Observation to an understanding of feeding difficulties in infancy. *International Journal of Infant Observation and its Applications*. 1(3): 44–59. Editors Lisa Miller, published by Tavistock Clinic Foundation and the University of East London Press.

Cardenal M. (2022) Children in a world in war. *COCAP Blog*, IPA website.

Cardenal M. and Williams G. (2020) La observación de bebés y el trabajo sobre las ansiedades de pérdida. In Monica Cardenal and Marcelo Redonda (Eds.), *Territorios postkleinianos. Una actualización de la tarea psicoanalítica* (61–80). Teseo, Buenos Aires, Argentina.

Meltzer D. and Harris Williams M. (1988) *The Apprehension of Beauty: The Role of Aesthetic Conflict in Development, Art and Violence*. Clunie Press.

Meltzer D. and others (1975) *Explorations in Autism. A Psycho-Analytical Study*. Clunie Press.

Chapter 11

The silenced scream
'Under anorexia nervosa'

Jeanne Magagna

Introduction

A baby is conceived with a biological necessity for a mother in utero and to stay alive after birth. Bion (1959) says the baby has a preconception of there being a 'good mother', 'a good breast' to nurture, protect, and understand the baby. However, as Cardenal (2025, this book) has suggested, the infant's emotional bond with the mother can be ruptured so severely that the infant has to find his own ways to avoid the devastating anxiety including the fear of death. There are many possible ways for the infant and child to survive intense fear when there is a ruptured bond with the mother. In the most extreme situation, the child retreats into a comatose state, not keeping the self awake to the external world (Cardenal 2025, in this book). Such a comatose state present in 19 children is described in our book *The Silent Child: Communication without Words* (Magagna 2012).

When an infant is born prematurely and resides in a neonatal intensive care unit or is physically ill in hospital, there is a great risk of pathological defences arising. Without the mother or father present, the baby feels both physically and psychologically unheld. Porges (2017) in his polyvagal theory suggests that in order for healthy psychological and physical development to occur the baby has to feel safe and trust another human being. But in the absence of a containing parent *what can the terrified baby do*? Porges suggests that fight-flight and comatose states are the baby's survival mechanisms. The NICU baby develops primitive protections against the fear of annihilation and that of spilling endlessly into space (Bick 1968). These primitive protections are also used under normal experiences during infancy when there is a brief separation between the mother and infant.

Having trust in the mother and father and feeling safe, protected, emotionally understood and physically nurtured leads to introjection of the good mother and father.

With 'good internal parents' to trust and to rely upon the child lets go of adhesive mechanisms, the omnipotent tools to survive *ruptured links* with the parents. Bion (1959, 1962) points out that *containment* of the baby's crying enables the cries to be transformed into thoughts suitable for thinking about emotional experience.

DOI: 10.4324/9781003647317-14

Likewise, on a physiological plane, if the parents consistently bear the emotional brunt of the baby's different anguished cries, take them seriously and comfort the baby, then a highly effective stress response system can be established in the neurophysiological brain. These stress response systems will enable the child to cope well with stress in later life (Helm et al. 2007).

All anorectic children's and young peoples' symptoms involve excessive reliance on adhesive mechanisms, on *primitive omnipotence*. The symptoms are accompanied by the children's omnipotent illusion that these activities *save the self* from catastrophic anxieties including fragmentation, dissolution, spilling out endlessly (Bick 1968). I am not describing boys suffering from anorexia nervosa, although 1/3 of the young people referred to us at Great Ormond Street Hospital in London were boys whom I describe in my audible book, *A Psychotherapeutic Understanding of Eating Disorders in Children and Young People* (Magagna 2022).

Anorectic symptoms

Anorectic symptoms used in lieu of introjection of emotionally containing parents include:

1 *Overwhelming anxiety leading to closing the mouth to food*
   In infancy the mouth is the bridge between internal experience and the outside world represented by the mother. When there is no adequate internal mother to help bear anxiety, when the link with the internalized good mother is broken, the bridge to her, the mouth, stops opening to food. This anorectic child omnipotently closing the mouth to food leads some young people to die of starvation and/or the effects of starvation on the body (Bryant-Waugh and Lask 2004).
2 *Non-stop exercise*
   Babies when left alone often kick in non-stop movement to hold themselves together emotionally in lieu of a good internal mother. Anorectic athletes and dancers use these non-stop movements in lieu of emotional containment of their anxieties.
3 *Filling the mind with obsessive calorie counting and calculating one's weight*
   This represents a wish to omnipotently control that which feels overwhelming: one's greed, one's hunger for understanding, an overwhelming sense of undigested emotions and fears, and a sense of disgusting physical fatness connected with the overwhelming feelings and sensations.
4 *Omnipotent control of bodily developments* such as menstruation, development of breasts, body hair, change in hip shape. Ordinary sexual developments are replaced by a stick thin body and adhesively holding onto the 'hard bones' protruding through the skin. A neuter identity or masculine identity might be felt to be necessary to avoid and staying away from identification with a hated and subsequently persecuting internalized mother damaged by one's aggression towards her. This may occur because of misattunement between mother and one's infantile self and/or mother's potential lack of protection or intrusion into the baby with projections of hate, depression, neediness, or some mental illness.

5 *Adhesively adhering to the cruel superego in the absence of containing good internal parents.* Having to get perfect grades, acknowledging only loving feelings with hating feelings being repressed through the activity of the cruel superego, and various obsessive mechanisms such as obsessive washing and controlling of time may accompany this.

6 *Forbidden by the cruel superego* may be pleasurable activities such as keeping warm, receiving presents, and engaging in enjoyable activities.

7 *The anorectic feeling of fatness is very linked with autistic anxieties regarding formlessness and loss of shape.* Such experiences of falling forever, losing orientation, liquefying, and spilling out or falling into bits all contribute to the anorectic feeling of fatness (Tustin 1986).

In her book *Good Girls*, journalist Hadley Freeman writes about her experience of spending three years suffering from anorexia nervosa in psychiatric hospitals. She said, 'I felt like a china doll, sitting on a bookshelf, *protected and perfect ...* and suddenly, who knows what, maybe age, maybe atmospheric pressures, maybe just an internal weakness, a crack scores across her face. Just like that' (Freeman 2023: 16).

So, what emotional conflicts and anxieties contribute to 'the crack' scoring across the porcelain face of the 'good girl' suffering from anorexia nervosa? The mask of anorexia nervosa conceals a 'starving self' with 'a silenced scream' for a trusted person who can bear the brunt of one's psychological pain, one's dependence, one's love and one's hate, and make those feelings 'thinkable'. Anorexia nervosa consists of a masked conglomeration of omnipotent strategies which conceal a wide variety of psychopathologies and uncontained physical and emotional experiences. We need to understand that unique girl whose scream for understanding and care has been silenced. The omnipotent control, perhaps arising from early infancy, forms the mask of anorexia nervosa. The young person's physical starvation actually represents a self starved of compassionate comprehension by the self and significant others.

Now through research, we understand that in addition to sexual or emotional abuse, family conflicts, external social turbulence or depression, and autistic and social anxiety states may also prompt girls to develop anorexia nervosa. In fact, one-third of anorectic girls are anorectic (Tchanturia 2021). Removing the 'porcelain mask' of anorexia nervosa must be simultaneously accompanied by the provision of a compassionate individual psychotherapist. Absolutely essential is also the provision of a psychotherapist working with the parents to *provide* 'a couple's cradle of containment' to help their child to eat as well as to deeply receive and understand their child's projections of love and hate into them (Magagna and Piercey 2020). Because anorexia nervosa affects the body, it is crucial to enable parents, through weekly parent work, to develop effective ways of bearing their child's anxieties, phobias, and conflicts about eating before, during, and after mealtimes, in order to help their child eat. This needs to be done with supervision by professionals experienced in being with individuals with eating disorders; otherwise, abusive coercion and criticism may occur during the mealtimes. Parents need to understand that their child is anxious rather than bad, but parents often they feel their child is simply wilfully disobeying their wishes and that makes them very angry. In fact, the child's projections of previously split off feelings of anger and hate will increase as the child begins to eat and the child's 'porcelain mask of anorexia nervosa' is removed. The child's negative feelings which arise can be very shocking, disturbing, and dysregulating for parents and nursing staff. Hopefully the psychotherapist/psychoanalyst will protect the parents somewhat by 'gathering the infantile transference' as described by Donald Meltzer (1975) in his book, *The Psychoanalytic Process.*

What does recovering from anorexia nervosa involve?

First, we need to say what is wounded in the anorectic young person. I will take my clue from a 14-year-old anorectic girl, Maria, who said, "You don't know what it is like to be near this black hole!" The black hole is a wound from loss of attunement in early infancy.

Likewise, in a 9–18-year-old prepubertal or adolescent boy or girl, closing the mouth and mind to experiencing overwhelming noxious and hostile feelings occurs to protect the self from becoming emotionally overwhelmed. Therefore, we can assume that anorexia nervosa is 'a mask' concealing trauma, conflict, and the loss of a satisfying and containing relationship with 'the other' and with the self'.

Omnipotent control

Anorexia nervosa involves the use of omnipotent control when there is a profound loss of security derived from an intimate relationship with containing good internalized parents.

Anorexia nervosa also involves harming the parents' child, and it is therefore also filled with hostility to the parents who are designated as the people who should provide an emotionally supportive and understanding nurturing relationship.

Is the anorectic young person healed because their weight is restored? I don't think so

Here is an anorectic girl's poem suggesting what in her inner world requires a deeper repair:

I really need some help,
because my life is in a mess.
…

I'm trapped in a crazy world
of either fat or thin.
…

Figure Two

Figure 11.1 Girl imprisoned.

> So, as I said I feel trapped,
> like I've been left behind,
> for me skinny is attractive
> and nothing can change my mind.

Suggested in these lines is a kind of euphoric feeling about being thin. Although there is a statement about being trapped, implied is a sense of triumph, of feeling that her SELF is elevated by joining the anorectic propagandizing self. There is both a manic denial of the sense of loss and a denial of the girl's underlying depression. Refusal of food or dieting makes the omnipotent destructive SELF feel like a superior expert (Rosenfeld 1987). Most crucially, the danger of death from anorexia is completely absent!! There is one important sentence however: 'I really need some help, for my life is in a mess' (Figure 11.1).

I ask you again: what needs healing? (Figure 11.2)

Obsession about food and omnipotent control replace the loss of a good containing object, a resilient psychic structure internally, that would enable the child to hold feelings and lend thought to them. No thinking is present, but instead we observe denial, obsessional control, and intellectualisation in which the vulnerable self is

Figure 11.2 Omnipotent control.

split off and not easily accessible. Therefore, the SELF cannot adequately mature (Figure 11.3).

In therapy the anorectic girl often initially says:

I don't want to think about my feelings.
I don't know anything about my feelings.
I don't have dreams.
I don't want to be with people.
I don't want food.

During the therapist's summer holiday, Maria, the patient mentioned earlier, barely slept or ate and her suicidal thoughts became stronger. For these three weeks Maria had also secretly stopped taking her olanzapine. Returning from the holidays, Maria's eyes were filled with alarm and suspicion. She sighed and smiled tightly. The therapist said, 'It looks like you are trying to hold on even though your strength is running out. You seem to be trying to put on a mask of politeness and passivity.' Maria plaintively replied, 'There's no hope and never was, it was all a mask! I'm a weakling, I can't even die. That would be the best thing I can do! I'm crazy, I'm completely sick and hopeless.' The therapist said, 'I want to support this little Maria who hasn't given up despite all the pain and darkness inside and give her the opportunity to continue living and our working together.'

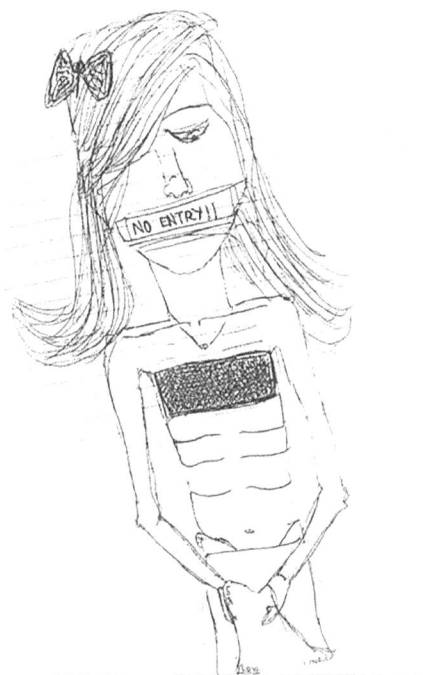

Figure 11.3 No entry girl.

Maria boomed, 'Why are you here saying that you care what happens to me? Let's face it, it's just convenient for you to get a decent sum of money from me every month! You're comfortably settled!'

The therapist said,

I'm here in the room with you right now, because I can hear someone inside you who is very small, scared and alone, who is paralysed by the huge propaganda that is looming, bringing terror and hopelessness, propaganda that is sucking out everything good inside you, like a black hole.

The therapist added,

I will stand here with this little girl and hold her hand so that she will not be left alone in this horror. If my presence won't banish the propaganda at least I won't turn my back on this little girl and I shall be with her where she is now.

'You don't need to know what it's like to be near this black hole,' responded Maria in a hushed voice.

The therapist replied, 'Nevertheless, I have made a decision to work with you and I will try to understand what it's like for you to be with this black hole inside.'

So, what needs healing in this anorectic girl, Maria?

Inside Maria, and many anorectic young people, is not simply a hurt, a disappointed self. Over time there has developed a very hard and cruel voice which is directed against the self and the therapist. A part of herself is damning her with the words, 'You are fat, you are ugly, you are greedy and unlovable, you shouldn't eat, you shouldn't have any pleasure.' And one could add, 'Also you are not allowed to experience the beauty of an intimate understanding relationship with your therapist.'

Cumulative trauma or a severe trauma, some basic fault, at a deep unobserved level, has occurred. Subsequently the trauma of loss threatens the continuation of therapy for it will arise again during separation after the patient has begun to depend upon the therapist. Young anorectic boys and girls in our weekly inpatient therapeutic group almost always became aware of a sense of loss and a lack of inner development. Also, they mentioned that, despite the outward appearance of femininity or masculinity, anorexia nervosa also often involved a lack of sexual identity. For them often only the hard muscle and bones of the omnipotent destructive part are part of their identity. For the girls there is often an obliteration of the feminine self. This is linked with the fact that an identification with a good mother taking care of the infant self has been damaged by an attack on the internalized mother. The natural development of the child has been impeded by 'the good friend', the omnipotent destructive part of anorexia which is often associated with a hard, bony, male structure. The boys feel 'disgusting and fat' and just want muscle and bone for they too have damaged internal parents.

My book on eating disorders (Magagna 2022) describes the complexity of the therapist's own personal need for his/her emotional development. Trying to be emotionally present while being rejected and projected into by a part of the young person is extremely difficult. Trying to remain aware of the huge responsibility for the dependency of the young person's emerging, vulnerable self is often a difficult task, particularly for new, young therapists, who are perhaps not feeling ready to have a baby, but are actually encountering a very primitive infantile part of the anorectic young person who is forming a bond with the therapist.

Different tones of voice, different parts of the therapist's self are required for addressing different parts of the young person. 'You're useless,' is a feeling frequently projected into the therapist. When Maria goes 'tch' in a superior way, saying, 'You almost never get it right,' I know she is in her omnipotent combative soldier self which is silencing me. I am to feel small, unimportant, and stupid. I need to take the projections through an analyst-centred interpretation as recommended by John Steiner (1993) in *Psychic Retreats.* While at times acknowledging one's lack of understanding, the therapist has to acknowledge to oneself that one is being drawn into a sado-masochistic relationship with the omnipotent destructive part that is not only protecting the vulnerable self from being wounded but also, as Di Masi (2003) says in *The Sadomasochistic Perversion,* attempting to move into the exciting controlling sadomasochistic relationship with the therapist in an attempt to avoid psychic pain.

Most importantly, I think it is useful to keep the different aspects of the ano- rectic person alive in the discussion: For example, the therapist can address, with different tones of voice, firmness to the propagandizing self, tenderness to the 'lit- tle girl', collaborative thoughtful, and mature voice to the 14-year-old needing to take responsibility for protecting and understanding 'the little girl' both inside and outside the session. This technique is described by Donald Meltzer (1994) in *Tem- perature and Distance.*

The anorectic child's links with the parents /therapists is filled with hostility about misattunement between the child and significant others. It is important for the child to be able to acknowledge rather than deny hostility. The therapist and parents' compassionate reception of the child's loving dependence and hostility allows healing of 'the cruel voice' of the anorectic young person.

Healing of the anorectic young person involves developing a trusting link between therapist and young person. It is only gradually that the person in therapy can bear to appreciate the therapist's unconditional containment of all her feelings of love and hatred. It is terrifying to let go of the protection of 'the gang filled with propaganda against dependence' (Rosenfeld 1987) and move into the anxiety pro- voking situation of bearing to trust the therapist. In the past, trusting a 'significant other' has involved feeling pain and rage about unmet needs and experiencing per- sonal traumas. Now they are likely to arise again in the transference relationship to the psychotherapist.

Only slowly can the young person begin to face her hidden sense of loss as well as perhaps the destructiveness of her greed, possessive jealousy, and destructive envy. Only with time can the healing anorectic patient regain, acknowledge, and mitigate this psychic pain and accompanying split-off and projected hostile feel- ings towards primary figures. It is this hurt and accompanying hostility which has created 'poison food' and 'terrible fat', 'a sense of ugliness' and a feeling of being unlovable, rejected and 'no good'.

The process of the anorectic young person's healing involves gradually trusting the therapist and struggling to let go of the protection of omnipotent control using of denial. Only then can the young person internalize the therapist's capacity to receive and understand feelings of dependence, love, hostility, possessiveness, and hurt.

The therapist's empathically receiving and understanding the child's multitude of feelings allows the child to have some sense of forgiveness towards themselves and towards the parents for just being human beings with their own deficiencies rather than having to be perfect.

The anorectic child has been starved emotionally because the link with the vul- nerable self has been broken by the omnipotent self which creates denial of vulner- able and painful feelings.

Healing of the young person involves developing sufficient emotional strength in the mature self to reunite emotionally with the vulnerable feelings inside themselves. Later, in therapy, Maria said, 'I feel relieved when I can feel sad or angry rather than numb to my feelings.' Here we see the link between Maria's mature self and her vulnerable self has been restored. In this way maturation of the infantile self can ensue.

Healing involves relinquishing the isolating, constraining, numbing impediments 'to becoming oneself' alone and with others.

References

Bick, E. (1968) The experience of the skin in early object relationships. *International Journal of Psychoanalysis*, 49: 484–486.

Bion, W.R. (1959) Attacks on linking. *International Journal of Psychoanalysis, 30*: 309–319.

Bion, W.R. (1962) *Learning from Experience.* London: William Heinemann.

Bryant-Waugh, R. and Lask, B. (2004) *Eating Disorders: A Parents' Guide.* East Sussex: Brunner-Routledge.

Cardenal, M. (2024, September 27) COCAP Presentation: *Self-harming in early life and the difficulty in living for some infants.* Chapter 10 (in this book).

Di Masi, F. (2003) *The Sadomasochistic Perversion.* London: Routledge.

Freeman, H. (2023) *Good Girls.* London: 4th Estate.

Helm, J.L., Saxbe, D. and Adam, E.K. (2007). Stress reactivity and parental caregiving: The development of healthy physiological regulation in infancy. *Psychoneuroendocrinology*, 32(8–10): 997–1005.

Magagna, J. (2012) *The Silent Child: Communication without Words.* London: Karnac.

Magagna, J. and Piercey, J. (2020) Collaborative Work with Parents. *British Journal of Psychotherapy* 36(2): 177–189. ISSN: 17520118.

Magagna, J. (2022) *A Psychotherapeutic Understanding of Eating Disorders in Children and Young People.* Abingdon: Routledge.

Meltzer, D. (1975) *The Psychoanalytic Process.* Perth: Clunie.

Meltzer, D. (1994) Temperature and distance as a technical dimension of interpretation. In: A. Hahn (Ed.) *Sincerity and Other Works* (pp. 374–387). London: Karnac.

Porges, S. (2017) *The Polyvagal Theory.* New York: W.W. Norton.

Rosenfeld, H. (1987) *Impasse and Interpretation.* London: Tavistock.

Steiner, J. (1993) *Psychic Retreats.* London: Routledge.

Tchanturia, K. (2021) *Supporting Autistic People with Eating Disorders.* London: Jessica Kingsley.

Tustin, F. (1986) *Autistic Barriers in Neurotic Patients.* London: Karnac.

Chapter 12

Self-harm behaviors in adolescents

Psychoanalytic understanding

Humberto Lorenzo Persano

Introduction

Self-harm is a pervasive and multifaceted clinical phenomenon that continues to challenge mental health professionals worldwide. This behavior, defined as the deliberate infliction of injury upon oneself without suicidal intent, often emerges during adolescence and young adulthood—a developmental period marked by heightened vulnerability, identity formation, and social inclusion changes. Alarmingly, recent years have witnessed a troubling increase in self-injurious behaviors, a trend intricately linked to the broader existential malaise among youth in contemporary societies. Addressing self-harm necessitates an interdisciplinary approach that incorporates psychoanalytic, psychosocial, and neurobiological perspectives.

This rise is particularly pronounced in Western societies and those influenced by Western ideals, where adolescents face immense societal pressures, fragmentation of identity, and an overarching loss of meaning. Julia Kristeva described this phenomenon as a crisis of meaning, asserting that modern individuals grapple with an unbearable emptiness in the absence of shared symbolic frameworks (***Kristeva, 1980). The dissonance between societal expectations and the lived realities of young people often manifests itself in self-destructive behaviors, as they struggle to reconcile these pressures with their internal worlds.

Moreover, self-harm is not merely a symptom of psychological distress; it serves as a critical marker of future risk. A substantial body of research has established self-harm as a predictive indicator of suicidal ideation and behavior, particularly among vulnerable populations. According to the World Health Organization (***WHO, 2023), suicide remains the second leading cause of death among adolescents and young adults globally, surpassed only by unintentional injuries such as road accidents. The strong correlation between non-suicidal self-injury (NSSI) and suicide attempts underscores the urgency of addressing self-harm within clinical and community-based interventions.

The sociocultural context further complicates the phenomenon of self-harm. In a hyperconnected digital age, young people are subjected to relentless comparisons and online scrutiny, amplifying feelings of inadequacy and alienation. Peter ***Fonagy et al. (2002) have highlighted the role of early attachment disruptions

DOI: 10.4324/9781003647317-15

and deficits in mentalizing capacities in the etiology of self-harm, emphasizing that self-injury represents a failure in the individual's ability to manage emotional pain through adaptive means. These insights are crucial for clinicians, as they underscore the need for interventions that foster resilience, enhance emotional regulation, and rebuild meaningful connections. Philippe ***Jeammet (2007) underscores the importance of understanding the symbolic dimensions of self-harm, viewing it as a desperate attempt to assert control and restore a sense of agency in the face of overwhelming internal chaos. Similarly, Marsha Linehan's research offers evidence-based tools for helping individuals develop healthier coping mechanisms, reducing the frequency and severity of self-injurious behaviors (***Linehan, 1993).

The SARS-CoV-2 pandemic forced individuals to make profound and sudden adjustments to their daily lives. These disruptions not only reshaped routines but also had far-reaching effects on mental health, significantly altering the landscape of psychopathology that clinicians encounter. Among the most concerning trends has been the alarming rise in eating disorders (EDs) and Non-Suicidal Self-Injury (NSSI) among adolescents (***Scita & Artoni, 2022).

This increase highlights deeper psychological and societal dynamics, suggesting a shared thread that links these two psychopathological manifestations. At the core of both behaviors lies the intersection between the body and self-harming gestures, reflecting profound struggles with identity, control, and emotional regulation. These disturbances can also be understood in the context of our modern, consumerist society, which privileges immediacy, productivity, and external validation over introspection, reflection, and emotional processing.

The temporal dimension and the experience of self

One critical factor that ties these behaviors together is the experience of time. Adolescents, today, particularly during the pandemic, have faced an abrupt disconnection from structured routines and social interactions, amplifying feelings of uncertainty and emotional instability. This disruption has been exacerbated by a cultural shift that prioritizes speed, instant gratification, and performative success. The loss of slower, contemplative, and introspective time—essential for emotional processing and identity formation—has created a vacuum in which impulsive actions, such as restrictive eating and self-harm, offer an illusion of control and immediacy.

As adolescents grapple with the pressures of rapid digital communication and social media, they often experience heightened anxiety and self-comparison, leading to cycles of shame and inadequacy. In this context, the body becomes a site for enacting distress, where EDs and NSSI serve as attempts to externalize internal chaos and reassert control over fragmented identities.

The rise in adolescent psychopathology during the pandemic underscores the urgent need for clinicians to address the underlying emotional and societal factors that drive these behaviors. Recognizing the temporal disruptions and cultural shifts that influence self-perception and emotional regulation can help inform more effective interventions. By fostering slower, reflective therapeutic spaces, clinicians can help adolescents reconnect with their internal worlds, develop healthier coping mechanisms, and build resilience against the pressures of modern life.

In conclusion, self-harm is a multifaceted issue rooted in complex interactions between individual vulnerabilities and sociocultural dynamics. It demands a nuanced understanding that integrates theoretical insights with practical strategies for intervention. The rising prevalence of self-harm among adolescents is not only a pressing clinical concern but also a reflection of the broader challenges faced by a generation grappling with unprecedented societal changes and existential uncertainty.

Psychoanalytic approaches to self-harming behaviors in adolescents

From a Freudian psychoanalytic perspective, self-harming behaviors can be understood as unconscious expressions of internal conflict and unprocessed trauma. Freud's concept of *repetition compulsion* provides a valuable lens: individuals who self-harm repeat traumatic patterns to gain mastery over them, albeit unconsciously. Freud observed, *"The patient cannot remember the whole of what is repressed in him, and what he cannot remember may be acted out"* (***Freud, 1912). Self-harm thus becomes a form of *acting out*, whereby psychic pain—unarticulated in language—is discharged through the body.

There is an intricate and profound relationship between emotions—particularly anger—and self-harming behaviors. When anger dominates the psychic scene, it often lacks an appropriate outlet for discharge, leading the subject to unleash this rage upon themselves. This inward-directed aggression serves both as a release and a form of relief from the tension that overwhelms the Ego as a psychic organization. Freud's foundational insights on the psychic economy shed light on this process, as he claimed that when painful or traumatic experiences reach an intolerable intensity, they surpass the psyche's threshold of containment within the representational world (ψ). In such circumstances, the psychic apparatus resorts to an archaic mechanism: discharging the tension through the *motor pole* (φ) (***Freud, 1920). Self-harm thus represents an externalized expression of unmanageable internal pressures.

Freud further elaborated on this phenomenon in *The Economic Problem of Masochism* (***1924), where he connected the release of tension to the *Nirvana Principle*—the death drive's striving toward a state of absolute quiescence, devoid of all stimulation. This drive, deeply connected to masochism, manifests itself as a paradoxical form of pleasure derived from self-inflicted suffering. However, what distinguishes self-harm from masochism is that aggression is not directed toward external objects in the environment but rather turned inward, onto the *body ego*. Freud described this mechanism as "turning against the self," an archaic defense that reflects both regression and primitive psychic functioning (***Freud, 1917). In adolescence, such mechanisms become particularly salient, as the adolescent psyche is still in a maturational process and remains highly susceptible to regression under pressure.

This regression—whether temporary or persistent—reveals the adolescent's profound psychic suffering and the failure of more mature defenses. Self-harm emerges as a desperate attempt to gain mastery over unprocessed emotions and unbearable affects. As Otto Fenichel noted, the aggression turned inward upon oneself can relieve unbearable tension momentarily, though it comes at the cost of harming the self and perpetuating the cycle of psychic pain (***Fenichel, 1945). Self-harming behavior thus represents a failure to symbolize and process emotional states through language and thought; instead, the adolescent resorts to acting out, wherein the body becomes the canvas for unspoken pain.

Winnicott's work further deepens this understanding by framing self-harm as an attempt to preserve the "true self." For Winnicott, when the environment fails to provide a "holding" experience, adolescents may resort to self-injury to *feel real*. As he profoundly notes, *"It is a joy to be hidden, and disaster not to be found"* (***Winnicott, 1965). Self-harm, then, emerges as a paradoxical act of self-preservation—a desperate effort to reconnect with the fragmented or hidden self in the face of overwhelming psychic disintegration.

The impact of early attachment disruptions

When early bonds with caregivers are disrupted, the effects extend far beyond neglect or emotional deprivation. These disruptions can expose the child to passive aggression or emotional invalidation, leaving profound imprints on their psychological development. According to ***Kernberg (1992), such relational dynamics often lead to the internalization of aggression through a process of identification with the aggressor. The child, unable to challenge or escape the source of aggression, unconsciously adopts hostile attitudes and behaviors directed toward them, turning these dynamics inward and fuel patterns of self-criticism and punitive behaviors. Disordered eating behaviors thus become an expression of the adolescent's attempts to manage these unconscious conflicts, externalizing their emotional pain onto the body. This internalization process establishes a foundation for self-directed aggression, where the child begins to mirror the criticism, rejection, or invalidation they experienced in their primary attachments. As ***Winnicott (1960) noted, the absence of a consistent and empathetic caregiver leaves the child vulnerable to developing a *"false self"* as a defense against feelings of worthlessness. The false self—an outwardly adaptive but inwardly disconnected part of the personality—attempts to maintain relationships while masking deep emotional pain. This protective facade often manifests itself as perfectionism and hyper-control over the body, masking profound insecurities and emotional fragility.

Over time, internalized aggression may take the form of harsh self-criticism, perfectionism, and punitive behavior directed at the self. Such patterns often surface in adolescence, a period marked by heightened vulnerability due to developmental transitions and the consolidation of identity.

Jessica Yakeley explores the unconscious meanings and functions of self-harm within a relational and attachment framework. She emphasizes that self-harm often serves as a means of expressing unarticulated emotions, managing internal conflicts, and exerting control over overwhelming feelings (***Yakeley, 2010).

Yakeley highlights the importance of understanding self-harm as both a physical manifestation of internalized distress and a defensive strategy to ward off feelings of helplessness and fragmentation. From a psychoanalytic perspective, self-harm can be seen as a form of communication, a symbolic language of pain that conveys what cannot be spoken aloud. Adolescents who engage in self-harm often struggle with mentalization, the capacity to reflect on and make sense of their emotional experiences (***Fonagy et al., 2002).

According to this author, self-harm also reflects disruptions in early attachment relationships, where emotional needs were inadequately met. These experiences leave adolescents prone to internalizing aggression and resorting to bodily acts to manage affect. The act of cutting, for example, may function to transform emotional pain into physical sensations that feel more manageable, while simultaneously punishing the self for perceived failures or inadequacies (***Yakeley, 2010).

Expanding the scope of self-harm

Self-harm is not limited to cutting behaviors; it also encompasses disordered eating patterns such as restrictive dieting, binge eating, and purging. These behaviors often emerge as physical manifestations of unresolved attachment insecurities and emotional distress. Adolescents with fragile self-regulation may resort to these practices as mechanisms to assert control or enact self-punishment, externalizing internalized aggression through their bodies.

***Fairbairn (1943) highlighted that disruptions in early attachment relationships can lead to a profound psychological split between the *"ideal self"* and the *"despised self."* This internal division fosters cycles of shame, self-loathing, and punitive behaviors, ultimately reinforcing patterns of self-directed aggression and emotional dysregulation.

The body as a site of control and punishment

For adolescents grappling with feelings of inadequacy and emotional turmoil, disordered eating behaviors often serve as a means of regulating overwhelming affects. By controlling food intake or engaging in purging rituals, these individuals attempt to transform intangible emotional pain into tangible actions, achieving a temporary sense of mastery over internal chaos.

> I hate the way I look. Not eating makes me feel like I finally have control over something.

Such statements reveal how the body becomes a battleground where internal conflicts are enacted. The adolescent's efforts to assert control through restrictive eating reflect a desperate attempt to calm down feelings of inadequacy, guilt, and self-loathing.

The interplay between self-directed aggression and disordered eating behaviors reflects deeper issues related to identity and emotional regulation.

Attachment insecurity and fragmented self-regulation

The inability to develop secure attachments during early life stages undermines the child's capacity for emotional regulation and self-soothing. ***Fonagy et al. (2002) emphasized the importance of mentalization—the ability to understand one's own and others' mental states—in the development of secure attachments. When caregivers fail to mirror the child's emotional experiences, the child may struggle to develop this reflective function, leaving them prone to emotional dysregulation and impulsive behaviors.

In cases of EDs and self-harm, the body becomes the site where unprocessed emotions are enacted.

> Not eating gives me a sense of control. It helps calm the storm I feel inside
> When I cut, it makes everything feel more real—like my body is bearing the pain my mind can't process

These statements reflect the adolescent's reliance on somatic expressions to manage emotional pain, underscoring the role of disrupted attachment in shaping their coping strategies.

***Kernberg (1992) and ***Bowlby (1969) emphasized that early relational trauma affects the development of the self, creating vulnerabilities to pathological defenses such as splitting, projection, and projective identification. By recognizing the symbolic nature of self-harming and disordered eating behaviors, clinicians can help adolescents process their unresolved pain and develop healthier modes of emotional regulation and focus on rebuilding the capacity for integration and mentalization, allowing the fragmented self to be repaired and reconnected.

The role of emotional regulation is central to the constitution of an integrated Ego and a stable sense of self. Peter ***Fonagy et al. (2002) describe mentalization as the ability to "reflect upon and understand one's own and others' mental states," a capacity that develops only when caregivers provide a secure and attuned relational environment. This relational exchange fosters intersubjectivity, which is essential for the development of self-regulation mechanisms.

When early relationships fail to provide this secure and responsive emotional holding, the infant is left unable to internalize adequate strategies for managing affective states. As a result, the emotional turbulence that ensues may be expressed through archaic motor behaviors, particularly under conditions of distress. In adolescence the inability to regulate negative affects often leads to emotional impulsivity, which in its most extreme form, manifests itself in self-harming behaviors, which, paradoxically, serve as a maladaptive attempt to contain unbearable psychic tension.

In *Beyond the Pleasure Principle* (1920) Freud postulated that when the psychic apparatus is overwhelmed, the drive tension—particularly aggression—demands discharge. In masochistic expressions, this aggression relies on *primitive defense mechanisms* such as splitting and "turning against the self," with no conscious foresight of its consequences.

In clinical practice, self-harm is frequently observed in individuals with borderline and narcissistic personality organizations, depressive states, eating disorders, and substance abuse. Otto Kernberg's psychoanalytic theory of borderline personality highlights the role of *splitting*—the inability to integrate good and bad aspects of the self and others—which results in overwhelming emotional dysregulation. For these individuals, self-harm may function as an effort to manage dissociative states, unbearable affects, and feelings of emptiness. ***Kernberg (1975) describes this as a *"primitive defense"* against annihilation anxiety, where the act of self-harm creates a temporary, albeit destructive, sense of control.

In patients with EDs, the body serves as a central arena for psychic conflict—a symbolic battleground where struggles over identity, control, and self-worth are enacted. Philippe ***Jeammet (2009) insightfully describes self-destructive behaviors in adolescence as a means of survival, emphasizing that *"the adolescent feels trapped between their need for independence and their dependency on others."*

Self-harm, in this context, reflects a breakdown in the capacity to symbolize and verbalize internal conflicts. Instead, these unprocessed emotions are displaced onto the body through somatization and physical acts.

Self-harm as embodied communication

Psychoanalytic perspectives emphasize that self-harm is also a deep form of communication, a language expressed through the body when words fail. It is an enactment of unspoken trauma, emotional pain, and unresolved conflicts. ***Ferenczi (1932) explored the concept of the body expressing psychological truths, particularly in the context of trauma and psychosomatic symptoms. For instance, in his work on the "confusion of tongues" he discusses how unprocessed traumatic experiences can manifest physically when they cannot be articulated verbally. *"The patient's body speaks the truth that the mind has silenced."* This perspective compels clinicians to look beyond the observable behavior and decode its symbolic meaning, tracing it to relational, historical, and unconscious dynamics (***Ferenczi, 1932).

The body as a site and expression of conflict

The adolescent body thus becomes both a battleground and a canvas where psychic pain is enacted and made visible. Julia ***Kristeva (1990) captures this violent choreography as follows: *"the adolescent turns inward against the self, acting as both tormentor and tormented, a violent dance between punishment and relief"* (***Kristeva, 1990: 8–23).

   She underscores the role of self-harm as both a physical manifestation of psychic pain and a symbolic attempt to assert agency over internal fragmentation. The adolescent's use of the body as a medium reflects an effort to reclaim control and make sense of emotional chaos, even as these acts perpetuate cycles of shame and self-punishment (***Kristeva, 1989).

Key phrases in adolescents who self-harm: the fragmented self

A recent study identified three recurring phrases expressed by adolescents who engage in self-harm: *"I deserve the pain," "I don't want to feel anything,"* and *"I feel hurt, and no one cares."* These statements shed light on the psychic structures and emotional conflicts underlying self-harming behaviors. According to ***Stänicke et al. (2018) and ***Persano (2022), these phrases reflect fragmented self-representations that emerge during adolescence, particularly among those who struggle with self-injury.

1   *"I deserve the pain."* This phrase reveals a representation of a *"self that deserves to be punished."* Adolescents expressing this belief often internalize a punitive Superego, shaped by experiences of guilt, shame, and perceived failure. The act of self-harm functions as both punishment and release, providing temporary relief from unbearable psychic tension.

   I hate myself for being weak. Hurting myself makes me feel like I'm paying for it.

   Freud (1923) explored this phenomenon through the lens of the Superego, emphasizing its harsh, critical nature in driving masochistic tendencies (Persano, 2022).

2   *"I don't want to feel anything."* This phrase points to the emergence of *"unknown aspects of the self"* and reflects dissociation and emotional numbing. Adolescents who voice this sentiment are often overwhelmed by affective states they cannot articulate, leading to a defensive disconnection from their emotions.

3   ***Winnicott (1965) noted that adolescents facing emotional fragmentation may resort to bodily enactments to create a paradoxical sense of control. One patient explained, *"When I cut, it makes me feel real, even if it's just for a moment."* The act of self-harm externalizes this internal chaos, functioning as a defense against overwhelming feelings and as an attempt to stabilize a fragile sense of self. *"I feel hurt, and no one cares."* This statement reflects a *"self that feels damaged"* and underscores a profound sense of emotional isolation and relational disconnection. Adolescents who feel unseen or invalidated by others

use self-harm as both a cry for help and an attempt to externalize psychic pain when verbalization is impossible.

No one listens to me. When I hurt myself, at least I know that my pain is real

The body as a mirror of psychic pain

Ultimately, the body in self-harm acts as a mirror reflecting psychic wounds that cannot yet be spoken. By acknowledging self-harm as a form of embodied communication, psychoanalytic approaches illuminate its symbolic dimensions and create pathways for healing. Adolescents who harm themselves are not merely seeking attention; they are expressing profound emotional truths that demand to be heard, understood, and integrated into their evolving identities.

The role of self-representation in adolescent development

Adolescents are tasked with forming a coherent sense of self while navigating intense emotional upheavals, changes in relationships, and emerging autonomy. When these processes are disrupted by trauma, relational neglect, or internal conflicts, self-representation remains fragmented and does not become integrated.

***Freud (1923) conceptualized the Ego as a mediator between internal drives and external reality, trying to maintain cohesion amidst conflicts. In cases of self-harm, however, the Ego struggles to contain and process unbound affect, leading to the emergence of archaic forms of self-representation rooted in shame, guilt, and aggression.

As Marsha ***Linehan (1993) explains, self-harm often serves as an attempt to regulate overwhelming affects by imposing physical pain that is more manageable than emotional distress. Similarly, ***McDougall (1989) views such behaviors as psychosomatic enactments, where the body becomes a stage for expressing unarticulated psychic pain.

I need to make myself pay for all the mistakes I keep making. Hurting myself feels like a way to set things right

My emotions feel too intense to handle. When I hurt myself, it helps me calm down, even if just for a little while

It feels like no one understands how much I'm hurting. When I harm myself, it's proof that my pain is real and can't be ignored

These statements highlight the critical need for therapeutic spaces where adolescents can explore and integrate fragmented aspects of the self, transforming destructive enactments into reflective understanding.

The phrases illustrate the complex interplay between self-representation, emotional regulation, and identity formation in adolescents who engage in self-harm

(***Stänicke et al., 2018; ***Persano, 2022). Psychoanalytic and relational frameworks, combined with other psychodynamic psychotherapies like mentalized based therapy (MBT) (***Bateman & Fonagy, 2004, 2019) or transference focused psychotherapy (TFP), offer pathways for addressing these deeply rooted issues and promoting healing through symbolic expression of internal conflict (Yeomans et al., 2015).

Self-harm functions as a non-verbal form of communication, a silent cry for help that is inscribed upon the skin (***Lemma, 2010). As Christopher Bollas writes, the body becomes the site of the unthought known, a place where the unspeakable finds expression, where the individual unconsciously communicates trauma or emotional pain through somatic expressions rather than through language (***Bollas, 1987).

I harm myself, therefore I control my pain

This mechanism often reflects the adolescent's unconscious struggle with their dependency needs and a defensive reaction to feelings of helplessness. Philippe Jeammet observes that self-destructive behaviors are less a wish to die than a desperate attempt to escape psychic disintegration and intolerable emotional states (***Jeammet, 2009).

The body in self-harm also becomes a symbolic site where traumatic experiences are externalized. The wounds inflicted upon the skin often stand in for unprocessed psychic wounds, revealing a profound conflict between the adolescent's need for communication and their inability to verbalize emotional states.

In sum, self-harming behavior reflects the interplay of multiple psychoanalytic dynamics: the discharge of uncontainable psychic tension, the turning of aggression inward, the failure of symbolic articulation, and the use of the body as a means of communication. For adolescents, who navigate the delicate threshold between dependence and autonomy, self-harm becomes a way of expressing vulnerability while simultaneously asserting control. It calls for clinicians to listen to what Winnicott described as the *"hidden self"* behind the destructive act, providing a safe and empathic space where unspoken pain can be symbolized, contained, and ultimately healed (***Winnicott, 1965).

Adolescents with borderline personality organizations are particularly susceptible to self-harming behaviors due to their fragile ego structures and impaired emotional regulation. Otto ***Kernberg (1975) identified emotional dysregulation as a core feature of borderline personality organizations, noting that aggression often overwhelms the Ego's integrative functions. In such cases, self-harm provides temporary relief from the intensity of unregulated negative affects but comes at the expense of the self's coherence. Kernberg describes this because of Ego fragility, where primitive defenses such as splitting dominate: the adolescent oscillates between idealized and persecutory states of mind, unable to integrate conflicting emotional experiences.

Furthermore, emotional dysregulation and self-harm in adolescence reflect a failure in the symbolization process. Self-harm thus emerges as an archaic *acting-out* behavior that externalizes internal chaos.

The adolescent's inability to regulate emotions can also be linked to disruptions in attachment. Attachment theory, particularly as elaborated by ***Fonagy and Target (1997), emphasizes that disruptions in the attachment bond during early life compromise the development of mentalization and affective regulation. Adolescents who experienced neglect, trauma, or inconsistent caregiving may lack the capacity to understand and modulate their emotions, leading to impulsive acts such as self-harm as a means of coping. Mentalization theory suggests that such dissociative experiences arise when the adolescent's capacity to reflect upon their mental states collapses under emotional distress. In these moments, the *pre-reflective self* takes over, and the act of self-harm becomes a way to reclaim control over overwhelming affect through bodily sensation.

The manifestation of aggression—both toward others and turned against the self—underscores the narcissistic vulnerability inherent in adolescents who engage in self-harm. Narcissistic fragility often stems from failures in early mirroring relationships, as described by Heinz Kohut's self-psychology. Kohut posited that deficits in empathic attunement leave the individual unable to sustain a coherent sense of self, leading to fragmentation under stress (***Kohut, 1971). Self-harm, in this context, becomes a means of achieving temporary relief from feelings of emptiness, fragmentation, or unbearable shame.

Thus, self-harm in adolescents reflects a complex interplay of impaired emotional regulation, archaic defenses, and relational failures. The act serves as a maladaptive attempt to reduce psychic pain and regain control over overwhelming emotional states, yet it perpetuates a cycle of dysregulation and self-destruction. Clinicians must recognize that self-harm is both a symptom and a communication—an externalized expression of internal chaos. As Winnicott poignantly stated, the capacity to be alone is a developmental achievement; without it, oneself can only exist in reaction to pain (***Winnicott, 1958).

Self-harm as a primitive and archaic mode of expression

Understanding self-harm within the framework of psychoanalytic theory highlights its function as a primitive and archaic mode of expression. According to ***Freud's (1920) economic model, unbound affect—raw, unprocessed emotional energy—is discharged through motor activity when the psychic apparatus cannot contain or elaborate it.

The act of self-harm represents a short-circuit between the unbound energy and the motor pole, bypassing mental processing.

I couldn't find the words to explain it—I just had to do something to make the feeling go away

For psychoanalytic treatment, the aim is to prevent these short-circuits and create conditions where raw affects can be transformed into verbalized mental content. This transformation requires a therapeutic framework that blocks impulsive motor discharges and provides a containing space for the expression of mental states.

Addressing self-harm in adolescents thus requires an empathic, psychoanalytically informed approach that explores the relational, developmental, and unconscious dimensions of the behavior. By creating a therapeutic "holding environment," clinicians can facilitate the adolescent's ability to integrate conflicting emotions, develop healthier forms of self-regulation, and gradually replace self-destructive acts with meaningful symbolic expression.

References

Bateman, A., & Fonagy, P. (2004). *Psychotherapy for Personality Disorder. Mentalization-based treatment*. New York: Oxford University Press.

Bateman, A., & Fonagy, P. (2019). *Handbook of Mentalizing in Mental Health Practice*. Washington: American Psychiatric Association Publishing.

Bollas, C. (1987). *The Shadow of the Object: Psychoanalysis of the Unthought Known*. Columbia University Press.

Bowlby, J. (1969). *Attachment and Loss: Vol. 1. Attachment*. New York: Basic Books.

Fairbairn, W. R. D. (1943). The Repression and the Return of Bad Object. In *Psychoanalytic Studies of the Personality*. London: Routledge.

Fenichel, O. (1945). *The Psychoanalytic Theory of Neurosis*. London: Routledge.

Ferenczi, S. (1932). Confusion of Tongues between the Adults and the Child. In *Final Contributions to the Problems and Methods of Psycho-Analysis*. London: Karnac Books.

Fonagy, P., Gergely, G., Jurist, E., & Target, M. (2002). *Affect Regulation, Mentalization, and the Development of the Self*. New York: Other Press.

Fonagy, P., & Target, M. (1997). Attachment and Reflective Function: Their Role in Self-Organization. *Development and Psychopathology*, 9(4), 679–700.

Freud, S. (1912). Remembering, Repeating, and Working-Through (Further Recommendations on the Technique of Psychoanalysis). In Mark Solms (Ed.), *The Standard Edition of the Complete Psychological Works of Sigmund Freud* (Vol. 12, 145–156). London: Hogarth Press, 1991.

Freud, S. (1917). *Mourning and Melancholia*. In James Strachey (Ed.), *The Standard Edition of the Complete Psychological Works of Sigmund Freud* (Vol. 14, 237–258). London: Hogarth Press, 1986.

Freud, S. (1920). Beyond the Pleasure Principle. In Mark Solms (Ed.), *The Standard Edition of the Complete Psychological Works of Sigmund Freud* (Vol. 18, 3–64). London: Hogarth Press, 1991.

Freud, S. (1923). The Ego and the Id. In Mark Solms (Ed.), *The Standard Edition of the Complete Psychological Works of Sigmund Freud* (Vol. 19, 3–66). London: Hogarth Press, 1991.

Freud, S. (1924). The Economic Problem of Masochism. In Mark Solms (Ed.), *The Standard Edition of the Complete Psychological Works of Sigmund Freud* (Vol. 19, 157–170). London: Hogarth Press, 1991.

Jeammet, P. (2007). *L'adolescence*. Paris: Solar.

Jeammet, P. (2009). El yo frente a la libertad. Evolución social y adolescencia. *Revista de Psicopatología y Salud Mental del Niño y del Adolescente* (13), 31–40.

Kernberg, O. F. (1975). *Borderline Conditions and Pathological Narcissism*. New York: Jason Aronson.

Kernberg, O. F. (1992). *Aggression in Personality Disorders and Perversions*. New Haven: Yale University Press.

Kohut, H. (1971). *The Analysis of the Self.* International Universities Press.

Kristeva, J. (1980). *Powers of Horror: An Essay on Abjection*. New York: Columbia University Press.

Kristeva, J. (1989). *Black Sun: Depression and Melancholia*. New York: Columbia University Press.

Kristeva, J. (1990). The Adolescent Novel. In J. Fletcher & A. Benjamin (Eds.), *Abjection, Melancholia, and Love: The Work of Julia Kristeva.* Routledge.

Lemma, A. (2010). *Under the Skin: A Psychoanalytic Study of Body Modification*. Routledge.

Linehan, M. M. (1993). *Cognitive-Behavioral Treatment of Borderline Personality Disorder.* Guilford Press.

McDougall, J. (1989). *Theatres of the Body: A Psychoanalytic Approach to Psychosomatic Illness*. London: Free Association Books.

Persano, H. L. (2022). Self-Harm. *The International Journal of Psychoanalysis, 103*(6), 1089–1103.

Scita, F., & Artoni, P. (2022). Corpo e autolesionismo: spunti di riflessione sui disturbi dell'alimentazione e sull'autolesionismo in tempi di pandemia da SARS CoV-2. *Rivista sperimentale di freniatria: la rivista dei servizi di salute mentale, CXLVI*(3), 105–123.

Stänicke, L. I., Haavind, H., & Gullestad, S. E. (2018). How do Young People Understand Their Own Self-Harm? A Meta-Synthesis of Adolescents' Subjective Experience of Self-Harm. *Adolescent Research Review, 3*, 173–191.

Winnicott, D. W. (1958). The Capacity to be Alone. *International Journal of Psychoanalysis, 39*, 416–420.

Winnicott, D. W. (1960). Ego Distortion in Terms of True and False Self. In John D. Sutherland (Ed.), *The Maturational Processes and the Facilitating Environment: Studies in the Theory of Emotional Development* (140–152). London: Hogarth Press and the Institute of Psycho-Analysis.

Winnicott, D. W. (1965). *The Maturational Processes and the Facilitating Environment: Studies in the Theory of Emotional Development*. New York: International Universities Press.

World Health Organization. (2023). *Preventing Suicide: A Global Imperative*. Geneva: WHO.

Yakeley, J. (2010). Understanding Self-Harm: Psychoanalytic Perspectives. *Advances in Psychiatric Treatment, 16*(3), 189–197.

Yeomans, F. E., Clarkin, J. F., & Kernberg, O. F. (2015). *Transference-Focused Psychotherapy for Borderline Personality Disorder: A Clinical Guide*. American Psychiatric Publishing.

Chapter 13

Self-harm behaviors in adolescents

Understanding the role of social media, family and society: therapeutic implications

Humberto Lorenzo Persano

The role of social media in the rise of self-harming behaviors

In today's digital age, the proliferation of social media platforms has profoundly influenced adolescent behaviors, particularly self-harming tendencies. The widespread sharing of self-injury images, personal testimonies, and related content on platforms like Instagram, Tumblr, TikTok, and specific self-harm forums has significantly contributed to the increase in self-injurious acts. These platforms often act as spaces where adolescents, already grappling with fragile identities and intense emotions, encounter content that normalizes, validates, or even romanticizes self-harm.

The adolescent psyche, characterized by its search for identity, belonging, and autonomy, is particularly vulnerable to the influences of these virtual spaces. Adolescents who feel isolated or misunderstood may engage with self-harming content to form connections with others who appear to share their pain. This identification process fosters a sense of community but simultaneously reinforces masochistic tendencies and externalizes internal conflicts through harmful acts.

Identification and social contagion: a psychoanalytic framework

Freud's early observations on identification (1921) provide a crucial framework for understanding the influence of social media on self-harming behaviors. Freud described identification as an unconscious process whereby an individual internalizes aspects of another—whether admired, envied, or perceived as similar. In the context of social media, adolescents unconsciously identify with peers engaging in self-harm, not as direct imitation but as a means of alleviating their own isolation. Identification serves a relational function, aligning the adolescent with a perceived group identity, while also acting symbolically to externalize their inner turmoil.

Winnicott's (1960) concept of the "false self" further elucidates this phenomenon. Adolescents who lack a coherent and stable sense of self may adopt destructive behaviors to "feel real" or to fill the void of psychic fragmentation. As

DOI: 10.4324/9781003647317-16

Winnicott states: It is better to feel bad and real than to feel nothing at all. Self-harm, when displayed and mirrored in online spaces, becomes a distorted mode of self-affirmation, where the body is used to externalize otherwise unbearable emotions.

The "contagion effect" of self-harm content

The phenomenon of social contagion—where behaviors spread through shared exposure—is significantly exacerbated in the digital era. Adolescents, in their quest for connection and belonging, engage with self-harming images and content not as passive observers but as participants in a shared masochistic enactment. This exposure creates what can be termed a "contagion effect" where self-harm behaviors are normalized, even glorified, through online communities and repetitive visual representations.

This dynamic is aptly described as a "masochistic choreography" wherein adolescents unconsciously replicate behaviors they see online, performing their psychic pain through acts of bodily harm (Persano, 2022).

As Marsha Linehan (1993) states: Self-harm becomes both a performance and a ritual, a way of externalizing unbearable emotions while creating a fleeting sense of agency over chaos. Adolescents derive a paradoxical sense of relief and control from these rituals, but the normalization of self-harm within these spaces deepens their suffering and reinforces the cycle of destructive behaviors.

The double bind of social contagion lies in its contradictory effects: it provides temporary relief and a sense of shared experience but ultimately isolates the adolescent further. By normalizing harm as a coping mechanism, these online spaces discourage healthier means of emotional regulation and perpetuate a destructive feedback loop.

Clinical observations and adolescent experiences

The following statements from adolescents illustrate the profound influence of social media on their self-harming behaviors:

> I came across a post where someone shared their scars, and it made me feel understood. I wondered if doing the same could help me feel better.
>
> There are so many people online discussing self-harm that it feels more normal now—like I'm not the only one dealing with this.
>
> I began following accounts where people opened up about their struggles, and it made me feel less isolated. But over time, I couldn't stop thinking about hurting myself too.

These accounts reveal the dual nature of online self-harm communities: they provide a sense of shared experience but simultaneously amplify and reinforce harmful behaviors through social mirroring.

Therapeutic implications and interventions

Addressing the role of social media in adolescent self-harming behaviors requires a nuanced therapeutic approach that incorporates psychoeducation, mentalization, and boundary-setting around digital exposure. Key strategies include:

1 *Psychoeducation on the influence of social media*: Adolescents must be helped to understand the ways in which social media normalizes and amplifies destructive behaviors. Therapists can provide psychoeducation to increase awareness of the "contagion effect" and its impact on their emotional states.
2 *Mentalization-Based Therapy (MBT):* Mentalization techniques, as outlined by Fonagy et al. (2002), can help adolescents reflect on their thoughts, emotions, and behaviors, reducing impulsive acts of self-harm.
3 *Encouraging alternative coping mechanisms*: Therapists should work with adolescents to develop healthier coping strategies that replace self-harm. Creative and expressive outlets, such as art therapy, journaling, and physical activity, can help externalize psychic pain without resorting to bodily harm.
4 *Parental and peer involvement*: Involving family members and trusted peers in the therapeutic process can help adolescents feel supported offline, counteracting the isolating effects of harmful online communities.
5 *Digital hygiene practices:* Encouraging adolescents to limit exposure to self-harm content and to curate healthier, supportive online environments is essential.

Social media as a double-edged sword

Social media and self-injury websites play a paradoxical role in adolescent self-harming behaviors. While these platforms provide connection and validation, they also amplify social contagion and normalize destructive acts. Understanding the psychoanalytic dynamics of identification, social mirroring, and the "contagion effect" is essential for clinicians working with adolescents. By fostering mentalization, encouraging healthier coping mechanisms, and addressing the digital influences on their behavior, therapists can help adolescents break the cycle of self-harm and develop more constructive ways of managing their emotional pain.

Intrapsychic, familial, and social dynamics

From a psychoanalytic perspective, several potential intrapsychic, familial, and social dynamics contribute to the emergence of self-harming behaviors in adolescence. At the intrapsychic level, self-harm often reflects a regression to archaic defense mechanisms such as splitting, turning against the self, and acting out (Persano, 2019).

Freud (1917) identified turning against the self as a mechanism in melancholia, where internalized aggression is redirected inward onto the Ego. This mechanism is particularly evident in adolescents who describe dissociative states during self-harm episodes. Patients often report being unable to remember the event fully, saying:

> I'm not sure what came over me—I just couldn't handle it anymore, so I cut myself. It only hit me when I saw the blood.

This narrative reflects a breakdown in the ability to symbolize and mentalize emotional pain, leading instead to somatic enactment.

At the level of family life, domestic aggression and trauma play a critical role in shaping self-harming behaviors. In families where aggression is normalized—whether overtly through violence or covertly through neglect and emotional unavailability—children often internalize this aggression (Persano, 2022).

Freud (1923) described this dynamic as the *cathexis of aggression* over libido, where the child's developing Ego becomes infused with hostile energy that later manifests as self-destructive impulses. Jeammet and Bochereau emphasize that when aggression cannot be directed outward or verbalized, it turns inward against the self, attacking the body as a stand-in for the internalized object. These authors further highlight that this suffering reflects the adolescent's desperate quest for autonomy in the face of dependency, leaving them vulnerable to cycles of shame, guilt, and self-punishment. Therapeutic interventions must address these symbolic meanings, helping adolescents transform destructive impulses into reflective understanding and adaptive emotional expression (Jeammet & Bochereau, 2007).

Moreover, families and broader societal structures often fail to establish an effective protective shield to contain the child's developing psyche (Persano & Goldberg, 1995).

On a societal level, the increase in disturbed interpersonal relationships—fueled by disconnection, social media pressures, and cultural fragmentation—further disrupts the adolescent's ability to regulate aggression. Society's failure to contain aggression through functional relational structures results in the adolescent's psychic regression to archaic coping mechanisms.

The interplay of social contagion, intrapsychic regression, familial aggression, and societal fragmentation creates fertile ground for the rise of self-harming behaviors among adolescents. The act of self-harm reflects the adolescent's attempt to regulate overwhelming emotions, achieve a fleeting sense of control, and externalize psychic pain. However, this relief comes at the cost of deepening the cycle of dysregulation and perpetuating feelings of shame and isolation.

As clinicians, understanding these behaviors requires us to adopt a psychoanalytically informed approach that integrates the adolescent's relational history, unconscious processes, and socio-cultural influences. By providing a therapeutic holding environment where the adolescent's pain can be symbolized and articulated, we facilitate the development of healthier mechanisms for emotional regulation and self-expression.

Violence in contemporary societies and its influence on adolescents

In contemporary society, violence has become a pervasive force that manifests itself in multiple forms—physical, psychological, and social. Among adolescents, violence often emerges not only as a direct experience but also as a broader cultural phenomenon. The recognition of violence and its varied expressions is critical for understanding self-harming behaviors in this age group. While physical violence remains prevalent, modern society has seen the rise of more insidious forms of violence, such as social discrimination and cyberbullying, which exacerbate feelings of alienation and vulnerability among adolescents.

Cyberbullying, amplified by the ubiquitous presence of social media, has transformed peer interactions and introduced new modes of aggression. The anonymity and accessibility of digital platforms have enabled relentless attacks on adolescents' self-esteem, body image, and identity.

> They posted awful things about me online—I felt trapped with no way out. I was so overwhelmed with shame that I cut myself just to make it stop.

These instances of cyberbullying and peer discrimination act as powerful catalysts for self-harming behaviors, turning external violence inward. Adolescents internalize the aggression directed toward them, often viewing themselves as deserving of punishment. This reflects a collapse of the boundary between external and internal violence, transforming societal aggression into self-directed masochism.

The subject's aggression toward specific body parts reflects an intrapsychic struggle between the Ego and the Ideal of the Ego. This dynamic highlights a narcissistic conflict where the Ego is perceived as failing to meet the rigid demands of an idealized self-image. As observed in clinical practice, adolescents frequently target areas such as the abdomen, thighs, arms, hips, and breast, regions symbolically linked to body image and self-worth.

> I feel so big. I hate the way my thighs look.
> My hips aren't the shape they should be. (while pointing to a self-inflicted cut)

Ephemeral relief and split-off aspects of the self

Self-harming behaviors provide temporary relief through both psychic and somatic discharge. In these moments, split-off aspects of the self—parts that remain unintegrated and alien to conscious awareness—emerge forcefully. These split-off parts often carry feelings of shame, self-loathing, and aggression that the adolescent cannot process or verbalize. Despite the masochistic nature of these acts, self-harm can paradoxically offer an opportunity to acknowledge these previously unfathomable aspects of one's psyche.

I don't know what came over me. It felt like I was watching someone else instead of myself.

I felt completely disconnected. Seeing the blood flow gave me relief, I couldn't even feel the pain.

This experience of dissociation underscores the fragile boundaries between self and non-self, a psychic split that is often rooted in early relational traumas and unresolved conflicts.

Masochism, aggression, and identification with the aggressor

Self-harming behaviors are frequently tied to affective aggression, which is triggered by overwhelming emotions such as anger, sadness, and emptiness. These emotions often stem from experiences of abandonment, whether real or imagined, and the subject's inability to manage the associated psychic pain. Archaic forms of masochism frequently underlie these acts, representing a form of identification with an internalized aggressor (Freud, 1924; Kernberg, 1975). Through masochistic behaviors, individuals unconsciously recreate painful relational dynamics as a way of managing their intrapsychic conflicts, albeit unsuccessfully (Persano, 2022).

In clinical practice, self-harming behaviors often emerge following moments of perceived rejection or abandonment. Adolescents may use immature and archaic defense mechanisms, such as splitting and projective identification, turning their aggression inward. This internalized aggression becomes intertwined with impulsivity and violence, manifesting in self-directed harm.

I was overwhelmed with anger, but instead of taking it out on someone else, I turned it on myself.

The role of early object relations in aggression and masochism

The regulation of aggression and masochism is deeply rooted in early relational experiences, where ambivalent emotions—love and hate—are first encountered. According to object relations theory, early interactions with primary caregivers shape the child's internal world and self-representations. The incorporation of relational patterns—particularly those dominated by aggression—becomes a core aspect of the child's identity and temperament traits (Klein, 1946; Kernberg, 1984, 2004; Fonagy et al., 2002; Persano, 2022).

When early object relations are marked by aggression or emotional neglect, these experiences are internalized as enduring templates for future relationships. Adolescents who self-harm often reenact these relational modalities in their interactions with others and with themselves. In these cases, self-harm becomes an unconscious attempt to relieve and resolve unprocessed childhood traumas.

Unpleasant affective states, such as shame, rejection, or abandonment, trigger self-harming behaviors as the adolescent turns aggression against the self.

When my mom left, I felt completely lost. It was like my body was overflowing with pain, and cutting was the only way to quiet it

Here, the body becomes the battleground for psychic pain, a space where aggression, despair, and masochism converge.

Understanding self-harm in adolescents requires an integrative approach and must be conducted with sensitivity and a focus on building trust. Adolescents often fear judgment and shame, which may hinder open communication. By validating their experiences and helping them recognize the symbolic meaning of their actions, clinicians can assist in fostering insight, emotional regulation, and healing.

Impulsiveness and its masochistic connotations

Impulsiveness in adolescents often carries an unconscious masochistic connotation, as the consequences of impulsive actions can lead to unintended and sometimes self-destructive results. Self-harming behaviors exemplify this duality, where impulsive acts serve as both a discharge of unbearable emotional tension and a reenactment of internalized aggression. Acting without regard for consequences is a hallmark of impulsiveness, which is frequently observed in adolescents with self-harming tendencies.

Impulsivity is shaped by both constitutional (temperamental) predispositions and early relational experiences. The capacity to tolerate painful and frustrating situations brought on by reality requires the development of impulse control, which emerges through healthy Ego development. When this function is impaired, impulsive manifestations occur as immediate evacuations of psychic tension. Freud's *economic model* (1895) elucidates this process, describing how the transformation of quantity (raw affective energy) into psychic complexity—a task of the secondary function of the psychic apparatus—becomes disrupted. In these cases, the Ego, as the organizational center of complexity, fails to function adequately, leading to deficits in the ability to symbolize, mentalize, and regulate impulses.

Deficits in Ego function and impulse control

As Freud (1923) stated, "The Ego is first and foremost a bodily Ego," emphasizing how the psyche is anchored in somatic experiences. When the Ego's organizational capacity is compromised, as seen in self-harming adolescents, raw impulses are discharged through the body rather than transformed into words, symbols, or mental representations.

Impulse control is a key function of Ego organization. Deficits in this function are often evident in adolescents who engage in self-harming behaviors. The inability to contain and process raw emotions results in motor discharges such as cutting, burning, or other forms of self-injury. These impulsive acts bypass psychic elaboration and operate as archaic mechanisms for tension release. This impairment in Ego function has several associated features:

1 *Limited capacity for sublimation:* Adolescents who struggle with sublimation—the redirection of drives into socially acceptable outlets—often rely on primitive, motoric expressions of psychic pain. For example, one adolescent stated:

> When I feel overwhelmed, I can't think straight—I just need to do something, like cutting, to make it stop.

2 *Archaic defense organization:* Instead of utilizing mature defenses such as repression or intellectualization, self-harming adolescents often rely on splitting, projection, or acting out as mechanisms to manage intrapsychic conflicts. These defenses reflect a more archaic stage of development, where tension is discharged through action rather than mental processing.

3 *Alexithymia and affect regulation difficulties:* Alexithymia—the inability to recognize and articulate one's emotional states—is frequently observed in individuals who self-harm. Their internal experiences are reduced to polarities governed by the pleasure principle, such as calm/tension or well-being/discomfort. Unable to identify or symbolize their emotions, these individuals act on their feelings through impulsive motor discharges. As one adolescent described:

> I can't figure out what I'm feeling, I just know I need it to go away

4 *Impairment in self-representation:* Adolescents with Ego's deficits often struggle to maintain a stable sense of self. Their self-representations are fragmented, unstable, and dominated by overwhelming affective states. This impairment contributes to their reliance on somatic modes of expression, where the body becomes the primary site for managing internal chaos.

The role of Ego instability and archaic mechanisms

An unstable Ego organization facilitates the use of archaic mechanisms for emotional and drive discharge. This instability reflects deficits in early development, often resulting from inconsistent caregiving, traumatic experiences, or relational disruptions during critical developmental stages. The early failure to integrate ambivalent emotions and to develop a coherent internal world leaves the adolescents vulnerable to impulsive actions as a means of managing psychic pain.

Clinical Implications and therapeutic considerations

Understanding the relationship between impulsiveness, masochistic tendencies, and Ego deficits is crucial in the treatment of self-harming behaviors in adolescents. Therapeutic interventions must address the underlying deficits in impulse control, affect regulation, and self-representation. By fostering the adolescent's capacity to mentalize and symbolize their emotional experiences, clinicians can help reduce their reliance on self-harm as a coping mechanism.

Self-harming and its addictive dimension

Self-harming behaviors in adolescents are closely associated with addictive phenomena, where repetition compulsion and an unconscious pursuit of relief or reward play a central role. Addictive behaviors, whether they manifest through repetitive cutting on the wrists and forearms, ingestion of substances, or suicidal gestures, share common dynamics: the subject engages in a compulsive act that temporarily alleviates psychic pain, even at the cost of bodily harm. The sense of reward derived from these acts is often amplified by external care or attention received afterward, creating a reinforcing cycle that encourages repetition.

This addictive aspect can be linked to the death drive (*Todestrieb*), as Freud (1920) theorized in *Beyond the Pleasure Principle*. Through the infliction of pain and punishment upon the body, the subject submits to the drive for non-existence, a pull toward the dissolution of tension and a state of inanimate calm.

> I felt awful, and I just couldn't handle it anymore, so I started cutting. I don't know why, but seeing the blood made me feel calmer.
> At first, I didn't think I could deal with it, but after it was over, I felt a sense of relief. Now, it's what I turn to whenever I feel overwhelmed.

These quotations reflect a complex interplay between the desire for release, the addictive cycle of behavior, and the momentary relief provided by self-harm, a form of somatic discharge that bypasses psychic elaboration.

The ethical conflict: Ego, Superego, and self-punishment

Self-harming behaviors often arise as a response to an unbearable ethical conflict between the Ego and the Superego. The Superego, as the internalized voice of ideals and prohibitions, exerts immense pressure when the individual perceives failure in meeting perfectionistic demands. Adolescents who struggle to adhere to idealized goals—such as achieving a desired weight, maintaining rigid diets, or controlling binge-purge cycles—may experience intense self-loathing and feelings of failure. This failure is then externalized as aggression, impulsively directed toward the self in the form of cuts, burns, or other self-inflicted injuries.

> I just couldn't handle it any longer
> I overate and felt so ashamed. I thought I deserved to hurt myself because I felt worthless

The masochistic component of self-harm reflects an unconscious fantasy of a body or self that deserves to be punished, a manifestation of the destructive conflict between the Ego and the Superego. Narcissistic elements also emerge, where the attack on the self reflects a sense of grandiosity turned inward, coupled with an unrealistic demand for omnipotent control over the body and its drives. This psychic dynamic aligns with Freud's (1923) understanding of the Superego as a harsh, punitive agency that intensifies self-directed aggression when ideals are not met.

Self-harm, femininity, and emerging sexuality

Self-harming behaviors are observed more frequently among adolescent females, suggesting a link between self-directed aggression, emerging sexuality, and the adolescent process. The body, as a site of femininity and burgeoning sexual identity, becomes the target of attacks driven by ambivalence toward sexuality, identity formation, and perceived inadequacies. Cutting the body can be interpreted as a symbolic rejection of feminineness or a defense against the anxieties associated with the transition to adulthood and womanhood (Kernberg, 2004; Persano, 2022).

Clinical expressions such as "I hate my body" or "I don't want to be seen" highlight the body's central role in self-harming behaviors and the rejection of emerging sexual characteristics.

Malignant aggression and self-destructiveness

Self-destructive aggression is a uniquely human phenomenon, with its most extreme expression being suicide. Erich Fromm (1973) described this as *malignant aggression*, an inherently human form of destructiveness that combines cruelty and self-directed violence. In narcissistic personalities, dysregulation of the self, self-esteem, and affective states can lead to self-harming behaviors as a maladaptive response to perceived failure, shame, or loss of control. The body becomes the battleground for this dysregulation, reflecting deep psychic suffering and an unconscious enactment of destructive fantasies.

Narcissistic wounds and the role of humiliation

The violence experienced in society does not remain external; it penetrates the adolescent's psychic world, where it interacts with their own narcissistic vulnerabilities. Adolescence is a critical stage for identity formation and the consolidation of self-esteem. Experiences of social rejection, bullying, or cyberbullying strike at the core of the adolescent's self-image, leading to what André Green (1986) termed the *narcissistic wound*. These wounds, marked by humiliation and shame, generate feelings of worthlessness and self-loathing that adolescents often express through self-harming behaviors.

> When they mocked me in front of everyone, I just wanted to vanish. Hurting myself felt like a way to punish myself for being so worthless.
> When my friends betrayed me, I felt completely invisible. Cutting made me feel real again, but it also felt like I deserved it for being so foolish.

I don't feel like I can rely on anyone anymore. Hurting myself is the only thing that gives me a sense of control.

Humiliation becomes intertwined with narcissistic offenses, creating a cycle where self-harm serves as both a punishment and a release. This behavior reveals the masochistic dimension of self-injury, where the subject unconsciously submits to self-inflicted pain to resolve unbearable psychic tension.

Therapeutic approaches

Given the complex interplay between societal violence, narcissistic wounds, and self-harm, psychotherapeutic interventions must address both individual and relational dimensions. The initial stages of treatment involve creating a therapeutic alliance that provides a safe, containing space for the adolescent's emotional expression. This requires a precise explanation of the treatment framework to prevent further self-harming behaviors and to channel psychic energy into constructive, symbolic forms.

Understanding the symbolic meaning of phrases that adolescents express is crucial in clinical practice, as they provide entry points for exploring the adolescent's internal world and emotional conflicts. Therapists must approach these expressions with empathy, validating the underlying emotions while helping the adolescent develop healthier modes of affect regulation.

Therapeutic interventions must address these patterns by:

1 *Providing containment and validation:* Creating a safe therapeutic environment where emotions can be verbalized rather than enacted.
2 *Promoting mentalization:* Helping adolescents develop the capacity to reflect on their emotional states and integrate fragmented aspects of the self.
3 *Exploring relational patterns:* Examining how early attachment dynamics influence current behaviors and self-perceptions.
4 *Encouraging symbolization:* Facilitating verbal expression of emotions and conflicts, allowing adolescents to replace somatic enactments with reflective understanding and into verbal and symbolic forms of communication.
5 *Exploring early attachment patterns:* Understanding how disruptions in caregiving have shaped the adolescent's internal world and relational dynamics.
6 *Building emotional regulation skills:* Helping adolescents develop healthier ways to manage affective states without resorting to self-punitive behaviors.
7 *Strengthening the self:* Supporting the integration of fragmented aspects of identity and fostering a more cohesive and resilient sense of self.

Therapeutic approaches to symbolization and integration

Recognizing self-harm as both a cry for help and an attempt to reconnect with a fragmented self allows for deeper therapeutic engagement. Clinicians must provide a "holding environment" (Winnicott, 1965) where patients feel safe enough to verbalize and symbolize their pain. The therapeutic process aims to transform unbound affects into meaningful psychic content, enabling adolescents to process their trauma without resorting to bodily enactments.

Comprehensive interventions for treating self-harm

Self-harming behaviors in adolescents require integrative therapeutic approaches that address both the emotional distress underlying these actions and the maladaptive coping strategies used to manage them. Effective treatment approaches focus on promoting emotional regulation, enhancing reflective functioning, and fostering healthy interpersonal relationships.

Key interventions include:

1 *Mentalization-Based Therapy (MBT):* MBT emphasizes strengthening an adolescent's ability to mentalize, which involves understanding and reflecting on their own emotional states as well as those of others. By improving mentalization, adolescents can better regulate affects and reduce impulsive enactments (Fonagy et al., 2002). MBT helps adolescents replace somatic expressions of distress with verbal articulation, enabling healthier emotional processing (Bateman & Fonagy, 2004, 2019).

2 *Cognitive-Behavioral Therapy (CBT):* CBT focuses on identifying and restructuring negative thought patterns that contribute to self-harming behaviors. It helps adolescents reframe beliefs such as "I deserve pain" into more adaptive, self-compassionate thoughts (Linehan, 1993). Techniques such as cognitive restructuring, problem-solving, and distress tolerance training are used to build healthier coping mechanisms.

3 *Transference-Focused Psychotherapy (TFP):* TFP, developed by Kernberg (1992), is particularly useful for adolescents with difficulties in emotional regulation and identity integration. It addresses internalized aggression and fragmented self-representations that often underlie self-harming behaviors. Through therapeutic relationships, TFP helps patients explore and resolve unconscious conflicts, transforming destructive patterns into healthier relational modes. By examining transference dynamics, adolescents can gain insight into their internal struggles and develop more stable and integrated self-concepts (Yeomans et al., 2015).

4 *Expressive Therapies:* Art therapy, music therapy, and narrative approaches encourage adolescents to externalize emotions in symbolic and creative ways. These therapies provide alternative forms of expression, helping patients represent their pain without resorting to physical harm. By engaging in expressive practices, adolescents can process trauma and build emotional resilience.

5 *Relational Approaches*: Establishing a strong therapeutic alliance is essential in treating self-harm. Relational approaches emphasize building trust, validating emotions, and fostering connection. When adolescents feel seen and understood, it reduces feelings of isolation and reinforces healthier patterns of attachment and self-regulation (Winnicott, 1965).

6 *Psychoeducation and Support Networks:* Involving families and peers plays a critical role in reducing stigma and reinforcing treatment goals. Psychoeducation helps caregivers understand the underlying psychological dynamics of self-harm, promoting empathy and more effective support systems. Group therapy settings can also provide adolescents with a sense of community, breaking the isolation that often perpetuates self-destructive behaviors.

7 *Trauma-Focused Therapies:* For adolescents whose self-harming behaviors are rooted in trauma, approaches such as Eye Movement Desensitization and Reprocessing (EMDR) and trauma-focused CBT provide structured techniques for processing traumatic memories. These therapies focus on reducing hyperarousal, increasing distress tolerance, and transforming maladaptive beliefs related to trauma.

8 *Dialectical Behavior Therapy (DBT):* Originally developed by Linehan (1993) for borderline personality disorder, DBT is highly effective for managing emotional dysregulation in adolescents. It combines cognitive-behavioral strategies with mindfulness techniques to improve distress tolerance, emotion regulation, and interpersonal effectiveness.

An integrative framework for healing

Addressing self-harming behaviors in adolescents necessitates a comprehensive, interdisciplinary framework that acknowledges both intrapsychic and relational dimensions of distress. An effective therapeutic approach combines psychodynamic methods, such as Transference-Focused Psychotherapy (TFP), with evidence-based practices, including Mentalization-Based Therapy (MBT), Cognitive-Behavioral Therapy (CBT), and Dialectical Behavior Therapy (DBT). These modalities enable clinicians to tailor interventions to the specific emotional and developmental needs of each adolescent.

Psychodynamic and evidence-based approaches

Psychodynamic therapies, such as TFP, delve into unconscious processes, exploring internalized conflicts, attachment ruptures, and patterns of self-directed aggression. These approaches aim to restructure maladaptive relational patterns and strengthen identity integration. In parallel, evidence-based treatments like MBT, CBT, and DBT address affect regulation, cognitive distortions, and behavioral impulsivity, providing adolescents with tools to manage distress and reduce reliance on self-destructive behaviors.

Expressive therapies and psychoeducation

Expressive therapies, including art, music, and narrative techniques, encourage adolescents to externalize and symbolize painful emotions in creative and non-verbal ways. These therapies foster self-awareness, resilience, and emotional expression, helping adolescents process trauma and develop healthier coping mechanisms.

Psychoeducation, involving both adolescents and their families, reduces stigma, enhances communication, and builds support systems. By involving caregivers in the therapeutic process, clinicians can promote a deeper understanding of self-harm and reinforce the development of emotional regulation strategies at home.

Group settings and relational interventions

Group therapies and "off-the-couch" psychoanalytic approaches provide adolescents with opportunities to form meaningful peer connections, breaking cycles of isolation and alienation. Group settings create a supportive space where adolescents can verbalize affective states, share experiences, and process trauma collaboratively. These interactions introduce new relational modes that can be internalized, fostering integration of previously fragmented parts of the self.

Multidisciplinary collaboration

An effective treatment model also emphasizes interdisciplinary collaboration among psychiatrists, psychologists, social workers, art therapists, and educators. A team-based approach ensures that both biological and psychosocial factors are addressed, combining medication management, trauma-informed care, and family interventions to support holistic healing.

Restoring integration and resilience

Treating self-harming behaviors in adolescents requires a multidimensional and integrative approach that weaves together psychodynamic, cognitive-behavioral, and expressive therapies within a relational framework. By addressing the underlying emotional pain, promoting mentalization, and strengthening interpersonal connections, clinicians can help adolescents transition from patterns of self-destruction to resilience and self-discovery.

Through interdisciplinary collaboration, therapeutic containment, and tailored interventions, adolescents can reclaim a sense of agency and coherence. This process not only alleviates immediate symptoms but also lays the foundation for long-term psychological growth, enabling adolescents to build healthier relationships with themselves and others.

Conclusion: self-harm, a psychological landscape

Many adolescents who engage in self-harming behaviors are survivors of traumatic situations that have left deep psychological scars. Adolescents struggling with self-harm frequently rely on primitive defenses, such as splitting and projective identification, to cope with overwhelming emotions and fragmented identities. Intensive therapeutic approaches focus on stabilizing emotional states, fostering self-regulation, and promoting the internalization of healthier relational patterns.

Violence in contemporary society, particularly in forms such as bullying, cyberbullying, and social discrimination, plays a crucial role in the emergence of self-harming behaviors. These external stressors exacerbate internal psychic vulnerabilities, including narcissistic wounds, impaired affect regulation, and fragile self-esteem. The interaction between societal pressures and internal conflicts creates conditions ripe for self-directed aggression, where adolescents enact their distress upon their own bodies.

Self-harming behaviors in adolescents reflect profound struggles with trauma, identity, and emotional regulation. These behaviors are often rooted in early relational disruptions and exacerbated by societal pressures, leaving adolescents vulnerable to cycles of shame, aggression, and disconnection. Effective treatment must address both the intrapsychic and interpersonal dimensions of self-harm, offering adolescents a space where their pain can be symbolized, verbalized, and ultimately integrated.

By fostering emotional containment, enhancing reflective capacities, and rebuilding relational trust, psychotherapy provides adolescents with the tools to navigate their inner conflicts without resorting to self-destructive behaviors. Through compassionate, structured, and integrative approaches, clinicians can guide adolescents toward healing, resilience, and the development of a cohesive sense of self.

References

Bateman, A., & Fonagy, P. (2004). *Psychoterapy for Personality Disorder. Mentalization-based treatment*. New York: Oxford University Press.

Bateman, A., & Fonagy, P. (2019). *Handbook of Mentalizing in Mental Health Practice*. Washington: American Psychiatric Association Publishing.

Fonagy, P., Gergely, G., Jurist, E., & Target, M. (2002). *Affect Regulation, Mentalization, and the Development of the Self*. New York: Other Press.

Freud, S. (1917). *Mourning and Melancholia*. In James Strachey (Ed.), *The Standard Edition of the Complete Psychological Works of Sigmund Freud* (Vol. 14, 237–258). London: Hogarth Press, 1986.

Freud, S. (1920). Beyond the Pleasure Principle. In Mark Solms (Ed.), *The Standard Edition of the Complete Psychological Works of Sigmund Freud* (Vol. 18, 3–64). London: Hogarth Press, 1991.

Freud, S. (1921). Group Psychology and the Analysis of the Ego. In Mark Solms (Ed.), *The Standard Edition of the Complete Psychological Works of Sigmund Freud* (Vol. 18, 67–143). London: Hogarth Press, 1991.

Freud, S. (1923). The Ego and the Id. In Mark Solms (Ed.), *The Standard Edition of the Complete Psychological Works of Sigmund Freud* (Vol. 19, 3–66). London: Hogarth Press, 1991.

Freud, S. (1924). The Economic Problem of Masochism. In Mark Solms (Ed.), *The Standard Edition of the Complete Psychological Works of Sigmund Freud* (Vol. 19, 157–170). London: Hogarth Press, 1991.

Fromm, E. (1973). *The Anatomy of Human Destructiveness*. New York: Holt, Rinehart, and Winston.

Green, A. (1986). The Dead Mother. In *On Private Madness* (142–173). London: Karnac Books.

Jeammet, P., & Bochereau, D. (2007). *La souffrance des adolescents*. París: La Découverte.

Kernberg, O. F. (1975). *Borderline Conditions and Pathological Narcissism*. New York: Jason Aronson.

Kernberg, O. F. (1984). *Severe Personality Disorders*. New Haven: Yale University Press.

Kernberg, O. F. (1992). *Aggression in Personality Disorders and Perversions*. New Haven: Yale University Press.

Kernberg, O. F. (2004). *Aggressivity, Narcissism, and Self-Destructiveness in the Psychotherapeutic Relationship: New Developments in the Psychopathology and Psychotherapy of Severe Personality Disorders* (Chap.13, 205–219). New Haven: Yale University Press.

Klein, M. (1946). Notes on Some Schizoid Mechanisms. *The International Journal of Psychoanalysis, 27.*

Linehan, M. M. (1993). *Cognitive-Behavioral Treatment of Borderline Personality Disorder.* Guilford Press.

Persano, H. L. (2019). Mecanismos de Defensa. In H. L. Persano (Ed.), *El Mundo de la Salud Mental en la Práctica Clínica* (Chap. 27, 319–338). Buenos Aires: Akadia Ed.

Persano, H. L. (2022). Self-Harm. *The International Journal of Psychoanalysis, 103*(6), 1089–1103.

Persano, H. L., & Goldberg, C. M. (1995). Internal World Its Configuration Through the Family. In *International Psychoanalytic Studies Organization, Proceeding s of the XIIIth International Congress* on July 29th, 30th & August 2nd, 50–65. San Francisco.

Winnicott, D. W. (1960). Ego Distortion in Terms of True and False Self. In *The Maturational Processes and the Facilitating Environment: Studies in the Theory of Emotional Development* (140–152). London: Hogarth Press and the Institute of Psycho-Analysis.

Winnicott, D. W. (1965). *The Maturational Processes and the Facilitating Environment: Studies in the Theory of Emotional Development*. New York: International Universities Press.

Yeomans, F. E., Clarkin, J. F., & Kernberg, O. F. (2015). *Transference-Focused Psychotherapy for Borderline Personality Disorder: A Clinical Guide*. American Psychiatric Publishing.

Chapter 14

Discussion of self-harming from a French psychoanalytic perspective

Panos Aloupis

The author, a psychosomatician belonging to the Psychosomatic Institute of Paris Pierre Marty, discusses the clinical vignettes presented at the COCAP Conference of September 2024 that demonstrated different aspects of Self-Harming by building a common thread inspired by the Paris Psychosomatic School. Psychosomaticians often consider somatization as the consequence of a psychic process, which for lack of adequate means, assaults the body. In such cases, we are dealing with complex unconscious mechanisms, despite the obvious, largely conscious phenomena of aggression on the body by the baby, child, or adolescent in some clinical presentations. It can be stated clearly that the common factor in the emergence of these destructive processes is the presence of trauma, as shown in almost all the clinical vignettes.

The Freudian child is born with a need for self-preservation, and it is the encounter with the maternal environment, which progressively transmits to the infant the way in which human beings invest the other and the world. Psychoanalysts refer to the primary bond and to archaic mechanisms of the first period of life when the child discovers a world that meets the baby on its own ground but in a significant somatopsychic asymmetry. Jean Laplanche (1997) has called this situation the "fundamental anthropological situation."

In this situation, the baby meets the maternal object and/or its substitutes via his/her body, which thus becomes the arena for the exchanges with the surrounding world. He/she has left the environment of the mother's womb, whose living conditions helped him/her to grow and be ready to confront the outside world. Freud defined self-preservation as a state with specific properties and capacities, designed to preserve what has been created during pregnancy, and at the same time to develop means of facing the demands of human life. In their first years of childhood, men and women build an unconscious and acquire a way of thinking that remains all through life closely connected to word representations and their affects. First the baby, later the child and adolescent, all will meet conflict with the drive manifestations of childhood and adolescence, and only gradually invest their own way of cathecting their internal world – the self – and the external world, i.e. others, society and culture. The body, from the outset, remains a daily mediator, even if we

DOI: 10.4324/9781003647317-17

often forget it, given our status of thinking beings. Besides, in psychoanalysis when we say "mind," frequently we mean "psyche."

In Freud's invention of psychoanalysis, the duality of the principles of pleasure and reality is fundamental. The search for pleasure takes two forms: on the one hand, satisfaction, and on the other, the reduction or extinction of tension. This is how frustration, displeasure, pain, and suffering become our lifelong compan-ions. They inhabit the unconscious continent as they express the unacceptability of perceptions; this is probably the meaning of Freud's phrase that the object is born in hatred. Absence, loss, and lack make the baby, and human in general, inscribe internal object representations to replace what is missing.

This is how our psychic world becomes inhabited, through experience and the unique way for each of us in which this experience becomes an object of represen-tation and affect. When Humberto Persano (Chapter 12 in this volume) refers to tension, it is this tension that, perhaps even from pregnancy onwards, becomes an important clue that excitation is slowly and surely driven to be transformed into a human psychic construction. The psychic apparatus, in Freud's terms, stores the product of experiences and perceptions, transforming excitations and stimuli as far as possible. It is exactly when this process of transformation – which itself is con-tinually changing – encounters stumbling blocks, interruptions, and breakdowns, that the situation is experienced as traumatic.

We could say that trauma is always potentially present, but psychic vulnerabil-ity is not the same at all ages and in all circumstances. A baby, whose world is cataclysmic, lives in a state of dependence and helplessness and thus requires the presence and mediation of the other. An adolescent, because of the bodily changes and impulsive demands he or she is passively and inexorably undergoing, is also confronted with traumatic situations. A child, because of the discontinuity in the construction of his or her psychic defences, is more vulnerable to situations that he or she cannot yet psychically approach and internalize. In all cases, trauma affects the body when transformation processes fail to integrate deeply experienced affects and representations into unconscious fictions and fantasies. The anxiety then cir-culates freely and becomes diffuse because the body lacks a strong link with the psychic organ.

The search for pleasure and the need to keep tension far away are unavoidably accompanied by a reaction to displeasure and the demands of reality. Babies and children make use of their motricity and their growing capacity to be able to wait. The hallucinatory satisfaction of desire as well as masochism both reinforce the human being's ability to tolerate and transform ultimately suffering into expecta-tion. The capacity for thinking, for dealing with conflict and transforming absence, frustration, and loss into objects of mourning and mentalization is what makes the neurotic man a complex being, constantly defending him or herself against trau-matic perceptions, whether from internal or external sources.

The aggression and destructiveness that ensue in these circumstances were elab-orated and conceptualized by Freud (1920) after the horrors of the First World

War. During this period, he was personally affected as was the society collectively. The clinical reality of trauma led him to propose the duality of the life and death drives. which he formulated as "beyond the pleasure principle." In these situations, thought processes are sometimes stunned, leaving the way open for acting (*agieren*), and when acting is no longer sufficient, the body suffers the full brunt of the traumatic effects.

This theoretical introductory framework aims to discuss how the other authors (Monica Cardenal, Jeanne Magagna and Humberto Persano, see Chapters 10–13 in this volume), all followed their own way of this Freudian thread in their case-presentation and theoretical elaboration. Whether it's the desire to disappear, or the desire to control a life-threatening experience, or the desire to put a stop to a persecuting drive, each case shows how displeasure becomes unbearable, and how aggression against the body appears to be the only way to escape a murderous object. This is often, but not always, a subjective experience, both mentally and bodily, that is linked to traumatic situations within the early attachment relationship or in the face of a situation (e.g. illness, aggression, war, loss) that proves difficult to metabolize psychically.

Two founders of the Paris psychosomatic school, Pierre Marty and Michel Fain (1995), presented a report to the French-speaking congress of psychoanalysis in 1954 entitled "The importance of the role of motor skills in the object relationship." A sensori-motor dimension, as part of the psycho-motor activity, accompanies all of us throughout life, thereby integrating the vicissitudes of the primary relationship, and reflects the distance from the external object as this becomes progressively inscribed in the psychic apparatus. Psychomotricity is the seat of auto-eroticism and of our bodily narcissistic investment. However, it can also become the seat of defence and constitute a protective armour to face a threatening internal or external world. In these cases, one is often confronted with the inability to accept and integrate passivity, which results in forcing an active motor pathway, whether bodily or mental. Self-aggression, insomnia, anorexia, attention deficit disorders, and addictions are all part of this active search for flight and conjuration from an object that threatens the child's narcissistic and vital integrity. Monica Cardenal (Chapter 10 in this volume) illustrates this remarkably well in her clinical vignettes of babies who have trouble living. She talks about tension and the use of musculature as a bodily defensive expression of the experience of traumatic relationships in a context of suffering. Between the desire to disappear in an experience of annihilation, probably already felt, and a destructiveness that strikes the baby's body with visible and invisible lesions just as much as the mother's body, we can estimate the risk for the primary bonding relationship.

Braunschweig and Fain (1975) have clearly differentiated between the calming mother and the satisfying mother. The satisfying mother builds a relationship with her baby, mostly unconsciously, in which shared pleasure results in the psychic acceptance of the object and the investment of passivity facing the active mother-object. In this way, the absence, estrangement, and aggression of the primary object can be psychically transformed to become the subject of dream work and of masochistic elaboration, in which the two drives, life and death, remain intertwined. This negative side of the object relationship thus gives access to representation and to the hallucinatory satisfaction of desire, which are essential elements for the growth of a solid and rich ego. Fain (1971) speaks of a primary hysterical identification, insofar as, faced with the absence and withdrawal of the mother, who leads her maternal life in parallel with her identity as a woman, the baby learns to identify with his or her mother's desire as much as with the object of her desire. This is the basis of human life, where the investment of life boils down to a question of desire and lacking, with all its vagaries.

In contrast to the satisfying mother, Fain described the clinical situation of what he referred to as the calming mother, who soothes her infant like a tranquilizer tablet sedating concretely instead of helping psychically to accept the missing or failing. For example, a mother who rocks her agitated baby by shaking it, without any connection to her tenderness, or even her anger. We are close to Spitz's hospitalism. In such cases, the baby can only identify with an absence that may even become a vacuum of life, in which it risks or even seeks to disappear. Even more, in this type of relationship or experience, an experience of unbound death drive is transmitted, because of the impossibility of emotional sharing. In these cases, the internalization of the death drive can make relying on passivity very difficult as well as the investment of and by the object, which results in projection via the musculature. The body becomes rigid, the baby will not let itself be touched or cuddled, and abandonment in sleep can only happen as a result of exhaustion or of a fierce resistance against a mortifying experience of breakdown. Therefore, pleasurable sensorimotor cathexis as a privileged way of dealing with the object has become difficult, and the death drive is more at the service of exhausting internal and external destructiveness than for the transformation of excitement and tolerance of the cataclysm of life.

The cases of anorexia illustrated by Jeanne Magagna (Chapter 11 in this volume) show convincingly how a child, in its struggle to avoid impingement and aggression by the other, has no other means to avoid contact but by responding aggressively or by actively fleeing away from it. In this context, the child develops defences that were originally designed to reassure it that it is no longer in danger. If it has grasped that feeding is important for the mother, or that it is the preferential way of exchange with her, then "closing the mouth to food" becomes a radical solution for protection of the feeling that it has finally controlled a violent situation of intrusion and unpredictability.

How about self-preservation? It is true that different functions of self-preservation, such as eating, are important for survival, but life presupposes also a libidinally invested exchange with others. This is why, psychoanalytically speaking, eating is transformed into a sexually and aggressively invested function. We no longer eat simply because we are hungry, but according to the vagaries of our pleasures and social customs. The drive for eating thus becomes part of the interactive relationship with the other. In many cases of anorexia, it takes the place of an almost silent acting out, attacking the pleasure of the body, the self and above all the other, as a cry for radical independence in a state of total dependence. The anorexic patient created in this way an illusion of mastery in trying to free her/himself from the impact of the other through becoming free of food, but paradoxically, anorexia puts him/her in a state of constant, tyrannical submission. In this sense, the function of eating becomes a perverse solution that denies suffering. Jeanne Magagna calls it a sado-masochistic relationship with the omnipotent destructive part in an attempt to avoid psychic pain. Indeed, anorexia resembles a mask that veils a passionate traumatic story of the relationship, in which accepting loss and depressiveness was not possible because of the underlying destructiveness. This is why many anorexic girls, later women, are generous and active, while their bodies are rigid and impenetrable, both physically and sensually. Therefore, feminine receptivity is not allowed, as this is perceived as intrusive and dangerous. Hyperactivity thus remains the only effective defence, both motor as well as mental hyperactivity, with significant intellectual achievements. Jeanne discusses the presence of a tyrannical superego, but in the French psychosomatic clinic and its theoretical thinking, it is rather understood as a matter of a demanding, perfectionist ideal ego. These patients do not always follow a path that compels them to act in a way that one would recognize as the effect of a prohibiting superego for protection and punishment according to parental and societal laws. Instead, part of the ego chooses to follow a demanding road to perfection and match an imago of a perfect, ideal ego. It is not a forbidding voice but a totalitarian one, which hides and even denies difference, separation and loss. This is why, when anorexic patients start to feel depressed and sad, approaching and helping them often becomes easier. It is the pathway through depression that promotes acknowledgement and working through of hostility and aggression.

Anorexia attacks the body. It often appears during adolescence as a sign of taking control over impulsive jolts that are experienced as persecutory and dangerous, uncontrollable and unpredictable. Humberto Persano (Chapter 12–13 in this volume) talks about "self-harming" behaviour, which extends to self-aggressive actings. Although it is observed that often the skin is attacked, we can also witness behaviours that seek out the limits of physical viability, of the adolescent's own psychic and/or somatic life. Even though the self-harming is intended as "a mode of relief of suffering," the bodily suffering becomes the object of denial to mask psychic pain. These are defensive mechanisms that try to stop the excited destructiveness, but in a perverted way—by treating the body and skin as if they were inanimate objects—and in doing so, they seek the limits of life. On the one hand, adolescents attack themselves as if nothing can hurt them; on the other hand, through this behaviour, they scream for help from the other. Although the other has an unconscious place in fantasy of being an executioner, the self-harming adolescent continues to hope for a perfect, saving other. Body and self are being treated in the same paradoxical way.

The paradox in self-aggression means that the patients attack themselves to stop what is attacking them – in other words, they want to survive – while at the same time to end suffering, they are destroying themselves. Through this self-inflicted motor aggression, the teenager seeks to find a way out of the experience of annihilation, as if in a sense he or she becomes the death drive that extinguishes the excitation, and also the agent of this attempt at reorganization. However, like night-mares, these anti-traumatic defences are often compulsive, as long as the trauma remains active. They can fade away with the vicissitudes of life, changes in the body, or with therapy that helps the patient to metabolize his or her destructive excitation and become more able to cathect the other and himself or herself without the anxious anticipation of an active, disruptive dangerousness.

When pleasure carries traumatic traces or when passivity is experienced as intru-sion, then active aggression of the body becomes a compulsive and self-punishing gesture of paradoxical verification of a self that wants to triumph and survive beyond destructiveness.

References

Braunschweig D. and Fain M. (1975) *La nuit, Le jour*. Paris, PUF.

Fain M. (1971) Prélude à la vie fantasmatique. *Revue française de psychanalyse*, vol. XXXV, no. 2–3: 291–364.

Freud S. (1920) Beyond the pleasure principle. *SE*, vol. 18 (1955): 7–64.

Laplanche J. (1997) The theory of seduction and the problem of the other. *International Journal of Psychology*, vol. 78: 653–666.

Marty P. and Fain M. (1955) Importance du rôle de la motricité dans la relation d'objet. *Revue française de Psychanalyse*, vol. 19, no. 1–2: 205–322.

Chapter 15

A 'superstructure' for holding on to or for self-destroying?

Anouk Meurrens

Using two clinical vignettes, I propose to explore the development of an internal structure of hypercontrol with a paradoxical double purpose: survival and self-destruction.

In this short text, the author will shift from one patient to another, focusing on some aspects in which they are similar. Not much will be revealed about their history, mainly to preserve confidentiality.

Two young women of strong intellectual capacity will be presented, both of them devote a great deal of psychic energy to building and maintaining a "superstructure."

Lucie counts, classifies and arranges series of numbers, grams, kilometres, calories that are ingested, consumed, taken or spent, all this in mental arithmetic sheets, like the Little Prince's businessman on his tiny planet who was lost in the icy universe (de Saint Exupéry, 1943). The numbers are lined up, arranged, subtracted and multiplied. It seems confusing, but it's very clear. It seems very clear, but it's confusing. The numbers flutter around her like tiny insects producing a continuous sound around her brain. Two hundred calories ingested minus fifty steps climbed, plus one hundred and fifty grams of milk chocolate, multiplied by 28 days without breakfast, plus an uncontrollable crying fit, plus the fear of emptiness.

"At first it was my solution, now it's become my problem." Emma explains that she has set up this mechanism to control something in her body, and now it's the reverse: it's this same mechanism that is controlling her. It's like a robot program, an AI designed to control everything to do with her body, and which has applied the algorithms so well that it has taken control over its creator.

But losing this control represents a great threat, firstly because the body, if let go, is both threatened and threatening, but also because we can sense an immense abyss hidden behind the structure.

"When I enter a space," Lucie explains, "there's always the question of the place my body can occupy in that space. She visualizes the air she moves, the number of cubic centimetres her body occupies, she imagines what others see when they look at her."

The fear of an uncontrolled expansion of the body directly echoes the absence of a sufficiently containing psychic envelope, with the fear of overflowing playing out at both bodily and psychic levels. The superstructure therefore seems to fulfil

DOI: 10.4324/9781003647317-18

a function equivalent to that of the 'second skin' developed by Esther Bick (1981), by maintaining the integrity of the ego in the face of the anxiety of an unbearable overflow.

> Sometimes I feel like I'm made of dark, slimy, gooey stuff. I know it's absolutely invisible, but part of me is convinced that it's only because of my 'superstructure' that it's invisible. If I got rid of it, I'd fall apart like a puddle of foul-smelling tar.

Emma describes how she feels that her body is only made up of bones, muscles and kilos of fat. The idea that 90% of her body is made up of water petrifies her. When she cries, she feels empty.

She wonders how we can be asked to be solid when we are fundamentally liquid?

This fear of liquefaction is reminiscent of Frances Tustin's work on primitive fears (1990,1992), and the role of the body in the search for reassurance and a sense of existence. Here, rigid control is marked by constraints linked to the body, and not just by mental obsessions. The continuity between the bodily sensation of dissolution, liquefaction and overflowing, and its psychic echo, seems essential to me.

These patients cling to their superstructure, which supports them and crushes them at the same time. As time goes by, the superstructure becomes more and more demanding. In exchange for a semblance of solidity, it demands more and more sacrifice from my patients. Out of loyalty to this mechanism, my patients renounce many bodily pleasures, but the direct benefit is masochistic satisfaction in the pleasure of the effort and the victory of control. They also benefit from punishing themselves for unconscious guilt. In both clinical situations, something is going on around family dramas in their early childhood for which they may have felt responsible.

They hold on to this cracked viaduct, suspended between the need for self-punishment and the need to feel alive. Self-violence builds a bridge between these two psychic demands, self-punishment serves to withstand an intense feeling of guilt, and survival carries the idea of holding on to the body so that it doesn't fall into the void like a slimy puddle.

This superstructure is described by the young women themselves as cracked concrete, rotten wood. It's a kind of hollow hyper-skeleton, both rigid and fragile. It is noticed that when the patients describe this mechanism, there are always contradictory terms in their descriptions: solid and fragile, indispensable and obsolete, heavy and hollow, supportive and crushing.

Although they recognize the rigidity of this mechanism, they do not see it as solid. And yet it contains and prevents all the fluid movements of the body and, of course, all the impulsive life.

Sexual impulses are crushed by tons of reinforced concrete, and aggressive impulses that are turned against their own bodies.

But it's also about touching the other person, the parent. As Jeanne Magagna puts it, "hurting your parents' child." There is an undeniable hostility towards the parents who have left them to fight for themselves at the worst times, the anxieties of sleepovers, the comparisons between girls in the dance class, the first menstrual periods, the dreadful inevitability of a transformation of the body as a natural catastrophe against which nothing can be done and which they silently have to undergo.

Those moments in the bath or in front of the mirror when they discover with horror the size of their thighs.

The rage of having been brought into the world, in such a brutal world, with a body that had become so deformed, and of having to take sole responsibility for managing this horrible body in this horrible world, which evokes the desire to destroy that body.

So the solution of hypercontrol is imposed, and here again a paradox emerges. Since the "healthy passivity", described by Michel Fain (2001) or Catherine Chabert (2003), could not be integrated, any giving away of control would give lead to a dangerous passivity in which these women would be at the mercy of both an external and internal world full of chaotic impulses. This mechanism enables us to maintain an active position and not give in to a letting go that would open the door to desire and lack; a passivity that would open the door to an encounter with the object and its loss. But this attempt at omnipotent control paradoxically leads them to total submission to a destructive ideal of perfection, as Panos Aloupis (Chapter 11 in this book) points out in his analysis of the role of the perfectionist ego ideal in anorexic patients.

This mechanism was initially built in the secret chamber of their minds and nobody knew of its existence. It is almost like an imaginary friend, accompanying them everywhere. It stood between them and the world, providing security and a barrier, but it also made things possible by preventing catastrophic anxiety. For example, it made going out for fast food with friends possible, because counting the number of chips reduced the young women's fear of turning into a shapeless mass of fat.

This mechanism aims to control the body and mind by imposing a quasi-permanent, codified, and painful relationship with food, physical exercise and everything to do with the body. Because of a limited anxiolytic efficacy, in cases of unbearable anxiety, it must sometimes be supplemented by more violent acts. At such times, it is necessary to injure oneself physically, so the relief is more direct. This is when the physical self-harming comes in for rescue.

After a few years of treatment, these young women can sometimes allow access into the secret chamber of their thoughts, explaining their internal machinery, their superstructure and their ambivalence towards it.

For a long time, the great fear of dependence on the analyst prevented them engaging in a therapeutic relationship. But the passage of time showed them that I was still there, and little by little they settled down. That's when I began to see the 'hungry self' that Jeanne Magagna talks about: "The mask of anorexia nervosa conceals a 'hungry self' that is silently crying out for someone they can trust to bear the weight of their psychological pain, their dependence, their love and their hatred, and to make these feelings 'thinkable'".

In the counter-transference, the analyst can become inhabited by very intense movements, death anxieties and then a kind of 'breastfeeding impulse' where suddenly the image of breastfeeding a baby appears. Sometimes both patients experienced a voracious movement towards their analyst and at other times a massive rejection, with very recurrent acts of absence.

Every time archaic scenes are approached, having to do with the early maternal bond, thoughts of death appeared. And, linked to them, intense feelings of guilt. These young women often have in common a particular contiguity between the early bond with the mother and something to do with death.

In images they may have expressed of themselves as children or babies, there is a very harsh judgement of their vulnerability. As if they had always been autonomous warriors capable of facing anything, and the parts of them that went against this strength had to be crushed and swept away.

Jeanne Magagna talks about the 'vulnerable self' that has been denied by an omnipotent and destructive ego. She explains that therapy could aim to reintegrate this vulnerable ego. To do this, trying to support these young women in the gradual integration a kind of non-judgemental internal parent who would be able to recognize the legitimacy of the vulnerable ego, is vital in the analytic treatment.

Of course, all this work is very slow and delicate because the robotic superstructure is invasive and often cuts off thought. But Lucie and Emma's strength is that their thinking is alive, luxuriant even, weaving branches through everything like a shrub thirsting to grow. Even when it's cut off by the superstructure, it always finds a small gap to slip through. It's a way of thinking that tolerates doubt and remains in an active quest to understand. This thinking, if it survives all attacks, can be one of the best allies in the difficult moments when the clinical work is invaded by destructive and powerful robots.

Bibliography

Aloupis, P. 2025. Discussion of Self-harming from a French Psychoanalytic Perspective. In *The Body and Compulsion from Infancy to Young Adulthood: New Perspectives on Addiction, Self-Harm and Suicide*, Chap 14 (in this book).

Bick, E. 1981. L'expérience de la peau dans les relations précoces (trad J.Capiaux). *Revue Belge de Psychanalyse*: 67–70. Brussels.

Chabert, C. 2003. *Le féminin mélancolique*. Paris PUF. Petite bibliothèque de Psychanalyse.

De Saint Exupéry, A. 1943. *Le Petit Prince* (Vol. 1). New York: Reynal & Hitchcock.

Fain, M. 2001. Mentalisation et Passivité. *Revue française de psychosomatique*, 19 (1): 29–37.

Magagna, J. 2025. The Silenced Scream: 'Under Anorexia Nervosa'. In *The Body and Compulsion from Infancy to Young Adulthood:New Perspectives on Addiction, Self-Harm and Suicide*, Chap 11 (in this book).

Tustin, F. 1990. *The Protective Shell in Children and Adults*. London: Routledge.

Tustin, F. 1992. *Autistic States in Children*. London: Routledge.

Winnicott, D. 1971. *Jeu et Réalité*. Paris: Gallimard.

Part 4

Introduction

Suicide and masochism in adolescence today

Fernando M. Gómez

Introduction

Suicide in childhood and adolescence constitutes a tragic act – profoundly enigmatic from both clinical and social perspectives. Understanding it requires a complex comprehension through a pluralistic theoretical and technical psychoanalytic perspective, conceived as a polyphonic dialogue that addresses the challenges posed by the 21st century. Adolescence is a developmental stage marked by a series of decisive psychic and bodily changes: the emergence of genital sexuality, the reorganization of narcissism, identity formation, and access to new freedoms and responsibilities. When these processes are unsuccessful or insufficiently supported, significant feelings of hopelessness, disillusionment, frustration, and inner emptiness may emerge, and sometimes suicide is presented as the sole solution. In this context, bodily experiences acquire particular centrality. For many transgender adolescents, the body becomes a site of deep psychic conflict – where identity tensions, narcissistic anxieties, and often violent and invalidating social gazes converge, increasing the risk of self-harm and suicide.

Youth suicide is one of the most alarming contemporary mental health concerns. Its emergence cannot be reduced to purely biological, social, or behavioral factors; it reflects profound subjective suffering that must be heard and understood in all its complexity. Depression, self-harm (cutting, burning, lacerations, etc.), and suicide appear with increasing frequency in clinical consultations, challenging our diagnostic and technical tools. UNICEF reports that anxiety and depression accounted for 40% of global mental disorders in 2021. Annually, 45,800 adolescents die by suicide – over one every 11 minutes (UNICEF 2021)[1] – and it remains the second leading cause of death among 15- to 19-year-olds (WHO 2019).[2] In the United States, suicide attempts among 12 to 17 rose 22.3% during the summer of 2020 and 39.1% in winter 2021, compared to the same periods in 2019 (Yard et al., 2021).[3] In Europe, Latin America and the Caribbean, in 2019, anxiety and depression represented 55% and 50%, respectively, of adolescent disorders; depression and suicide were the second and third causes of death among 15- to 19-year-olds. Common depressive experiences include: emptiness, hopelessness, and an inability

DOI: 10.4324/9781003647317-19

to envision a promising future. The persistent social stigma around mental health also hinders help-seeking, perpetuating suffering in silence.

How can a child or an adolescent – a figure associated with life, growth, desire, and the future – wish to end their life? What subjective features make adolescence particularly high-risk? Psychoanalytic work reveals complex unconscious fantasies: narcissistic immortality, idealized and omnipotent unions, freedom from object dependencies, incestuous fantasies, fantasies linked to bodily changes and their emotional impact, fantasies of hate and rage toward parental figures and the desire to attack or destroy them, often accompanied by feelings of guilt, humiliation, and shame. These phantasmatic elements can intensify anxiety and psychic suffering, especially when early object relations have been conflicted or deficient, triggering primitive defense mechanisms such as regression, splitting, and projective identification.

Psychic suffering was one of the core concepts in Sigmund Freud's work, particularly in his theorization of masochism and the death drive, which offered a conceptual framework to understand suicide. In "The Economic Problem of Masochism" (1924), Freud defined "primary masochism" as the core of drive constitution and a direct expression of the death drive (Thanatos) operating within the organism, resulting from the unbinding from the life drive (Eros). This unbinding may lead to acts of radical self-aggression such as suicide. Moral masochism – unconscious guilt in order to maintain a bond with an internalized punitive ideal in the Superego – can become devastating. Melanie Klein emphasized that the infant – in early psychic development – may experience intense persecutory and depressive anxieties related to fantasies of harming loved objects. These may underlie certain self-injury in children, representing an extreme expression of internal conflict between love and hate, infused with unbearable guilt toward primary objects. Jacques Lacan proposed that failed or defective symbolic inscription traps children or adolescents with death impulses, lacking a symbolic outlet – where suicide functions as an attempt to give symbolic closure to unrepresented anguish. André Green warns that severe fragmentations in narcissistic support and symbolic containment within the family environment contribute to failed or defective symbolic inscriptions and a weakened narcissism, constantly at risk of giving nothingness a value superior to life itself. This leads to a collapse in the ego's investment by the life-narcissism, installing a deadly void that pulls the subject toward acts of self-annihilation as a result of the loss of libidinal value in life itself ("Negative Narcissism", André Green).[4]

These perspectives highlight the link between suicide and masochistic aspects tied to the body, as a source of potential hate and pleasure contained within unconscious masochistic fantasies, which "inevitably reappears; like an unlaid ghost, it cannot rest until the mystery has been solved and the spell broken" (Freud, 1909),[5] thus creating a stage upon which these fantasies cannot be enacted. These fantasies involve the dual nature of drives (Life drive vs. Death drive), the conflictive dynamics among psychic agencies (Ego, Id, Superego, Ideal Ego), and between the internalized objects – both idealized and persecutory. These dynamics, along with the impossibility of mourning resulting from the relinquishment of infantile omnipotence – an instance we know is against recognition of finitude, the transition from infantile auto-erotism to the adult sexual body, and that can disrupt the reality test – often push adolescents to states of despair when confronted with the impossibility of loving and being loved. This profound need to love and be loved confronts them with powerful feelings of dependency, jealousy, and envy, which may intensify guilt and feed into a sadomasochistic loop – potentially culminating, in extreme cases, in the adolescent's suicide.

In this scenario, we cannot ignore the family's role, which – rather than providing care, protection, and love – can sometimes become the ambassador of death. From a broader perspective, hypermodernity exacerbates this subjective fragility: fragmented social ties, the idealization of happiness as a mandate, intolerance of suffering and pain, cultural pressure for success amplified by social media, and the crisis of the future as a symbolic horizon (climate crisis, wars, social violence, peremptoriness, etc.). These factors directly affect subjectivation processes, intensifying pre-existing vulnerability and generating new forms of psychic suffering. When these forms reach a significant magnitude – often linked to failures in narcissistic support, the impossibility of symbolizing pain, and subjective loneliness – they can give rise to dissociative processes of varying degrees, sometimes leading to moments of depersonalization that precipitate the suicidal act.

The texts in this chapter invite us to rethink the limits and boundaries of psychoanalysis with children and adolescents today on two critical topics: self-harm and suicide. Colleagues from diverse regions, cultures, and institutions bring their ideas, reflections, and knowledge, which result from their clinical experience. This plurality of voices fosters a dialogue among them, reinforcing the intertextual and dialogical nature inherent in any discourse, freeing it from the constraints imposed by orthodoxy and certainty. These, as we well know, tend to coagulate and fossilize the analyst's elasticity – a more open positioning, which recognizes that theory is alive and evolves within the clinical settings: concepts should not be crystallized into fixed definitions, but rather remain sufficiently "elastic" to adapt to the clinical context without losing coherence (Sandler, 1983)[6]; and the analyst's vital drive engagement – manifested through his presence fully engaged with his entire being and knowledge, with heart and soul, in the analytic task. Both qualities are essential for activating and preserving the analyst's imaginative, creative, and revitalizing capacities, which are so necessary for holding and analyzing these patients.

Notes

1 UNICEF (2021). Estado Mundial de la Infancia 2021. En mi mente. Promover, proteger y cuidar la salud mental de la infancia. Resumen Ejecutivo. https://www.unicef.org/es/media/108171/file/SOWC-2021-Resumen-Ejecutivo.pdf.
2 WHO (2019). Suicide in the world. Global Health Estimates. World Health Organization; [2019]. Licence: CC BY-NC-SA 3.0 IGO. https://iris.who.int/bitstream/handle/10665/326948/WHO-MSD-MER-19.3-eng.pdf.

3 Yard, E., Radhakrishnan, L., Ballesteros M. F. *et al.* Emergency Department Visits for Suspected Suicide Attempts Among Persons Aged 12–25 Years Before and During the Covid-19 Pandemic - Estados Unidos, 2019–May 2021. MMWR Morb Mortal Wkly Rep 2021;70:888–894. http://dx.doi.org/10.15585/mmwr.mm7024e1.
4 Green, A. (2001). *Life Narcissism, Death Narcissism.* Translated by A. Weller. London; New York: Free Association Books.
5 Freud, S. (1909). Analysis of a Phobia in a Five-year Old Boy. III. Discussion. In J. Strachey (Ed. and Trans.), The standard edition of the complete psychological works of *Sigmund Freud* (Vol. 10). London: Hogarth Press, p. 122.
6 Sandler, J. (1983). Reflections on Some Relations between Psychoanalytic Concepts and Psychoanalytic Practice. *Int J Psycho-Anal*, 1983; 64: 35–45.

Chapter 16

An endless tragedy

Attempts and suicide in childhood and adolescence

Silvia Flechner

Introduction

Suicide attempts or suicide in children and adolescents represent an extreme way of acting, placing the analyst in a difficult situation to resolve. These gestures and attempts deeply affect the analyst with unavoidable feelings of suffering and impotence.

The death of a child or adolescent by suicide is a tragedy, with profound and lasting effects on family, friends, and the larger community. Suicide is one of the leading causes of death among young people; it represents the extreme endpoint of mental ill-health. Many more young people either have suicidal ideation or attempt suicide, and a more considerable number still engage in self-harm.

Suicidal thoughts or actions, even in very young children, are a sign of extreme distress and should not be ignored. What is striking in cases where children and adolescents are caught up in this "life gamble" could be on one side, feel over-whelmed by the object, leading to various outcomes, most notably in violence either toward others or toward themselves, such as suicide attempts. On the other side, children and adolescents may display numerous anxieties, among which the anguish of abandonment and the agony of intrusion stand out. These earliest anxieties erupt during the structuring moment of Oedipus Complex, and their castration anxieties emerge. Oedipus and castration anxiety will be affected when some of the other anxieties develop, and it will remain a situation of primary concern due to their psychopathological consequences. The link between the Oedipus Complex and the anguish of the loss of an object of love is an essential motive for the drive movements; the dynamics of fantasies and identifications seal the future of psychosexuality.

I will highlight some factors that trigger situations of children and adolescents who have suffered dangerous situations at birth or throughout their first years of life.

Children can be sexually abused from birth onwards. Sexual abuse can have a devastating long-term impact on a young person's behavioral, emotional, social, and educational development. It often occurs alongside with other forms of child abuse, such as emotional and physical abuse, in many cases, the goal is to maintain

DOI: 10.4324/9781003647317-20

control and secrecy. Sexual abuse is not perpetrated solely by men; women can also commit the same acts.

A mother confronted with the birth of her child may have different reactions beyond those expected. For example, manic exaltation, depression or melancholy, puerperal psychosis, or other darker modes that make motherhood unbearable, even reaching infanticide (Munchausen syndrome). The myth of Medea already suggested that by killing her children, she also killed the mother in her, as well as how she was treated as a baby.

Children who witness continuous marital fights are exposed within the category of endangered childhoods. It will be necessary to understand the symptoms of each of the children exposed to spousal violence, as well as the transgenerational repetition of violence, treating each situation within a unique and unrepeatable story.

A specific "violence" is inherent to the human being, what Aulagnier (1975) has called "primary violence." The mother, faced with the baby crying without language, interprets the child's needs in her way. This translation of the mother is necessary for the survival of the baby who suffers such violence, but it builds from her the objects of a demand through words of language.

Bergeret (1984) evokes another violence called "fundamental," active during the Oedipal phase through fantasies of murder and desire for the paternal or maternal other.

A tyrannical father embodies and enforces the law instead of representing it, possibly because he wants to achieve perfection and the ideal. In cases where the child witnesses the violence of between their parents, the struggle can become a fight to the death. What the child will witness is this pathological bond with the other, excluding the third and exhibiting the violence acted.

The violence of the pair of parents, seen and understood by the child, strikes the infantile ghosts of Oedipal murder, transforming it into a nightmarish reality about that which should not have been imagined, mutating into blows, wounds, and screams, the fantasies that should only have been dreams of reverie. Beyond the trauma, it is challenging to dismantle, what can the child integrate concerning the bond with the other?

The "skin-self" (Anzieu, 2007) is based on the maternal function and the psychic containment of the maternal environment, allowing the child to create a psychic skin capable of protecting him from excess internal and external excitations. When the acted violence strikes the environment's capacity, it becomes one of the functions of the skin-self, which is the surface of separation that intends to mark the limit concerning the outside.

Children and adolescents show us intensely the force of attraction and power conferred by masochism and violence. It is a supreme defense of the Self, which, rightly or wrongly, feels powerless in a situation of being unable to do anything, of total passivity. Before disappearing, there is always something possible to destroy; at the last limit, if it cannot destroy others, it will destroy itself.

Death has occupied a privileged place in humanity's myths and rituals, as it represents the universal and irrefutable event par excellence. It is an outcome that is familiar as far as it happens daily, but at the same time and paradoxically, it is unknown and disturbing to us since while we are alive, the one who dies is the other. But the appearance of the "feeling of foreign," related to one's own death, nevertheless erupts and threatens narcissism.

About childhood

Most of the suicides occur in the child's home. The methods of suicide used most commonly used are hanging or suffocation, followed by firearms, which are usually stored unsafely in the child's home. School or peer-related problems are also present in cases of child death. The childhood suicide findings suggest that a progression toward suicide behavior accumulated over time and that an argument between the child victim and a family member (like incest cases) or disciplinary action was often the precipitating circumstance of the suicide. Currently, many cases of suicide in children have been linked to online games on the PC screen or cell phone, whether induced by a leader or situations in which there is no parental or adult supervision.

Part of the obsession that manifests in children and adolescents is the "fear of missing out" (FOMO). It means that something interesting or exciting is happening somewhere on the Internet that they can't miss. Anxiety has been increasing in children and adolescents, producing all types of physical and psychic disorders.

Increasing cases of pediatric suicidality highlight the ongoing mental health crisis among youth. Suicide attempts, ideation, and self-injury have become the most common mental health conditions seen in children's hospital emergency departments.

Children and adolescents also practice other attacks on the body that can be temporary or last over time, making them a symptom worthy of consideration. The examples are multiple and varied: Serious burns from leaving a child alone in the kitchen, as well as serious self-harm with knives, tell us about psychotic states where mental health professionals would have a predominant role.

Loving development runs parallel to the development of sexuality; both are associated with pleasure and are intimately related to corporeality. Children put their sexuality into action through erotic zones mainly. The psychic attributes of the child also undergo evolutionary changes concerning the development of sexuality. Emotions like anguish, guilt, joy, depression, shyness, apathy, nostalgia, and boredom stem from conflict and respond to anxiety.

The child's encounter with the familiar environment brings a sense of "home," which includes trust and tenderness, thus weaving the basis for the social bond. Its lack, whether by omission, absence, indifference, rejection, or an excessively intrusive presence, will be associated with experiences of non-existence and strangeness, thus opposing the familiarity to what Freud described as "The Uncanny" (*Heimlich-Unheimlich*) in 1919.

Based on the linguistic analysis of the German words, an analogy between the familiar and the sinister is suggested, considering the ambivalence of the colloquial word that turns toward the hidden or secret, connecting with the ominous. That familiar object is suddenly transformed, ceasing to be what it was, becoming terrifying, generating an unknowable anguish. What is destined to remain a secret becomes known.

Therefore, we could ask ourselves if the experience of ominousness occurs when an impression reanimates childhood traumatic situations or when primitive situations reaffirm them.

About adolescence

Adolescence is a time of profound psychic and body changes. It involves mourning the loss of childhood and the infantile body, as well as the fall and collapse of idealized infantile parents. It also heralds the appearance of a new, unknown body, quite different from what was expected. This period is marked by intense passions, where everything is played out in a single instant: life, love, sex, desire, crises, restlessness, boredom, depression, hatred, aggression, violence, and death.

Death is part of life. It becomes painfully cruel, incomprehensible, and unmanageable when it involves an adolescent. Hundreds of thousands of young people have not been able to face life, choosing to avoid the dark and overwhelming pain and suffering of a constantly changing psyche and body, where the narcissistic bases were not yet sufficiently secure.

The puberal process begins with the physical and psychic transformation that confronts the adolescent with the resumption of the conflicts pending during latency: a return to archaic phantasmatic conflicts, a reworking of the Oedipal conflict from the genital period, and a gradual positioning within a sexual identity.

Access to sexual identity leads him to mourn childhood omnipotence. The loss of this omnipotence can generate a confrontation with a strange and unknown world, trying to discover it. The adolescent faces important psychic work to the extent that the adolescent will be transformed, accepting the differences that separate him from his infantile self. Physical changes do not accompany psychic changes; they are generally not simultaneous.

During this period, adolescents can go through depression, which can range from severe rebellious and relapsing melancholic depression to simple affective conflict, deeply organized that includes a threat or a loss of love on the part of the object, thus triggering depression.

Green (2014) argues that the more we face a closed narcissism—impervious to relationships with the other, which also carries delirium as in melancholy—the more it signals the intervention of self-destructive forces.

What is the adolescent looking for through these attempts? Psychoanalytic clinical experience seems to indicate a need to destroy the apparatus of feeling and thinking, trying to escape from unbearable sensations and emotions.

The term "risk behaviors" designates a series of behaviors that expose oneself to a high probability of injury or death. Drug addiction, alcoholism, speeding, eating disorders, running away, or suicide attempts are the most frequent manifestations.

Each suffering adolescent has a history behind their risk behaviors, which can carry numerous meanings. Some of them can be unraveled as the adolescent accepts psychoanalytic help. Many of these behaviors originate in experience of abandonment, family indifference, or the feeling of not being considered. But they also include its reverse: maternal overprotection and invasive and suffocating behaviors (Flechner, 2010).

When boundaries have not been set, the adolescent may look for them on the surface of their body or jump right into acting out. It is a moment that we could call a hemorrhage of suffering that will destroy the limits of oneself, entering into vertigo that implies a feeling of falling, a loss of control and clarity, as if the thought had collapsed, producing a breakdown with reality. The diversion through bodily aggression is a paradoxical form of appeasement.

The maternal

In clinical practice, it is essential to refer to the pre-Oedipal stages of the mother–baby relationship in order to identify what we have called "maternal violence" (Flechner, 2005). It is about understanding the maternal relationship in its loving, aggressive, and violent dimensions, as Abensour (2011) considered it.

The maternal becomes the terrain where love and hate are played starkly, showing that the death drive is always present and linked in various ways with the life drive. The psychoanalytic clinical work could clarify the maternal, showing its singularity with each patient. The matrix of the maternal may seem a difficult concept to define because it produces a disturbing strangeness linked to the unknowable of the origins.

The maternal lies at the origins of the infant's psyche, including sexuality and danger in the face of the infant's defenselessness. Numerous aspects, such as love–hate, desire–rejection, and protection–abandonment, are disorganized and reorganized in the maternal psyche and transferred to the infant early on.

When children are abused or abandoned by parents or other significant adults, they often survive by developing antisocial behavior. They are often stigmatized as "violent," "offenders," "delinquents," and "drug addicts." We should consider whether these abnormal behaviors are generally due to an abnormal environment that often exists from conception. One consequence of maltreatment in children and adolescents is the storage of "traumatic memories" as discussed in Haydée Faimberg's (2007) paper on Telescoping Generations.

The suicidal instant

The suicidal instant is a massive reversal of self-destruction that is directed against the ego, observing itself in diverse situations. As analysts, it will be necessary to go through a narrow margin in which overflow situations arise, given the violence and impulsiveness of these acts. The death drive movements will be played in a peculiar way that largely materializes through action. An action that, in many cases, takes the form of an intrusive and violent act for the adolescent himself or for his environment.

The mirror image that secured and accompanied the self suddenly becomes unrecognizable, provoking a paralyzing terror. This physical and psychic paralysis arises in numerous self-elimination attempts, becoming the prelude to suicidal acts.

Shneidman (1992) wrote that suicide "is best understood as a combined movement toward cessation of consciousness and as a movement away from intolerable emotion, unendurable pain, unacceptable anguish." Multiple intensely distressing affects can contribute to this unbearable emotional experience, including anxiety, shame, self-hatred, and rage.

Analysts can frequently find "desperation," defined as a state of anguish accompanied by an urgent need for relief in previous sessions until the suicidal act. Among the many intense affects that can contribute to an unbearable suicidal state, the experience of aloneness deserves special consideration. Maltsberger (1988) likened it to "annihilation anxiety," driving a desperate need for escape. Aloneness feels outside time, as if it has always existed and will continue forever. It is qualitatively different from loneliness, which is contingent and time-limited. In loneliness, one may feel sadness and loss, but can still evoke images and memories of others, and maintain a feel of connection. In aloneness, by contrast, there is a loss of capacity to evoke soothing introjects or to experience the closeness and caring of others, even if they are present and available. Maltsberger also described the "descent into suicide" as a breakup of self-cohesion in the context of an overwhelming unbearable experience ("affect deluge") often triggered by a life crisis such as a critical loss or severe narcissistic injury.

Early developmental experiences, especially severe trauma and neglect, can increase vulnerability to unbearable affective states. The mother's capacity to recognize, appreciate, and reflect her infant/child's mental and emotional states is critical to the child's development of mentalization: the capacity to recognize and label emotional states and to appreciate and reflect on the mental states of others (Fonagy and Target, 1997; Fonagy et al, 2003). The child who is not recognized or held in mind by their parents will have difficulties with self-recognition and be more vulnerable to states of disorganization, overwhelming affect, and experiences of aloneness (Fonagy et al., 2003).

Clinical example

I will present extracts from an analysis of an adolescent patient, with a frequency of four weekly sessions that lasted ten years.

Max was the third child in a large family, mostly composed of boys. He was 17 when I met him. His father called requesting an interview, and both parents attended. His father was arrogant; his first sentence was: "How many more blank checks will I have to sign for this son? I have six children, but this one is unbearable. He has been undergoing two treatments, and no one can straighten him out…" *I come home from work, and my wife tells me to punish him*; "he has driven me crazy."

Indeed, he punished him with violence. In addition to approving of what the father was saying, his mother said about her son: "I have five children; I do not want this one."

This statement from the mother shocked me deeply. Was she too sincere? Was she a cold woman to the point of hating her son? I felt it as a condemnation of a young man I did not yet know. His father, on the other hand, was the one requesting a third treatment for his son since the two previous treatments had failed.

Max arrived at my consulting office in a high-speed pickup truck without a driver's license because he was a minor. However, his father allowed him to use it (my thoughts —remembering the phrases of his parents—were directed to another question: Would they want him to kill himself?)

When he arrived at the consulting room, I met a tall, thin boy with a good physique. However, he seemed to hide inside his ample clothing. His somber gaze corroborated his inner suffering. He was restless. His restlessness prevented him from remaining seated or lying on the couch. He walked around the office and talked while standing, thus showing great anxiety. He quickly drew my person and the objects in the consulting room.

Before I could ask him a question, he started to talk. His first sentences were direct against his parents:

> I don't know what they told you, but just in case, I'll tell you how they treat me at home; I don't get along with any of my siblings, my mother hates me, my father comes home from work, and my mother tells him to punish me, sometimes for no reason, he is violent, and I hate him.

A: What were the facts that he punished you?

P: Since they didn't allow me to enter the private school where all my siblings go, they began to make fun of me, treating me as a donkey and useless, my parents, too. I play with my brothers, but I know I'm aggressive. With the paddle, I break the lamps and everything that crosses my path, including my brothers.

A: Where does so much aggressiveness come from?

P: They mistreat me at home. I'm always the one who hits all the shots, even if I haven't done anything. My brothers know that if they say it was me, they won't do anything to them. They sent me to public school. I am not sorry at all. My classmates are much more similar to me than in that private school of theirs.

A: Do you feel that you were left with a lot of anger toward your parents because of this discrimination? Your siblings are in private school studying two languages, and you are in public school.

P: That was the least important because I felt good there. The worst thing is to be at home. They demand that I do all the errands. I am like a kind of "service person." They maltreat me, and I only have two paths: leaving home or disappearing.

A: What does "disappearing" mean to you?

P: Do you say kill me? I tried a few times, but I failed. Sometimes, I almost killed myself. That's why the doctor with whom I used to be treated decided to stop. He said I had suicidal tendencies, just because once I took my sister's car out with such bad luck that I was trapped between a bus and a truck; it is true that I almost killed myself... But my parents were angry that I had taken the car out without permission, not because of what might have happened to me.

A: Did you hurt yourself?

P: Ah, look! That question was never asked at home. Yes, I was hospitalized for fractures, but even then, my father just came to see me and came to pick me up when I was discharged, so they didn't give it too much importance.

A: I think it's essential.

P: Maybe for you, yes, but not for my family. It's not that I want to kill myself, but if it happens and I'm not to blame for what happened, I'm leaving this world.

Max impressed me with his speed and fluency in speaking, capturing my questions and answering them in a dialog that became agile despite his anxiety, which made it impossible for him to sit still. I was also struck by the years of mistreatment he endured from his family toward him. Jealousy and sibling rivalry were evident, but it was also apparent that Max reacted to aggression, identifying with his father and using the exact violent mechanisms, thus punishing his brothers.

We had numerous interviews with Max. I felt that I was embarking on a very complex situation. His actions were not limited to his family; outings with his friends also ended in street fights until late at night. These situations generated a particular fear in me, mainly the fear of also failing and being unable to predict the consequences. However, as several interviews continued, I had a different impression. His intelligence was more than enough to study two languages. Contrary to his parents' opinion, he even seemed to me too intelligent—despite having been diagnosed with dyslexia in childhood, which have never been treated. His low self-esteem played against him, as well as the fact that he felt abandoned, feeling great emptiness for not feeling loved by any member of his family.

Behind the restlessness he presented, his deep sadness was noticeable, as well as a depression that he transmitted even without speaking. Although he considered that it was not evident, as soon as he began treatment, he was able to express his deep discomfort and his feelings of emptiness and loneliness. He had not yet been specifically interested in other women; it gave the feeling of being a profoundly endogamic family, where only the opinions and facts of the family members counted.

The first year of treatment was tough for both of us. He refused to take medication, and the situation at home remained unchanged: his father continued to use extreme physical violence, throwing him to the ground and kicking him there, showing his brothers that everything he did was wrong. Added to this was the verbal violence of his mother. Meanwhile, each Monday session was marked with some bodily injury, from continuing to cut himself to sprains from having fought with his friends.

At the beginning of the sessions, Max was able to show me the numerous cuts on his forearms. He said that when his mother treated him as useless, cutting himself was more accessible to bear. In Max's words, "It didn't hurt so much."

While his family went on vacation, he was left alone at home. There, his failed suicide attempts took place, either by taking his mother's medication or trying to hang himself from a tree in the garden. This was why the previous therapist did not want to continue with the treatment. Having told his parents about these painful and intimate situations, Max did not want to return either.

I intended to have more interviews with his parents, but certain events made this impossible. Max told me his mother had been hospitalized again. When I asked him why, he said, smiling, "She is a psychiatric patient just like me." His mother was originally from another country than her father; supposedly, she emigrated for "love" of her husband. According to Max, she was a severe bipolar patient. From family stories, he learned that condition worsened after moving in with her husband. During her depressive episodes, she had been hospitalized due to risk of suicide.

A: Do you think you have your mother's illness?
P: Not me. Everyone says that I am the odd one in the family. I don't know if I have an illness. I want to be ordinary and to be treated well.
A: Being weird doesn't mean you have the same disease; in any case, you're weird because they let you drive a car without having an authorized license since you're a minor. You've told me you're going at a disproportionate speed in the city. Strange because your father, who does not have that disease, is violent with you, even in front of your siblings.
P: Yes, it may be, but I'm not going to take medication because wherever my brothers find out, in addition to the revulsion they have for me, they're going to say that I'm crazy much more than my mother. That was another reason the previous therapist did not want to continue treating me.

During the second year of treatment, the situation in Max's home remained the same or even worsened. We discussed the possibility of Max living elsewhere, but neither of his parents authorized him to leave from an economic reasons; even though this family had no financial problems.

Max turned 18 and obtained his driver's license. His father gave him an older truck than the one he had been driving; Max did not care; what did matter to him *was that it had slick tires*, and his father refused to replace them, saying it wasn't worth spending on an old truck. He quickly replied, "My father considers it not worth spending on me."

P: Do you understand that he doesn't care if I kill myself?
A: It may be that your father doesn't mind you killing yourself, but I need you to explain to me what you do to put yourself in such a complicated place.

> I think something leads you to put yourself in the position of a victim in front of your whole family.

P: Suppose so, and what do I fix with that?

A: We could understand a little more about that part of you that also causes this feeling of hatred for your whole family.

P: I have a hatred that won't go away. Sometimes, I regret feeling so strong.

A: What name would you give to remorse?

P: I don't know ... blame?

A: Yes, you could feel guilty; what is the reason for the feelings of guilt?

> Max remained silent while a tear began to fall, gradually, then another and another. He cried as if we had touched an old wound, and he felt that I was opening it more and more.

P: I need to understand why my mother doesn't love me. My father doesn't hate me that much; he follows my mother's orders.

A few months passed after this session, during which we were able to delve into the issue of his place and a certain masochistic posture-something he was quite aware of, especially since it come up repeatedly in his previous treatment.

Anzieu (2007) has stated that in some instances, the adolescent "can only possess control of his body by masking it in the position of the victim."

In the meantime, a certain feeling of esteem for his father emerged in him. Around that time, a friend of his father telephoned Max's home, reporting that he had suffered a severe accident at work. Max's mother answered the phone, saying she couldn't go, even less if he were injured. His brothers were shocked by the news and didn't know what to do. Max quickly took his truck and rush to the hospital to find out how his father was doing. He was in the intensive care unit, in a coma from a head injury, and visitors weren't allowed. Max managed to see him, took his hand, and said, "You're going to be fine."

As he recounted what happened, he began to cry again. Max added something he hadn't tell to his family. When his father heard his words, he squeezed his hand. It was a sign interpreted by Max as "something like a ray of hope" for improving their relationship.

It was a complex treatment. However, Max was still interested in recovering from years of suffering. Therefore, we finished when he had already been accepted to continue his studies abroad.

Considering Max's injuries, we can ask ourselves, is self-injury the symptom of our times? Injuries to the body can also be the preamble to a suicide attempt. It will be necessary for a disinvestment of one's own body to be able to attack or cut it so that when it is attacked, anguish is not registered.

The psychological distress experienced by an individual who self-injured is often fundamental and challenging to express. It is common among patients who have difficulty expressing a logical reason for their actions. They regularly refer to the sensation of feeling alive or simply feeling relief. It seems as if it were a matter of interrupting a primary representation with the limitation of a real sensation.

An essential issue throughout adolescent treatment is to avoid making premature diagnoses, unless there is clear evidence of psychosis or severe depression.

Suicide and its social environment

When Durkheim (1897) wrote his book *Le Suicide*, he highlighted the socio-structural character of 19th-century European societies, arguing that rather than psychological reasons, economic, military, and religious factors influenced suicide. Although his thesis should be revised, we can agree that the pressure of social life guided and determined by submission to unilateral models has caused constant forms of exclusion and anomie.

It is also important to remember that we are born with a propensity for violence, and that violence is not like a passing virus but is timeless and ever-present. Cruelty and destruction are always present, as Freud said in 1939, quoting Hobbes, "Man is the wolf of man" ("Homo homini lupus"). Each historical and social moment defines specific predominant modes of relationship between the human being, his own body, and the body of the other. In all of them, the social imaginary shapes bodies and is expressed directly through them and indirectly through how they are represented and conceived.

Suicidal gestures are also a social phenomenon; therefore, they cannot be examined as a predominant mode of relationship between the human being, his own body, and the body of the other. In all of them, the social imaginary shapes bodies and is expressed directly through them and indirectly through how they are represented and conceived.

The precariousness of intra-familiar and social ties, isolation, and loneliness led us to believe in the pseudo-intimacy of social networks. It has been reassuring throughout the pandemic; it allowed us, in many cases, to be close to our patients, but at the same time, it has isolated us. Especially adolescents, for whom the peer group is essential, grew even more distant. Space/time was narrowed for them, stoning their uncertainties, projects, and illusions. Unfortunately, many are no longer here to live through it.

Suppose societies with a significant degree of integration are capable of protecting their individuals from suicide. In that case, it may be because they instill in the subject the value of human life, values that also concern the group, the community, and culture.

We cannot ignore the Latin American context, characterized by social demands and increased poverty, which is also favored by the pandemic and governments of uncertain ideologies. Such situations lead us to ask ourselves repeatedly: Is there a way out? Do today's children and young people have a future?

We find ourselves in a frightening and turbulent post-pandemic world. The pandemic's impact on the mental health of children and adolescents has been fierce; consultations have multiplied worldwide, and mental health systems have failed to address this immense suffering adequately. Socio-economic and political uncertainty is rampant. We are increasingly aware of devastating inequalities and a lack of protection for many. Technology invades our daily lives, generating a perpetual spectacle of distraction that obstructs thought. Thrown onto the horizon of virtual communication in networks, the child and adolescent who self-harm exhibit their bodies subjected to the system of the networks, trying to make the screen affirm a corporal and subjective place. It is through destructive tendencies, whether attacks on the body, attempts, and suicides, that traces of discomfort woven from the fact of feeling transparent, incorporeal, and non-existent are also observed.

References

Abensour, L. (2011). L´ombre du maternel. *Revue Française de Psychanalyse*, 75 (5), 1297–1335.

Anzieu, D. (2007). *El yo-piel*. Madrid, España: Biblioteca Nueva.

Aulagnier, P. (1975/1995). *La violence de l'interprétation*. Paris, France: Presses Universitaires de France (PUF).

Bergeret, J. (1984). *La violence fondamentale*. Paris, France: Dunod.

Durkheim, É. (1897). *Le suicide Etude de sociologie*. Paris, France: Felix Alcan Editeur.

Faimberg, H. (2007). *El telescopaje de generaciones: A la escucha de los lazos narcisistas*. Madrid, España: Amorrortu Editores.

Flechner, S. (2005). On aggressiveness and violence in adolescence. *International Journal of Psychoanalysis*, 86, 1391–1403.

Flechner, S. (2010). *Psicoanálisis y adolescencia: Dos temporalidades que se interpelan*. Buenos Aires, Argentina: Paidós, 85–93.

Freud, S. (1919). *Lo ominoso*. En J. L. Etcheverry (Trad.), Obras Completas (Vol. XVII, pp. 219–252). [3.ª reimpresión castellana], Buenos Aires, Argentina: Amorrortu Editores. 1992.

Fonagy, P., Target, M. (1997). Attachment and reflective function: Their role in self-organization. *Development and Psychopathology*, 9, 679–700.

Fonagy, P., Target, M., Gergely, G., Allen, J.G., Bateman, A.W. (2003). The developmental roots of borderline personality disorder in early attachment relationships: A theory and some evidence. *Psychoanalytic Inquiry*, 23, 412–459.

Green, A. (2014). Suicidio(s): Patología y normalidad. En ¿*Por qué las pulsiones de destrucción o de muerte?* Buenos Aires, Argentina: Amorrortu Editores Buenos Aires, pp. 116–120.

Maltsberger, J.T. (1988). Suicide danger: Clinical estimation and decision. *Suicide & Life-Threatening Behavior*, 18, 47–54.

Shneidman, E.S. (1992). What do suicides have in common? Summary of the psychological approach. In *Suicide: Guidelines for Assessment, Management, and Treatment*. B. M. Bongar (Ed.). New York, NY: Oxford University Press, pp. 3–15.

Are the kids alright? Why is life unlivable?

Suicidal tendencies in gender disorders and trans identity

Patricia Gherovici

Context

Today's youth are clever, compassionate, yet increasingly burdened by anxiety and exhaustion. After accidents, suicide has become the second-leading cause of death among teenagers. This troubling reality raises critical questions: Could the so-called "gender trouble" of adolescence—an existential struggle touching on sexuality, the mind–body connection, societal taboos, family lineage, aspirational ideals, and the consumerist culture—actually underscore that, for many, transitioning is a matter of survival?

In the United States, adolescents were grappling with what was labeled as a "mental health crisis" even before the COVID-19 pandemic. Over the past decade, youth suicide and self-harm have soared exponentially. Parenting trends—either overly protective ("helicopter parenting") or intensely fear-driven ("paranoid parenting")—are often cited as contributors. A 2023 survey of 1,500 parents of children aged 3 to 17 painted a disconcerting picture: up to one in five children was described as struggling with a mental, emotional, developmental, or behavioral disorder. Nearly half of these parents reported that their children were battling anxiety, depression, attention-deficit/hyperactivity disorder (ADHD), or autism spectrum conditions. Overuse of screens—via social media, television, or other devices—was reported as a significant contributing factor, with approximately one in three teenagers deeply affected.

Notably, this crisis extends beyond the youth. Parents also report profound effects on their mental health, personal relationships, and work. Drawing on the sociological insights of Émile Durkheim and Arnold van Gennep, as well as the psychoanalytic work of Freud and Lacan, Carl Waitz (2025) argues that the erosion of social bonds, coupled with the disappearance of meaningful initiation rituals, has precipitated this crisis. The behaviors of today's youth, he contends, act as a distress signal—a mirror reflecting societal failures.

Social media and the internet further complicate matters. For instance, the widespread accessibility of pornography disrupts the development of a healthy space for fantasy, a crucial element of human sexuality. Without this imaginative engagement, sexuality struggles to integrate into the social fabric, hindering

DOI: 10.4324/9781003647317-21

young people's symbolic transition into adulthood. Early exposure to explicit content, paired with relentless consumerism, creates a generation adrift in meaning, detached from traditional social anchors.

The kids are telling us that something is wrong with them and with us. In other words, Waitz argues that the current youth mental health crisis is caused by the fact that our youth has lost their initiation rites that would ease the departure from childhood and allow entrance into the social link as adults. This deficit makes youth more vulnerable to self-harm and suicide. The COVID-19 pandemic's effects exacerbated these vulnerabilities on youth mental health on a global scale, intensifying existing challenges and creating new ones.

"Oppressed by gender"

I introduce here a clinical vignette of a teenager who, in our single session, described feeling "oppressed by gender" following a dramatic suicidal gesture. This will serve as an entry point into an exploration of what it means to move from death to life. Here death functions not as a final endpoint but as a generative force—a potential site of rebirth.

Clinical work reveals a path toward living with the death drive, a paradoxical force that, far from negating life, makes life possible. Within this framework, death is not the antithesis of life but rather its fundamental condition. This clinical fragment challenges prevailing perspectives among Lacanian and classical Freudian psychoanalysts by proposing that the wish to change one's gender is not an evasion or negation of sexual difference. Instead, it often reflects a profound preoccupation around sexual difference, where gender transition becomes a creative act of self-making and renewal. Drawing on Freud's case of the young homosexual woman, I explore the clinical stakes of suicidal tendencies in trans individuals and propose transition as an act of re-birth.

Jude was a 19-year-old college student who sought consultation after a desperate suicide attempt. They identified as non-binary and used "they/them" pronouns and were rescued from the edge of Philadelphia's Schuylkill River—a name eerily resonant with "school-kill" in English. Their university subsequently mandated a return to their parents' home in California, barring them from continuing their studies until they were "cured" of their suicidal depression.

Jude recounted a confluence of challenges shaping their life, navigating their identity as a trans and queer individual, coping with chronic Lyme disease and ADHD. In addition, they had shouldered adult responsibilities at a young age because of a fraught family history—growing up with parents battling addiction. The societal stigma surrounding their gender identity, coupled with these personal hardships, had pushed them to a breaking point. This is how they explained it:

> Starting this out is tough, but here goes. I start in the middle because I don't know where the beginning is yet. So, like, I've been dealing with a ton lately. ... My mom had a rough childhood herself and never really learned how to parent,

even though she practically raised her siblings. So, guess who stepped up to fill that role? Yep, me. It's like my childhood got fast-forwarded, you know? I was dealing with adult stuff way too soon, taking care of my younger siblings while my parents were dealing with their own demons.

...I've been battling since day one, and a big part of it is because of gender. No matter how much I try to own who I am, society still puts me in this box, you know? It's like I'm fighting two battles at once, and it's exhausting. No matter how much I changed—I changed my pronouns; I still feel oppressed because of gender.

Jude's attempt to leap into the river can be interpreted as a symbolic act of trying to "kill" themselves to be reborn. This was not merely a suicidal gesture but an act that spoke louder than words. What exactly Jude sought to destroy? Reflecting on their life at the time of the attempt, Jude described feeling overwhelmed by intense anxiety and profound dissatisfaction with their assigned gender.

Jude's ordeal echoes Samuel Beckett's famous complaint to his psychoanalyst, Wilfred Bion, that he had never been "properly born." Similarly, one might argue that Jude has only been "half-born." Jude themselves expressed a sense of lacking a beginning or origin when they said, "I start in the middle, because I don't know where the beginning is yet."

Jude's suicidal gesture was a symbolic act of annihilation with the aim of trans-formation, a desperate bid to "kill" a version of themselves to make space for rebirth. Despite positioning themselves outside the binary, they still found no framework for imagining a future in which they felt fully alive. Forced to assume adult responsibilities in childhood, Jude was denied the opportunity to have a clear starting point. They were trapped in a paradoxical yearning: a desire to find or create a beginning while grappling with the overwhelming sense that such a beginning has been lost or was never there.

The etymology of "gender" is revealing—the term comes from the Latin *genus*, meaning family, lineage, and difference. Aristotle used *genus* to categorize enti-ties, highlighting the early idea of belonging to a specific group. In late Middle English, gender developed from the Old French *gendre* (modern *genre*), which, like its Latin origin, was linked to birth, family, and nation. This connection also relates to words like "generation," reinforcing the ideas of origin and descent. Therefore, "gender" is historically tied not only to biological differences but also to social roles, belonging, and the continuation of cultural and familial identities.

Gender is commonly perceived as a social construct, while sexuality is more closely associated with the body and is influenced by various factors like class, race, ethnicity, and nationality. In everyday discussions, the concept of gender encompasses a wide spectrum of identities and expressions, indicating a more fluid understanding of the self. The modern perspective of gender as an identity or inner truth can be traced back to the pioneering work of psychoanalyst Robert Stol-ler, who introduced the concept of gender identity.[1] The academic differentiation between gender and sexuality often does not fully capture personal experiences, as many individuals find that the complexities of gender and sexuality challenge this separation, often emerging in issues that prompt them to seek analysis. The once clear distinction between gender identity and sexual orientation has become blurred leading to a shift from fundamental questions about gender to more immediate concerns about sexual orientation, reflecting a deeper confusion about identity. The struggle lies not only in exploring one's gender, but also in the interweaving of object-choice and sexual orientation, both of which play defining roles in shaping identity and are challenging to disentangle (Gherovici, 2010).

For Jude, this entanglement became far more than a theoretical question; it emerged as a life-or-death issue. They expressed feeling like a "parent-child," caught in a parentified role yet unable to situate themselves as either male or female. This sense of liminality, of being neither one thing nor the other, seemed to intensify their internal turmoil. After our only session, Jude returned to California to live with their parents—two functional addicts recently divorced. Despite their financial stability from successfully working in the film industry, Jude's parents continued to be heavily involved with drugs. Though Jude has dropped out of school for the time being, I know they are still alive, but the questions they face—about gender, identity, and survival—are far from resolved.

Unhappily, Jude's situation, although singular, is not exceptional. Between 2013 and 2018, a total of 14 students at the University of Pennsylvania tragically died by suicide, which led me to take Jude's case very seriously. Recent data reveal that suicide rates are particularly high among transgender youth. In a sample of 372 transgender youth, 56% reported a previous suicide attempt, and 86% reported experiencing suicidality.[2] A 2023 study conducted by the Williams Institute at UCLA School of Law reveals alarming statistics: 81% of transgender adults have contemplated suicide, while 42% have made attempts, and 56% have engaged in non-suicidal self-injury.[3] Findings indicated that interpersonal microaggressions significantly contributed to lifetime suicide attempts, while emotional neglect by family approached significance. Additionally, school belonging, emotional neglect, and internalized self-stigma significantly influenced past six-month suicidality.

In my clinical experience, transitioning often carries the weight of life or death, transcending mere gender expression or identity to become a matter of survival within their own bodies, where the presence of death is keenly felt. The struggle for many trans individuals is not just about how they are perceived, but about the profound challenge of existing within a body that feels profoundly disconnected from their sense of self.

Livable and unlivable genders

Freud avoided the need to choose between anatomy and social convention, recognizing the influence of both biological and social factors on the sexual and gendered subject. According to psychoanalysis, sex is not simply a natural occurrence, nor can it be solely attributed to a discursive construction. The sex/gender dichotomy is false. Sexual difference cannot be reduced to either term: gender requires embodiment while sex necessitates representation. It goes beyond conventional categorizations, indicating a deeper and more fundamental shift in the understanding of identity. This radical difference challenges traditional dichotomies while revealing a core element of negativity. Both sexual orientation and gender identity are considered as approximations for an indescribable aspect, referred to as "sexual difference" within psychoanalysis. To illustrate this, let's consider Freud's case of a suicidal 18-year-old homosexual woman.[4]

Margarete Csonka von Trautenegg, also known as Gretl and, in recent psychoanalytic literature, as Sidonie Csillag–described herself as having become "a celebrity in a grotesque way" (Rieder & Voigt 2019, xi).[5] In a deftly crafted fictionalized biography, Ines Rieder and Diana Voigt, under the pseudonym Sidonie Csillag, meticulously documented the remarkable life of the young woman briefly analyzed by Freud. Sidonie lived nearly a century, passed in 1999 at age 99, and concealed her true identity until after her death. Her real name was Margarethe von Trautenegg, née Csonka. While the pseudonym Csillag means "star" in Hungarian, her real maiden name Csonka translates as "mutilated." In October 2004, Rieder and Voigt entrusted the Sigmund Freud Museum in Vienna with a treasure trove of materials—an expansive photo collection, personal documents, and a wealth of interviews that together provide evidence of Sidonie's extraordinary life.

Thanks to Rieder and Voigt, we now have the opportunity of discovering the larger-than-fiction life of Sidonie Csillag, the protagonist of Freud's last published case, his controversial treatment of a "young homosexual woman." Freud treated Sidonie when she was an energetic 18-year-old girl from a well-respected, wealthy Viennese family of Jewish origin who converted to Catholicism. Her father brought her to analysis after her involvement in a love affair with a woman, which caused a social scandal and was followed by a suicide attempt. Freud did not assure Sidonie's parents that their daughter would become heterosexual as they hoped. He believed that psychoanalysis could not and was not intended to "cure" homosexuality, as he did not consider it to be a pathology, but rather a sexual orientation as contingent as heterosexuality.

Freud's decision (1920) to treat Sidonie despite her lack of overt illness since she "was not in any way ill—she did not suffer from anything in herself nor did she complain of her condition" (p. 150) may indeed stem from his interest in lesbianism, possibly spurred by his daughter Anna's situation, suggesting a desire to understand the nuances of female sexuality beyond pathology. However, Freud's broader conceptualization of female sexuality, as inherently linked to homosexual tendencies, allows for a more nuanced interpretation. By the time he penned this case history, Freud had begun to normalize homosexual feelings within neuroses, indicating an evolving perspective that recognized human desire beyond conventional social norms.

Freud acknowledged that Sidonie was not neurotic, arriving for analysis devoid of even a single hysterical symptom (p. 155). His task, therefore, was not to resolve a neurotic struggle but to navigate the complexities of her sexual orientation. For Freud, both homosexuality and heterosexuality emerged from the Oedipus complex; he noted that attempting to shift a fully developed homosexual to heterosexuality offered little promise of success, and yet he viewed bisexuality as the potential key to unlocking broader sexual expression.

Freud traced Sidonie's homosexuality back to a pivotal moment in her adolescence when her Oedipus complex resurfaced. This was sparked by her wish to bear her father's child coinciding with the birth of her younger brother. Although she harbored an unconscious resentment towards her mother for this situation, she ultimately renounced her femininity and, for a time, adopted a masculine identity, redirecting her affections toward her mother instead of her father as a means of compensating for her earlier hostility. Jacques Lacan described this dynamic as "reactive" (2004, p. 108). Freud also observed a stark contrast in the parental responses to Sidonie's homosexuality: her father was enraged and unforgiving, while her mother, who had always been her confidante, embraced the change with surprising ease. This maternal tolerance suggested an implicit understanding of Sidonie's choice, interpreting her disinterest in men to sidestep rivalry, especially given that the mother was still a relatively young woman who enjoyed male attention. In contrast, the father felt deeply betrayed; Sidonie's rejection of men symbolized a rejection of him as well.

Sidonie's situation resembles Jude's struggle in finding a place in the family genealogy, possibly contributing to the suicidal gesture. Many individuals who attempt suicide very often deny the finality of death and fantasize about a fresh start, imagining themselves still alive after the suicidal act, even if only to consider its impact on loved ones. When there is no clear origin, creating an end becomes necessary to establish a starting point, echoing Beckett's quote from *Endgame*— "The end is in the beginning." To summarize this nuanced case, let us mention that Sidonie insisted on maintaining a close relationship with a Viennese well-known noble demimondaine, a woman ten years her senior, whom Freud described as someone with a "distinguished name" but who was "nothing but a cocotte." The impoverished baroness was openly bisexual and rumored to be living in a ménage à trois with a married couple. Sidonie's parents did everything they could to end the relationship, fearing it would tarnish their daughter's reputation. But Sidonie remained steadfast—until one day, when the baroness, shaken by a disapproving glare from Sidonie's father, ended it. Devastated by the rejection, Sidonie attempted suicide by jumping from a railway overpass, resulting in serious injuries and an extended recovery.

Freud took her suicide attempt seriously and provided treatment accordingly. He remarked that the verb used to describe her fall was *niederkommen*, meaning both "to fall" and "to give birth to a child." The dual meaning of the German verb *niederkommen* was interpreted by Freud as linked to her adolescent wish for a child from her father—an urge that emerged just as her mother got pregnant with a baby brother. Freud (1920) argued that Sidonie experienced profound frustration in her yearning to bear her father's child, suggesting that her "fall" was a consequence of her father's influence (p. 162).

Lacan largely aligned with Freud's (1920) interpretation of Sidonie's attempted suicide, viewing it as both a punitive act and a manifestation of her desires—specifically, her wish to have her father's child, culminating in her tragic fall (p. 162). This desperate gesture encapsulated the significance of her predicament (Lacan 1962–1963, 106–110). Freud interpreted her fatal plunge onto the railway tracks as a symbolic representation of childbirth, likening it to *Niederkommen*–the act of a baby descending during delivery.

When Freud (1920) encountered Sidonie's intense "bitterness against men," he ended her treatment, referring her to a female colleague for reasons he called "obvious" (p. 164). Was this decision shaped by his difficulty accepting her rejection of men, or by his identification with her father, whom he described as "an earnest, worthy man, at bottom very tender-hearted" (p. 149)? Though he interpreted her renewed affection for her father as positive transference, her heterosexual "lying dreams" seemed to both gratify and unsettle him (p. 166). Freud ultimately concluded her "masculinity complex" by stating, "She was in fact a feminist" (p. 166)—a striking move that reframes her repudiation of men and defiance of masculine authority as an ideological stance.

While some women, like Anna O. (Bertha Pappenheim), successfully reinvented themselves as feminists, Sidonie lacked such support. As Adrienne Harris (1999) observed, "If 'she was in fact a feminist,' she was a feminist quite without the support of feminism" (p. 157). Though Sidonie may have been shaped by feminist ideals, her biography suggests she remained bound to her father's approval, showing little inclination to confront that dependence.

Freud's reaction to her same-sex love for an "older" woman—who was merely twenty-eight—raises questions about his own biases. His contradictions were evident, as he simultaneously conformed to and broke from patriarchal prejudices regarding femininity and homosexuality. Notably, Freud observed a critical distinction that remains relevant today: "The literature of homosexuality usually fails to distinguish clearly enough between questions of choice of object on the one hand, and of sexual characteristics and sexual attitude on the other" (p. 170). His abrupt termination of Sidonie's treatment can be interpreted as stemming from his skepticism about "treating" homosexuality, a doubt he reiterated, stating, "it is not for psychoanalysis to solve the problem of homosexuality" (p. 171). Perhaps he felt unable to address female homosexuality before unraveling the complexities of femininity that perpetually eluded him.

In a later hypothesis (1933), Freud posited that Sidonie's intense feelings for the baroness stemmed from a broken promise within a complex exchange—a gift economy of sorts. This raises a crucial inquiry: does the "symbolic gift of a child" equate to a woman's intrinsic desire for motherhood? It's noteworthy that Freud's exploration begins with the concept of homosexuality and concludes with motherhood (p. 66). Yet, curiously absent from this discourse is femininity—a term that eludes both Freud and the unconscious alike.

Born again

However, Sidonie's narrative can be reframed not as a longing to bear her Oedipal father's child, but as a quest to give birth to her own identity, positioning her outside the familial lineage. The biography by Reider and Voigt reveals numerous painful rejections that underscore this sentiment. In one particularly harrowing instance, just a year prior to her suicide attempt and subsequent treatment with Freud, a suitor of Sidonie's mother complimented her daughter's beauty. In a moment of deep humiliation, Sidonie's mother retorted that she was not her daughter, but merely "the child of an acquaintance" (Rieder & Voigt, 2019, p.42). Deeply hurt, Sidonie secluded herself for two days, crying and refusing to engage with her mother.

The rivalry expressed by her mother—who wished to be seen as the singular embodiment of beauty—effectively ostracizes Sidonie from the familial kinship system. This scenario echoes the struggles faced by Jude, the teenager I referenced earlier, who described their mother as childlike and indifferent, positioning Jude not as her child but as a caretaker for her siblings.

When Lacan revisited the case of the "Young Homosexual Woman" in 1963, he situated it within an exploration of the function of the object of desire, which he denoted as object "a" (2004, p. 129). This object manifested with startling intensity during Sidonie's initial suicide attempt, particularly considering the contrasting narrative presented in her recent biography (Rieder & Voigt, 2019, pp. 27–28). Lacan interpreted Sidonie's bold act of defiance—strolling down the street with her lady companion—as an "acting out," a moment when desires are "offered to be seen" (*donné à voir*). Freud had previously linked the suicide attempt to Sidonie witnessing her father's anger, which triggered the lady's subsequent rejection of her. However, the biography offers a different perspective: Sidonie and her companion encounter her father and a colleague from a distance, and upon seeing him, Sidonie panics and runs away, fleeing from the lady. By the time she returns, her father has left, having boarded a trolley, and crucially, he may not have even seen her. In this retelling, the father's "blindness" becomes a pivotal element, with the lady's reproach suggesting that Sidonie's flight indicated a lack of true love, thus serving as the catalyst for her tragic act.

It is quite plausible that Sidonie's father had indeed seen her, as Thomas Gindele (2003) notes, given that he was the one who brought her to treatment. This suggests that he might have provided Freud with an accurate account of the events (p. 397). However, Sidonie's own version adds emotional depth to her suicide attempt. While Freud depicts a disapproving paternal gaze as the trigger for her suicidal action, Sidonie recounts her father conversing with a colleague at the end of the street before hastily boarding a tram. Fearing the possibility of being seen by him, she fled from the lady without realizing that her father had already left. This uncertainty about her father's awareness—whether he had seen her with the baroness, chosen to ignore her, or simply hadn't noticed her at all—heightens the poignancy of her situation. Freud (1920) highlights a significant aspect of the lady's rejection that contributes to the complexity of Sidonie's emotional turmoil.

If, as the biography suggests, Sidonie's father stood too far away to recognize the two women, his furious glance would have been beyond her perception. Yet in throwing herself onto the tracks, Sidonie achieved three things: she obliterated the internalized paternal gaze, invoked the symbolic father through the potential of her death (since the dead father occupies that position), and publicly affirmed the depth of her love for the woman. The ambiguity—whether her father saw her—underscores the gaze as a pivotal object of desire. This theme resurfaces in Freud's parting comment on her "shrewd eyes," where he expressed unease at potentially facing her as an adversary (Rieder & Voigt, 2019, p. 55).

To be delivered of a child

Sidonie's case was analyzed by Diana Fuss (1995) who begins her analysis by scrutinizing Freud's cognitive framework of "falling," which he employs to rationalize female homosexuality (p. 57). Fuss argues that this "fall" should not be interpreted literally; instead, it represents a regression to a pre-Oedipal stage, characterized by a simultaneous desire for the mother and identification with the father. This perspective serves as a foundation for her critical examination of psychoanalytic theories that address female homosexuality. Fuss identifies a recurring theme in terms of "pre-" concepts—preoedipal, presymbolic, prelaw, premature, presexual, and even pretheoretical—portraying subjects "*as* foundational, primeval, primitive, and indeed as pre-subjects, before the normative, heterosexualizing operations of the Oedipus complex" (p. 58; italics in the original). She critiques Freud's framework, arguing that the issues he encounters stem from the Oedipus complex in all its manifestations, not solely from feminine sexuality.

Like Lacan, Fuss expresses skepticism regarding Freud's Oedipal explanation for Sidonie's transition from a maternal desire (the wish to become a mother) to a homosexual inclination (the desire to have a mother), attributing it to her mother's late pregnancy and the birth of a younger brother. This prompts her to question the significance of the substitute object promise, ultimately challenging Freud's evolving theory of femininity, which—initially outlined in this 1920 case, later developed in three pivotal works: "The Infantile Genital Organisation" (1923), "Some Psychical Consequences of the Anatomical Distinction Between the Sexes" (1925), "Female Sexuality" (1931), and "Femininity" (1933).

Fuss's project holds significant merit, as it addresses Freud's recognition of his theoretical limitations regarding gender identity, especially femininity. Initially, Freud posited that the Oedipus complex operated similarly across genders; however, his later writings on libidinal organization highlight distinctions in object choice, the castration complex's consequences, and the narcissistic investments associated with genitalia. In his final works, Freud acknowledges the mother as the primary object for girls, with subsequent variations influencing their ability to achieve a feminine identity through identifications that shape object choice. Fuss remains skeptical of Freud's interpretation of the daughter's shift towards the mother, which he described in 1920 as an "enigmatic disappointment" and later framed in 1932 as an "inevitable disappointment." This latter conceptualization emerged in his "Femininity" lecture, introducing the notion of a "masculinity complex" in women, suggesting a regression from the bond with the father. Freud (1933) posits that female homosexuality is not a direct extension of infantile masculinity. For a girl to navigate her sexual identity, it is essential that she initially regards her father as an object of desire and becomes enmeshed in the Oedipal scenario. However, as she experiences inevitable disappointments related to her father, she may regress into her earlier masculinity complex, reflecting a complicated interplay between her formative relationships and her sexual orientation (p. 130). Fuss (1995) questioned Freud's use of "regress," which she understood as "a retrenchment rather than an advance, a retreat *from* the father rather than a move *toward* the mother" (p. 64; italics in the original). Fuss critiques Freud's notion that displacement of incestuous desire from a heterosexual daughter towards her father onto the mother signifies a denial of the homosexual daughter's incestuous feelings for her mother (p. 64). She dismisses Freud's characterization of the "early masculinity complex" as rooted in daughter–mother incest. In contrast, Lacan posits that incest is inherently linked to the mother, who represents the first Other and the initial *heteros*. The mother is the sole incestuous object due to her fundamental role in the infant's survival, a bond reinforced by the newborn's dependence on her. Her status as the opposite sex introduces the potential for heterosexual desire. The profound psychological impact of maternal absence is underscored by Renée Spitz's (1945, 1966) studies on hospitalism. Similarly, Jenny Aubry (1983) found that children lacking sufficient maternal care exhibited autistic traits and self-destructive behaviors. John Bowlby's attachment theory posits that the bond between infant and caregiver is crucial for healthy emotional and psychological development. Bowlby viewed attachment as an innate biological mechanism and behavioral system designed to fulfill basic human needs. Mary Main, who studied under Bowlby and Ainsworth, developed this concept by suggesting that adults' representations of their own childhood experiences can significantly impact how parents form emotional bonds with their own children, shaping the next generation's attachment behaviors.

Lacan's analysis reinforces the idea that maternal deficits can have devastating effects on a child's development: "If the child is not the object of a particularized life desire, even if presented through the lack in the mother, it can neither develop nor get structured" (2001, p. 371 my translation). The repercussions of early maternal absence are profound, yet the challenge of separating from this primary affection is particularly daunting for girls. This concern echoes Freud's question: "How does a girl pass from her mother to an attachment to her father?" (1932, p. 147).

Fuss's critique can indeed be framed within the context of how castration reshapes the dynamics of maternal and paternal relationships for boys and girls. Initially, both share a symmetrical attachment to the mother. However, the introduction of castration complicates this relationship, adds a tertiary term—the phallus—that distinguishes the two genders. Consequently, the term "boy" becomes synonymous with possessing a penis and adopts associations with virility and masculinity, while "girl" acquires phallic significance that shifts away from anatomical definitions to embody traits such as mystery, demureness, and beauty. For boys, the phallus and castration serve to resolve the Oedipal complexities they face. For girls, the dynamics surrounding the resolution of the Oedipus complex are notably more intricate.

A change of sex

Both boys and girls are oriented toward a masculine position in this context, as they both love their mothers but ultimately must renounce that attachment. Serge André (1999) critiqued Freud's early theories on femininity, suggesting that to evade homosexuality and shift toward a male object of desire, a girl must undergo a "change of sex" in fantasy (p. 173). André explored the notion that homosexuality is embedded within the structure of the feminine Oedipus complex, arguing that a heterosexual object choice necessitates this fantasy transformation. He examined the case of a young homosexual woman to illustrate his point (pp. 173–184). Freud himself struggled to explain why not all girls transition to homosexuality, suggesting that the typical outcome of the Oedipus complex could instead represent a reiteration of earlier attachments to the mother.

Fuss challenges Freud's assertion that a daughter's desire for her mother reflects a regression caused by rivalry, suggesting instead that such rivalry is inaccurately framed. She poses a critical question: "Why, in short, is the daughter's 'rivalry' assumed to be with the mother and not with the father?" (Fuss, 1995, p. 62). Freud posited that in resolving the Oedipus complex, a girl resents her mother for the perceived loss of a penis and turns to her father in the hope of obtaining a child as a symbolic substitute. Fuss argues compellingly that Freud's theory of femininity ultimately leads to a dead end: the outcome of the feminine Oedipus complex merely results in a regression back to the pre-Oedipal bond with the mother.

Fuss' inquiry questions the efficacy of the Oedipus complex in fully elucidating femininity. While it appears to account for boys' sexuality with clarity, it falls short for girls. Lacan shifts the focus away from castration and its implications, emphasizing instead the divisions created by the primacy of the phallus for both genders. This perspective invites a reexamination of how female sexuality is constructed and understood within psychoanalytic theory, suggesting that the dynamics are not just about loss but also about the girl's complex positioning in relation to both parents.

For Lacan (1994), the girl's sense of lacking the phallus signifies a more profound absence of a symbolic object—the symbolic phallus itself. He argues that the notion of a missing penis is a symbolic construct imposed upon the Real, which, in its essence, is devoid of any true deficiency (p. 218). Consequently, the mother is seen as lacking an object she never possessed. What is perceived as absent is not merely the penis but rather the symbolic phallus, with the imaginary father serving as the agent of this sense of privation. This perspective challenges traditional interpretations of femininity and highlights the complexities surrounding female identity and desire.

In Sidonie's case, the girl redirects her resentment towards her mother—stemming from the perceived lack of a penis—onto her father when he fails to provide the desired child. Freud (1933) posits that this resentment drives women's desires for a penis in sexual intercourse, and for a child from a man. Lacan, however, argues that no object can fully satisfy this desire because the sense of privation is fundamentally imaginary. Regardless of how many children a woman may have, a lingering dissatisfaction can persist, as desire does not have a precise object. This dissatisfaction opens the possibility for the mother to pursue other desires beyond motherhood, such as a lover, career, or even mundane activities like watching television. The mother's ongoing dissatisfaction is crucial, as it introduces a dialectic of desire that enables the child to recognize desires beyond the mother, encouraging them to look outside the dyadic relationship.

Fuss's anti-essentialist stance, particularly her avoidance of the concept of the phallus, suggests a potential oversight regarding children's recognition of anatomical differences. Children typically become aware of these differences only after the symbolic event linked to the threat of castration. At this stage, anatomy—including chromosomes, gametes, and genitalia—transforms into a mythical Real that gains significance once the values associated with the gender assigned at birth are structured, leading to the establishment of a sexual positioning. Ultimately, this process culminates in an object choice, where the implications of gender and desire are solidified.

Of woman born

Adrienne Rich (1986) radically reexamined heterosexual object choice, asking: if the first erotic bond is with the mother, then could not the "natural" sexual orientation for both men and women be towards women? (pp. 23–75). Rich argued that neither heterosexuality nor homosexuality possesses any inherent "natural" quality. More recently, Judith Butler (1997) has commented on the pervasive "heterosexual matrix" in our society, which grapples with mourning the loss of homosexual attachment (pp. 132–150). Butler asserted that sexual positions are not merely acquired through mourning but often arise as a repudiation of homosexual attachments. Regarding femininity, they noted that "the girl becomes a girl through being subject to a prohibition which bars the mother as an object of desire and installs that barred object as a part of the ego, indeed, as a melancholic identification" (p. 136). Butler fundamentally challenges the idea that sexual identity is primarily constructed around object choice, suggesting that if one's identity as a girl is contingent upon not desiring other girls, then the desire for a girl inherently questions what it means to be a girl, indicating that within this matrix, homosexual desire poses a challenge to traditional gender constructs (p. 136).

If gender is not an inherent quality, then can it be considered an act? Philosopher Friedrich Wilhelm Joseph von Schelling conceptualized the act as a paradoxical phenomenon that transcends conventional boundaries within a symbolic framework. He argues that an act realizes what appears impossible in the existing symbolic universe, retroactively altering the very conditions that render its possibility feasible.

Applying this notion to gender as an act—an independent action that disrupts the typical cause-and-effect logic—we enter a realm where absolute freedom intersects with unconditional necessity. In this interplay, the subject navigates a precarious balance between existence and meaning, prompting profound questions about identity and agency. Viewing gender as an act could fundamentally alter the very landscape of possibility. It's crucial to differentiate between acting out and the passage to action, such as in suicide. An act signifies a transformative moment, akin to rebirth, whereas a passage to the act signifies a finality devoid of rebirth or return.

The kids are not alright

Our children are struggling. They are finding it challenging to transition from latency to adolescence, a time of identity reinvention and the negotiation of their sexual bodies. Importantly, gender incongruence should not be seen as a pathology; thus, sex realignment cannot be viewed as a cure or treatment. I distance myself from the historically pathologizing stance of psychoanalysis, instead invoking Lacan's concept of "sinthome" to propose an ethics of embodied desire that fundamentally reexamines sexuality, particularly through the lens of mortality inscribed within it.

For many pre-transition trans individuals, life can feel incomplete, and the journey toward a livable existence often mirrors a passage from a first birth to a second birth, which entails confronting death. T. S. Eliot poignantly captures this in the poem "The Journey of the Magi": "I should be glad of another death." The physical transformation and the choice to adopt a gender different from that assigned at birth emerge as acts of creation—rebirths that render life more bearable.

Sexual identity revolves around a specific body—one not merely born into but actively constructed. In a world where initiation rites are dwindling, leaving our youth to navigate their gender roles without guidance, only an act can introduce into the body the truths that the unconscious can either resist or fail to acknowledge—death and sexual difference. Since the unconscious struggles to articulate sexuality, gender is better understood not as an attribute or a noun but as a verb—representing action, occurrence, and state of being. The declaration of sex, a pivotal moment often occurring during adolescence, is an act that empowers the individual as an author of their own narrative. An act, in this context, encompasses not only personal agency but also legislative frameworks—what begins as a "bill" becomes law upon enactment. It is our responsibility, as psychoanalysts, to support these acts, recognizing them as forms of writing that inscribe experiences, agreements, and truths into existence.

Notes

1 Stoller, Robert; Sex and Gender: On the Development of Masculinity and Femininity, Science House, New York City (1968) and Stoller, Robert; Sex and Gender: The Transsexual Experiment, Hogarth Press (1968).
2 Austin A, Craig SL, D'Souza S, McInroy LB. Suicidality Among Transgender Youth: Elucidating the Role of Interpersonal Risk Factors. J Interpers Violence.

2022 Mar;37(5–6):NP2696-NP2718. doi: 10.1177/0886260520915554. Epub 2020 Apr 29. Erratum in: J Interpers Violence. 2020 Jul 29:886260520946128.

3 https://williamsinstitute.law.ucla.edu/press/transpop-suicide-press-release/.

4 Ines Rieder, Diana Voigt; *The Story of Sidonie C.: Freud's Famous 'Case of Female Homosexuality'*, Helena History Press (2019). The book had several editions before the English translation (under slightly different titles).

5 Rieder, Ines, Diana Voigt; *The Story of Sidonie C. Freud's Famous "Case of Female Homosexuality."* Trans. Jill Hannum, Ines Rieder, Saint Helena, CA: Helena History Press (2019).

References

André, Serge. (1999). *What Does a Woman Want?* New York: Other Press.

Aubry, Jenny. (1983). *Enfance abandonnée.* Paris: Métailié.

Butler, Judith. (1997). "Melancholy Gender/ Refused Identification." In: *The Psychic Life of Power: Theories in Subjection* (pp. 132–150). Stanford: Stanford University Press.

Freud, Sigmund. (1920). "Psychogenesis of a Case of Homosexuality in a Woman." In: *The Standard Edition of the Complete Psychological Works of Sigmund Freud*, translated by James Strachey (Vol. 18, pp. 145–172). London: Vintage, 1955.

Freud, Sigmund. (1923). "The Infantile Genital Organisation." In: *The Standard Edition of the Complete Psychological Works of Sigmund Freud*, translated by James Strachey (Vol. 19, pp. 141–145). London: Vintage, 1955.

Freud, Sigmund. (1925). "Some Psychical Consequences of the Anatomical Distinction between the Sexes." In: *The Standard Edition of the Complete Psychological Works of Sigmund Freud*, translated by James Strachey (Vol 19, pp. 248–258). London: Vintage, 1955.

Freud, Sigmund. (1931). "Female Sexuality." In: *The Standard Edition of the Complete Psychological Works of Sigmund Freud*, translated by James Strachey (Vol. 21, pp. 221–244). London: Vintage, 1955.

Freud, Sigmund. (1933). "Femininity." In: *New Introductory Lectures on Psychoanalysis, The Standard Edition of the Complete Psychological Works of Sigmund Freud*, translated by James Strachey (Vol. 22, pp. 112–135). London: Vintage, 1955.

Fuss, Diana. (1995). "Fallen Women: 'The Psychogenesis of a Case of Homosexuality in a Woman'." In: *Identification Papers: Readings on Psychoanalysis, Sexuality, and Culture* (pp. 57–82). New York: Routledge.

Gherovici, Patricia. (2010). *Please Select Your Gender: From the Invention of Hysteria to the Democratizing of Transgenderism.* New York: Routledge.

Gindele, Thomas. (2003). "Postface: Freud, Lacan, Sidonie." In: Ines Rieder and Diana Voigt *Sidonie Csillag: Homosexuelle chez Freud, lesbienne dans le siècle*, translated by Thomas Gindele (pp. 395–400). Paris: Epel.

Harris, A. (1999). "Gender as Contradiction." In: *That Obscure Subject of Desire: Freud's Female Homosexual Revisited*, edited by R. Lesser & E. Schoenberg (pp. 156–179). New York: Routledge.

Lacan, Jacques. (1957–1958). *The Formations of the Unconscious: The Seminar of Jacques Lacan, Book V*, edited by J.-A. Miller, translated by R. Grigg. Cambridge, UK: Polity Press, 2017.

Lacan, Jacques. (1962–1963). *On Anxiety, Book X, The Seminar of Jacques Lacan*, translated by A. R. Price, edited by Jacques-Alain Miller. London: Polity Press, 2004

Lacan, Jacques. (2001). *Autres écrits*, edited by Jacques-Alain Miller. Paris: Éditions du Seuil.

Rich, Adrienne. (1986). "Compulsory Heterosexuality and the Lesbian Continuum." In: *Blood, Bread, and Poetry: Selected Prose, 1979–1985* (pp. 23–75). New York: Norton.

Rieder, Ines & Voigt, Diana. (2019). *The Story of Sidonie C.: Freud's Famous "Case of Female Homosexuality"*, translated by Jill Hannum and Ines Rieder. Reno N.V. & Budapest: Helena History Press.

Spitz, Renée. (1945). "Hospitalism: An Inquiry into the Genesis of Psychiatric Conditions in Early Childhood." *The Psychoanalytic Study of the Child*, 1: 53–74.

Spitz, Renée. (1966). *The First Year of Life: A Psychological Study of Normal and Deviant Object Relations*. New York: International Universities Press.

Waitz, Carl. (2025). *Youth Mental Health Crises and the Broken Social Link: A Freudian-Lacanian Perspective*. New York: Routledge.

Chapter 18

Hosting strangeness

Self-harm and suicide in adolescence

Laura Accetti

As is well known, self-destructive behavior in adolescence may underlie different psychic functioning, each of which may be more or less compromised.

But what remains a central element in the clinical work with the suicidal adolescent is his relationship with the body. A body very often related to pain, but not so much to physical pain, but rather in terms of what Donald Winnicott describes as the fear of breakdown, an event not experienced and not accessible to psychic processing and therefore relegated to the realm of the body. In this sense, Winnicott posits the difference between the fear of death, and the fear of breakdown as the fear of disintegration of the personality and thus of annihilation. Regarding this perspective, Thomas Ogden offers us a personal interpretation: he understands it as the experience of a *"failure of the primary bond between mother and child" – a rupture of the experience of continuity, therefore, necessary for development – "which leaves the child alone and helpless on the brink of nonexistence"* (Ogden, 2016). Such a condition condemns the individual to a perpetual search for lost parts of oneself, which must be continually claimed in order to feel complete and to understand within oneself as much as possible of one's unlived life.

This rupture/discontinuity occurring in early psychic life becomes a rupture in the constitutive process of the sense of self in the body. It is determined by the "irruptions" (Fabozzi, 2024), albeit to varying degrees, by the object and their disruptive effect on the child's developing psyche. Traumatic impingements from the environment, which the child is unable to cope with, are "catalogued" as frozen in the body, waiting for the hope of transformation to open up.

Winnicott was convinced that everything we experience – from the trauma of birth – is remembered both emotionally and somatically. However, sometimes it is not merely a matter of remembering what has been frozen in the soma, but rather of an unconstituted memory that imprints itself on the ego, a deforming trace that leaves the subject deprived of a potential semanticization. I think this involves the incursion of a deforming presence that can be generative, creating modifications, alterations in the structuring of the thought.

What the parental couple is unable to transform will not only be deposited in the infant's developing mind but "will inevitably constitute a structural incapacity to transform and create connections" (Fabozzi, 2024). We might ask whether this

DOI: 10.4324/9781003647317-22

condition, in the clinic with the suicidal adolescent, does not leave the trace of a *non-sense* experience in the body, correlated with the sense of emptiness and nihilism that can characterize these patients.

Maria, a 15-year-old patient, is in analysis with me because of her "not feeling real," not being herself, not having a direction. Consequently, she disconnects, withdraws, and explodes as a response to the catastrophe that occurred – or was at risk of occurring – in prehistoric times, and which is always on the verge of happening again. Despair and terror can paradoxically push her to use violent ways toward herself, such as punching herself, thinking compulsively about dangerous activities, annihilating herself precisely to avoid disintegration.

However, if it is not possible to disembody pain at the same time, it is the pain itself that puts her in contact with the existence of a body, against the feeling of succumbing to apathy and absence.

In this case, self-hitting seems to represent a defense against the risk of catastrophe gaining strength again, and the body may become the last bastion to cling to in order to exist (Nicolò, 2021).

At the same time, it can represent the search for someone who can hold her, support her, process and transform her experiences, survive, and be there.

In this chapter, I will therefore attempt to formulate some reflections starting with the body – both physical and psychic, real and imaginary – as a site of early traces and memories, drawing attention to the psychic vicissitudes surrounding origins.

In particular I will focus on the importance of the *original imprint*, the presence of a psychic trauma resulting from the early disinvestment of the bodily Self by the mother, which is configured as an "insult to the child's Self" (Carratelli, 2016). A wound that originates from the experience of discontinuity of the sense of the Self "out of proportion" with respect to the various "physiological" experiences of discontinuity, proper to the various evolutionary passages, interfering with the constitution of the base of the Self in the body (which will have to be sufficiently integrated to cope with the pulsional emergence, whose renewed force in puberty could press or break what is precarious).

Another fundamental point concerns the vicissitudes of the primary scene, which I consider, as the foundation of the origin of the psychic subject, as the container of the "unconscious secret," i.e. all those primitive sexual fantasies of the sadistic fusion of parental bodies that resignify, and are continually resignified, by the wound to the bodily self and the original hole.

A paradigmatic example of these are the masturbatory fantasies that Laufer has explored extensively, and of which the primary scene represents the core, as the source of sexual arousal and thus as a fundamental contribution to infantile masturbatory fantasies.

But sometimes the lurking of unbearable regressive desires, guilt feelings, and the related anguish of being sexually abnormal can generate dissociated defensive fantasies or hallucinatory and delusional productions about the body as an expression of the rejection of internal contents. In these situations the disruptive quality of the anguish can feed self-destructive impulses.

The evolution toward delusional production suggests the powerful role played in the subject by the profound relationship with his own and others' *sexual* unconscious, with the sensory traces of the primitive and their inevitable reverberations on the imaginary (Laplanche, 1987, 2007).

At the same time, these secret and idiosyncratic productions are used by the adolescent to patch the "tear in the structure of the psyche" (Winnicott, 1971) resulting from failures in early relationships and to fill the void in the representational space of his mental proscenium, even if at the cost of a serious alteration in contact with reality, of which the body is the first representative.

The vital body

Analytical work with the suicidal adolescent reveals various situations in which the body can be obstructed in its expressiveness and vitality.

The feeling of *being alive* has a psychosomatic matrix. Winnicott describes the body as the foundation of the imaginative self resulting from the contact between mother and child. The creation of the "body as an internal object" (Laufer) is the ultimate result of this libidinal investment, and establishes the primacy of the other in fostering the development of a healthy integrative sensuality.

As we know, there are psychic and existential situations in which the transformative path from bodily sensoriality to psychic processing and thought is compromised.

When the new adolescent experiences "revisit" (Gutton, 2003) the earlier ones, especially the more original ones, the congruence or distancing between these experiences can lead to conflicts and discomfort in the symbolic reorganization of the body (Ruggiero, 2016).

All this can also be complicated by a phenomenon that is otherwise normal in adolescence: the reactivation of polymorphous perverse dispositions, which are also related to the reactivation of the Oedipus and which are characterized by bisexual confusions[1] (Meltzer, 1973). The later entry into Oedipal problems will be facilitated or hindered precisely by the characteristics of these events.

The child who has undergone traumatic experiences in the primary relationship may develop a powerful defense to keep dissociated or precluded the infant's aggressive–destructive reaction to the wound to the original self, attempting to maintain the "omnipotent phantasm of union or fusion with the idealized pre-oedipal body of the mother" (Laufer, 2005). This quest to re-establish fusion with the mother is a strenuous defense against the threat of object alterity, which makes the object relationship paranoid. The collapse of this defense due to the irruption of the reality of the sexual body will make the relationship with the body particularly persecutory.[2]

Clinical practice tells us that this sense of discontinuity can be well masked up to latency with recourse to the imaginary and dependence on the external object, as well as with hypertrophy of the ego (pseudo-autonomy). In early adolescence, this discontinuity is accentuated and emerges "on the surface" from the inescapable sexual transformations of the body and the difficulty in integrating it. The strangeness emanating from one's pubertal body functions feels uncanny (Freud, 1919): primary scene fantasies are reactivated under the banner of the strangeness of self and object.

As originally happened with the mother, in adolescence the boy will try to search for a new object that will allow him to identify himself, and to separate himself without giving in to what Laufer called the passive surrender to fusion with the mother's body.

In some cases, however, the struggle may be untenable and the adolescent will have to resort to what for him is the only available means, namely, a break with reality.

Then we will see situations where the body can become foreign, persecutory and extraterritorial as Philippe Gutton (2003) says. In adolescence, certain delusional constructs, such as suicide attempts and self-mutilation, can be framed in the formation of a "delusion in the body" (Laufer, 2011, personal communication), which is an act of denial of its sexual reality.

I have noticed in the clinical practice with adolescents with suicidal ideation how the vitality of one's own body can drain too much energy, to the extent that it activates a strong demand to control the body.

For example, one teenager stated that she had a strange relationship with her body, as if it were not hers, sometimes feeling almost foreign. She hated menstruation because it made her feel dirty and fearing to get dirty, thus she often forced herself to sleep motionless. This made her feel protected from the vitality of her body, which endangered her balance and equilibrium. The inability to cope with the internal turbulence caused by the "movements" of the body can lead to the onset of shame and cause fear and great discomfort. It can also prevent contact with some essential sources of replenishment of the sense of being alive and vital, for example: sexuality, the expression and enjoyment of affection, a positive relationship with one's own body and with other people. Often, on the contrary, one notices that the lack of vitality gives way to a "vitalism" (Neri, 2018), a pseudo-vitality determined by an anxiety that gives no respite.

The analytical work allows us to glimpse how in these patients a range of fantasies of annihilation of the self, transmitted by the traumatic nature of the relationship with the object, is declined. Also, it allows to make inferences about the vicissitudes of the object relationship and the underlying fantasies of the primary scene (Freud, 1914; Klein, 1928, 1932; Greenecre, 1973; Gaddini, 1974; Green, 1991; Ferraro & Garella, 2005), as we will see in the clinical case of Maria/Andrea.

Attacks on the vitality of the body: Mary/Andrea

Maria, 15, is an only child who has been living with her mother since her parents separated.

She was referred to me after several months of hospitalization in the outpatient ward at the Institute of Child Neuropsychiatry. Neighbors found her by chance as she was contemplating the void, with the intention of jumping from the 5th floor of her home. Maria had often committed self-harming acts including burning herself with a hot knife and punching herself in the face. She is haunted by the idea that she does not have the "right body": "I would have to be a completely different female in order to have a male" she says, or "I would have to be a tall, thin male in order to have a female", alongside the presence of these nagging fantasies, Maria feels isolated. Something very powerful prevents her from approaching others. She says she finds herself perpetually being with others the 'chickpea', which in slang means 'the third wheel' (a synonym for one who is *excluded from* the couple).

Maria's parents, Alba and Giulio, are a relatively young couple. They have been separated for about four years, and they make it clear that it was Alba who wanted the separation. They learned from the professors that on the first day of high school Maria stood up and told everyone that she wanted to be called Andrea,[3] – a request that was accepted by both her classmates and professors. Maria shared this communication only with her mother, establishing a kind of shared private message from which her father was excluded. An initial conflict emerges between the two in which the mother, perhaps to repair an experience of guilt in which she has felt absent and incapable in her relationship with Maria, seems to try to make an effort to pay attention to her. Perhaps also oriented to protect herself from any shocks that Maria might inflict on her, she presents herself as totally welcoming to her desire to be male, ready to accept any of her choices, but appearing fragile and prevented from making real contact. She bought a binder to bind her breasts, without Maria's request, anticipating it. The father continues to call his daughter Maria and does not believe it necessary to alter the relationship between them, indulging her in this madness. Contrary to what one might suppose, Maria prefers to be with her father who seems to guarantee her a less confrontational identification.

Throughout her life, her mother experienced long periods of depression, marked by a sense of emptiness and lifelessness. She describes herself lying in bed, enveloped in a deadly emptiness alternating with periods of weeping and intense despair. She recounts it as if from a sidereal distance. Gradually she withdrew herself, taking with her any investment in the external world.

As she speaks, an unexpressed emotional charge comes over me. I wonder what those words evoke in her husband, who appears to me almost *physically* stricken as he looks down. She uses words like bullets in their cold and distant nature.

To have better comprehension, I decided to see them separately.

Maria's father, Giulio, is quite resistant to telling his story. A native of southern Italy, he describes having an an-affective father, not very playful, closed and serious. His mother was a passive woman, she did not even try to be autonomous and her husband did allow her to, either. A family dominated by a "master father," who was deeply religious and devoted his life to the Church. Maria "happened" during a period of strong marital quarrel. Giulio was jealous of the autonomy Alba was gaining, and after the umpteenth quarrel, he had decided to close himself off in muteness. He received the news of Maria's arrival with detachment; throughout the pregnancy, he and Alba had never spoken to each other. Only a few months after the child's birth, Giulio decided to "forgive" her. "With my wife, I had imported my father's model," he admitted at the end of the interview.

Maria's mother, Alba, is a young and beautiful woman, though marked by hardship and austerity. During the interview, she tells me about her difficulties of growing up. She comes, like her husband, from a patriarchal family, consisting of a passive mother and a father she describes as vulgar, jealous, and capable of showing a great coldness. This is why she left home at the age of 20 as soon as she met Giulio. However, her husband soon became increasingly possessive, rigid, and aggressive like the father she had run away from, often withdrawing into herself in long periods of punitive muteness.

She was very depressed at various stages of her life, and also after Maria's birth during her adolescence. At those times, she needed to withdraw into a kind of sensory annihilation, in the darkness of her room.

When she found out she was pregnant, she felt trapped. She recounts the feeling of bewilderment and alienation at seeing the fetus in the first ultrasound image.

She never told anyone that she attempted suicide when she was growing up, ingesting large quantities of tranquilizers, from which she was saved. During her depression periods, her husband sexually abused her at night while she was dazed by the medication. She had never spoken of this situation to anyone. Unable to rebel against what was happening to her, she had tried to save herself by creating a secret inner space of denial and reticence, which had protected her from environmental stresses and intrusions that her fragile ego could not tolerate.

It seems, however, that the pregnancy, with all the associated fantasies, has caused her to relapse into a traumatic dimension, perhaps brought about by the great effort required to cope with the sensations in her body.

The analysis with Maria/Andrea

Maria presents a tall, slender physique, a very feminine face, quite depressed and leading a rather withdrawn life.

She asks to be called Andrea and to use male pronouns even although she is not sure yet who she wants to be. Presumably a male. I accept this to encourage mirroring. He says he feels out of place in a "pariolina" school[4] placing him in a different "background" which makes him feel embarrassed. A world of peers all moving, smoking, dancing and having sex that he feels unable to enter.

During our sessions, the body – whose changes I am often a "participant" observer to – is always the focus of "our" attention. Particularly prominent is Andrea's relationship with his hair, through which he seems to control the vitality of his body. Over time, he has presented himself with very short hair which he has cut himself with scissors. The visual impact denotes the "castrating" nature of his gesture, which often seems to me an action to block the emergence of a softer, more sensorial vitality. With this gesture, laden with meanings, Andrea seems to overturn the anxiety of exclusion and rejection of her origins in a counterphobic way, the fantasy of not being the female that her mother would have wanted and that would perhaps save her from her depression, and at the moment of puberty to control the fantasies arising from her growing body.

During her sessions, intense anguish emerges regarding his body image "deformed" by the sexual body. He cannot bear his "thighs" (in Italian, thighs have a semantic nuance in sexual terms) as those of his mother. Over time these will become, in the shared analytical dialogue that will be constructed, the "representation" of maternal elements deposited in the body and that loom large. This elaboration will only take place in the time of analysis; initially, Andrea seems to be unaware of any experience he has had with his mother, as if this has not been experienced and has been directly deposited in the body. Pubertal development began to torment him as these traces emerged, as an expression of the intrusion of ego-alien elements into his body, to the point that Andrea would like to forget and rid himself of them. At the age of 12, the age of menarche, the idea of suicide appears in relation to the death of his paternal grandfather, when Andrea says he first came into contact with the sense of finitude and the reality of death. He says that day he drew up his will. Puberty marked the end of his childhood body and made present strong anxieties of death brought about by the poor psychosomatic integration at the base of the Self. She seems openly struggling with her identification with her mother, aware of her fear of becoming like her hated mother because of the wound to the primary Self, now manifesting a struggle experienced in the relationship with her own body.

A body experienced as monstrous that she attempts to reconstruct through an infantile phallic self-representation. It seems that this choice protects her by allowing her to separate herself in the body from a cumbersome and confusing internal object such as the mother. At the same time, it allows her to be for her mother the sensitive male the father never was, through an inverted Oedipus. Finally, she attempts to deny the gap between her own representation of her body image and the drive body. But this fantasy is continually checkmated by pubertal sensations, causing it to vacillate and leaving her in contact with the paranoid rupture.

In the first phase of the analysis, he tells me of some dreams in which he reveals a deep understanding of the use of our space and the specificity of our work:

1 "I am in the car with my mother and an accident happens. We run over a person because we didn't see him. It was a very laughable dream."
2 "I used to go to the catacombs with Claudio, a friend, to hear Ultimo sing (Ultimo is a very popular singer among young people. He chose this name to define his belonging to the group of the "outcasts", the "invisible ones"). There was a reception with 2 girls. To hear him sing you needed 3 euros but we had 2. We walked down a dark, narrow street and there I felt myself falling. It felt like that feeling of falling that you get in your sleep. When I was little, I often dreamt of falling from above, and it was very scary, but then I would sprout wings and fly."
3 "While my mother was crying sitting on the bed, she turned into a black, slimy spider," she says with a disgusted face, "I drew it."

These dreams present complex depictions, of which I will not provide a detailed analysis, but I would like to focus on the landscape of his inner world.

In the first dream, the death of the third during the accident seems to represent the projection of Andrea's unconscious desire. But it also denotes, on the basis of the historical family vicissitudes that affected his birth, the ghost of his elimination, or equivalently, the return to his mother's womb. A hypothesis that the second dream seems to confirm. The dream depicts Andrea's struggle to join the peer group at the concert, trying to distance himself from the primary objects, an attempt which, however, fails. Instead of an opening to a space no longer familiar, but other, there is a deadly collapse of the new onto the old. It seems stuck in an unresolvable Oedipal dimension, which encourages regression. The collapse of an unreachable 3 into a 2 that becomes 1 is thus reproduced.

In this situation, we could speculate that in the presence of a third persecutory figure, the mother may have held her in an intense defensive attachment. An experience that dragged Maria/Andrea into a psychic state of non-life, burying part of her ego in the maternal "catacomb." I think of suicide, a theme indirectly represented in the dream as fear of falling, but the wings as an element of childhood omnipotence protect her.

In the third dream, the mother's sadness seems to reveal the failure of the mother's function as a protective anti-stimulus shield. She is transformed into a deadly black presence, which precipitates her into a dimension of a "cold core," as described by Green (*noyau froid*, 1983). Then the black spider emerges in the dream, which in its oneiric poignancy, seems to condense the image of the duplicated and tentacled mother, as a non-receptive and deadly mother connected with the father in the re-enactment of a dangerous primary scene.

It would seem that contact with a deadly, depressed, emotionally absent – though physically present – mother, a mother always on the verge of death (in Green's [1980] terms), compromised the elaboration of the primary scene and provoked an early trauma in the constitution of the self, a traumatic rupture, understood as a wound to the self

Comment

The story of Maria/Andrea seems to me emblematic of a "rupture" that has torn the pocket of illusion and primary fusion, where already the unveiling of the pregnancy to the ultrasound images provokes an instant reaction of widespread anguish in the mother. For Alba, a "traumatic situation" returns as the irruption of a highly disturbing, persecutory, deadly primary scene. At the same time, I think about Maria's bodily registering of strange bodily sensations (Gaddini, 1984).

The "feeling of being a stranger" to herself is then that irritating thorn that can drive Maria/Andrea in adolescence to dissociate from and deny the vertiginous bodily sensations of the excited genital zone, of her sexualized self that bears the sensory and perceptual signs of a persecutory and mortifying strangeness (Carratelli, Massaro, 2016). María operates a form of pseudo-manic reparation of rejection phantasies through establishing a fusional identity with her mother, rooted in a cold core that function as a suicidal primary identification. This is a powerful defense designed to keep the infant's aggressive–destructive response to the dissociated or precluded wound inflicted on the self at birth. At the same it shields her from the conscious hatred felt in adolescence toward the cold and rejecting mother.

But above all, I believe that María, having found herself at the mercy of objects that were both too absent and at the same time too traumatically present, had to become a mother of herself – looking after her infantile self made orthopaedically phallic, thus creating a perfect unity, without holes and shortcomings, in order to avoid collapse. This constitutes a form of self-holding that occurs as a defensive process of the ego due to early environmental failure, a concept that Winnicott defines as a defense against the primitive agony of falling forever (Winnicott, 1963).

The intolerability of the body and the desire to destroy it denote that the pressure of bodily transformations has not only activated on the psychic level all the Oedipal and pre-oedipal conflictuality, but has also intensified the force of attraction exerted by the register of the original, of a process that is alongside and precedes in its genesis the primary and secondary processes, conceptualized by Freud.

From Winnicott's perspective, then, it would not be a question of the castration anxiety typical of psychoneurosis, but of the collapse of the unity of the self, which has already taken place. That primitive agony that the infantile ego's organization had managed to bind and thus remain contained, on the condition of its splitting, finally ended up getting the better of the adolescent ego, inducing it, through suicidal acting, to attempt to "send the body to that death which had already taken place in the psyche" (Winnicott, 1963).

It would seem that the metabolizing work of the transforming pubertal body in transformation, required of the psyche, has intensified the force of attraction of the original and has more specifically reactivated an experience of "non-life" in close connection with the collapse at the origins. The search for a suicidal act seems in this sense an attempt to create an experience through bodily action. An attempt to establish an 'intimate' relationship with the collapse in order to represent it.

Conclusions

The specificity of the suicidal gesture and the analysis of the dreams observed in María/Andrea's clinical case allowed us to glimpse in the internal scenario a primary wound in the relationship between the mother and her child, in its infantile origin and its post-pubertal reactivation. These observations suggest that the metabolizing demands imposed by the pubertal body have intensified the force of attraction of the original and in particular of the original maternal imprint. On the intrapsychic level, the collapse results in an unthinkable state that provokes psychic pain, which, during puberty, manifests as *bodily action* (Aulagnier, 1975). In the second dream, we can observe a scene of a birth trauma and the anguish of falling, and losing oneself. It is to be hoped that the presence of the analyst and the analytic device itself can function as a container and allow and welcome the emergence of phantasmatic activity as an indispensable mediator. This allows the subject to protect themselves from reality when it becomes too close to the unthinkable and unrepresentable state, a state that could potentially lead to deadly actions. In the case of Maria/Andrea these functions manifested themselves very early on, and this is evidenced by the initial dream production.

Notes

1 The "zonal confusions" (mouth – vagina – ano combination and then nipple – tongue – fetus combination), which the child had already learned to distinguish, erupt at puberty sometimes accompanied by an idealization of the confusion (Meltzer, 1973).
2 Because of the accentuated experience of discontinuity of the sense of the excess self in these subjects due to the primary vicissitudes described above.
3 In Italy, Andrea is a masculine name but, because it retains feminine nuances, it is often chosen by trans adolescents. Maria/Andrea denotes her permanence in the middle between masculine and feminine, immobile and paralyzed, where masculine and feminine embody a primal scene.
4 Parioliolina means coming from the Parioli district (uptown area). Maria/Andrea seems to describe the sense of "disorientation" in finding herself in a neighborhood as foreign to where she comes from as she feels foreign in her body, to paraphrase Di Ceglie's (1998) words.

References

Aulagnier, P. (1975). *La violence de l'interprétation. Du pictogramme à l'énoncé.* Paris: PUF.

Carratelli, T., Massaro, V. (2016). Il bambino rosa: alla ricerca della leggerezza dell'essere. Note teorico-cliniche. *Rich&Piggle,* 24(4), 356–372. doi 10.1711/2604.26804.

Di Ceglie, D. (1998). *A stranger in my own body: Atypical gender identity development and mental health.* London: Karnac Books.

Fabozzi, P. (2024). *Dispiegare margini. Nei dintorni di Winnicott.E oltre.* Roma: FranoAngeli.

Ferraro, F., Garella, A. (2005). Scena primaria. *Rivista di Psicoanalisi,* 2, 593–621.

Freud, S. (1919). "The 'Uncanny'". The Standard Edition of the Complete Psychological Works of Sigmund Freud (Vol 17, pp. 217–252). London: Hogarth Press, 1955,

Gaddini, E. (1974). Formazione del padre e scena primaria. In *Scritti (1953–1985).* Milano: Cortina, 1989.

Gaddini, E. (1984). La frustrazione come fattore della crescita normale e patologica. In E. Gaddini (Ed.), *Scritti (1953–1985).* Milano: Rafaello Cortina Editore, 1989.

Green, A. (1980). « La mère morte » (1980), in Narcissisme de vie, narcissisme de mort (1983). Paris: Éditions de Minuit.

Green, A. (1983). *Narcissisme de vie, narcissisme de mort.* Paris: Éditions de Minuit.

Green, A. (1991). L'originario nella psicoanalisi. In Preta L (a cura di), *La narrazione delle origini.* Bari: Laterza, 1991.

Greenecre, P. (1973). The Primal Scene and the sense of reality. *Psicoanalisi,* 2(2), 106–130.

Gutton, P. (2003). *Le Pubertaire.* Paris: PUF.

Klein, M. (1928). I primi stadi del conflitto edipico. In Scritti 1921–1958. Torino: Boringhieri, 1978.

Klein, M. (1932). Primi stadi del conflitto edipico e della formazione del super-io. In *La psicoanalisi dei bambini*. Firenze: Martinelli, 1969.

Laplanche, J. (1987). *New Foundations for Psychoanalysis*. Ed. New York: The Unconscious in Translation, 2016.

Laplanche, J. (2007). *Sexual. La sexualité élargie au sens freudien*. Paris: PUF (English Translation.:

Lapalnche, J. [2011]. *Freud and the Sexual* [John Fletcher, Ed]. New York: The Unconscious in Translation, 2011).

Laufer, E. (2005). Le corps comme objet interne. *Adolescence*, 23(2), 363–379

Meltzer, D. (1973). *Sexual States of Mind*. London: Karnak Books. Neri, C. (2018). Aspetti vitali della vergogna. Frenis Zero. https://www.claudioneri.it/wp-content/uploads/2018/04/Resnik-vitalita-vergogna-2018-25.pdf

Nicolò, A.M. (2021). *Developmental Ruptures: The psychoanalysis of breakdown and defensive solutions*. London: Routledge.

Ogden, T. (2016). *Reclaiming Unlived Life: Experiences in Psychoanalysis*. London & New York: Routledge.

Ruggiero, I. (2016). *La mente adolescente e il corpo ripudiato*. A. M. Nicolò & I. Ruggiero (Eds). Roma: FrancoAngeli.

Winnicott, D.W. (1963). Fear of breakdown. In C. Winnicott, R. Shepherd, M. Davis (Eds.), *Psycho-Analytic Explorations* (pp. 87–95). London; Routledge, 1989.

Winnicott, D. W. (1971). *Playing and Reality*. London: Penguin Books.

Discussion on suicides and masochism in adolescence today through three clinical cases

Heribert Blass

All three authors: Silvia Flechner, Patricia Gherovici, and Laura Accetti, have presented rich papers that are full of clinical and theoretical thoroughness and offer a stimulating diversity of thought. It was a great pleasure to have the opportunity to listen to them at the COCAP Conference that took place last year. Now it is equally gratifying that all three lectures, in some cases in extended form, are available in this book.

The theme of the entire panel and the papers presented are highly topical. Just in September 2024, an analysis of the global state of adolescent mental health was published in the *Lancet Psychiatry*.[1] According to its results, "mental ill health […] of young people […] has entered a dangerous phase […] Unless treated effectively, mental illnesses are a major cause of premature death from physical illness and suicide." The authors confirm the existence of a scandal and "a form of self-harm inflicted by society upon itself." And the US Surgeon General, in view of the deteriorating situation, had called "for action to address youth mental health crisis."[2] Now in the papers presented, all three authors sensitively and intelligently describe what this youth mental health crisis can look like in individual cases, and all three show how important and significant psychoanalytical approaches to understanding and treatment are for both the individual and the society. They show that psychoanalysis is truly present in the community and the world, especially as the three colleagues are living and working in different countries and regions of the world. Nevertheless, in their clinical experiences, they are equally confronted with a range of physical and/or mental violence against children and adolescents and active actions of adolescent self-harm as well. In connection with the upheavals of adolescence and the crisis-ridden appropriation of one's own sexual body and sexual identity, two of these papers also deal in detail with the desire for self-determination of one's own gender in the context of a trans-identity, which is more frequently encountered today. All three papers address both passive traumatization and active self-destructive actions, and the spectrum of their focal points ranges from adolescent breakdown to psychological rebirth. As all authors described in their papers, this dialectic is not limited to certain cultures but can happen in all parts of the world. Even if we have to take the influence of individual cultures into account, it becomes evident that psychoanalysis has a cross-cultural approach.

DOI: 10.4324/9781003647317-23

The focus of my comment concentrates, despite the diversity and different orientations of the presentations, on their commonalities. I think there are at least three: firstly, the consideration of the role of parents as well as the social environment and culture; secondly, the central role of the biological and sexual body of adolescents; and thirdly, the psychoanalytic process.

Parents and social environment

All three authors recognize the eminently important role of parental fantasies, affects and actions for the child's mental development. The possibility of a traumatic parental presence *or* absence is emphasized in all three case studies. It is not the child or the adolescent alone who carries out self-harming or suicidal acts, but corresponding fantasies or actions always arise in the context of transgenerational transmission (cp. Faimberg 2005). We must not underestimate the role of parental violence – not only the crudest form of parental violence in the form of mostly paternal sexual abuse, but also the possible violence emanating from a mother in the form of deadly rejection, as tragically depicted in the mythological figure of Medea. I have not only treated patients who have been sexually abused by their father or brother, but also others who have heard their mother complain during her depressive crises: "Why didn't I drown you in the river?" or "Why didn't I kill myself together with you?" Not only this personal aggression, but also repeated observations of violence between parents obstruct the development and consolidation of a libidinal self-organization for the child. All three authors emphasize the contradictory simultaneity of *too much or too little* affective presence of the parents. A predominantly aggressive–intrusive quality of early object relationships or the lack of lovingly care in early attachments hinder coping with oedipal conflicts that could finally open the path to an identification with protective parental figures. On the contrary, the children are more likely to develop a *parentification* in which the generations are reversed, and they become parents to their own damaged parents. This is exactly described in all three vignettes. For instance, when the emerging skin ego of the infant is charged with experiences of parental violence and cannot become self-protective but is developing instead as a basis for attacks on one's own physical and erotic body to ward off powerlessness, like Silvia Flechner describes in the case of Max. Or otherwise, when the parents are perceived as too immature due to severe psychic conflicts and symptoms, as described in the case of Jude by Patricia Gherovici. Here the adolescent feels called upon to protect and parent their own mother. As Jude said in the only interview, they had to function as an adult for the mother. I think it is important to realize that this lack of a protective parental presence is associated with the unconscious presence of a persecutory, greedily envious parental couple. The adolescent is then torn between the search for adult parents and the sometimes-violent effort to expel the persecutory parents from within her-/himself and from her/his fantasized body. I believe that Freud's patient Sidonie, who is described by Patricia Gherovici in a subtle analysis, had to struggle with a similar dilemma in the face of a mother who both denied and competed with her. Under these circumstances, the development of an increasing independent self that becomes able to integrate and regulate external and internal options for action is being prevented. Thus, the path is paved for adolescent breakdown. Nevertheless, it is clear from all three papers that this severe crisis in adolescent development does not necessarily have to result in permanent collapse but can also open up the opportunity for a new beginning.

Another decisive parental influence is mentioned by Laura Accetti when she hints at the eminent importance of the parents' 'enigmatic messages' to their child according to Laplanche's concept of the *Sexual* (2014). As shown in her case of Maria/Andrea, not only sexual but also aggressive–destructive parental fantasies can become enigmatic for the child and start to shape the child's unconscious self-image and emerging identity.

I was touched by the fact that two ambiguous German terms used by Freud could illustrate the psychodynamically significant shift from one psychic quality to another. When Silvia Flechner speaks of the Ominous and thus refers to Freud's (1919) *The Uncanny* and to the opposition of *heimlich* and *unheimlich,* she takes up the potential double meaning in the German term *heimlich*. It contains the word *home* ('Haus' or 'Heim' in German), and in this sense, the term *heimlich* refers to one's own home as a place of protective retreat. But it can also become a hiding place from the world in the sense of a secret: what is happening at home, happens secretly, without public knowing. The step from protection to threat can become small: *unheimlich* does not designate a securing home anymore but marks a threatening place instead, and staying in one's own home can also become a threatening home. It becomes *unheimlich,* if the initially protective residents of the home have turned to persecutory characters, and if there is no longer a connection to a now protective public sphere. The same is true for one's own body: if not lovingly inhabited, the real and the fantasized body can become 'uncanny' and threatening. Patricia Gherovici refers to similar etymological context with her definition of *gender* as stemming from the Latin word 'genus'. All these terms: heimlich, unheimlich, and genus, already point to the connection between either the internalization of libidinal, generally erotic familial relationships or unconscious efforts to protect oneself from an inhospitable home and to seek salvation in the sacrifice of one's own body, be it through suicide or by an attack on one's own sexual body. However, I am impressed by the sensitivity how much the authors also take the parents' history into account and are able to adopt a transgenerational perspective without any attitude of reproach. I believe that this analytical attitude offers patients a basis for a repaired inner home instead of a broken home or for a better accepted and erotically valued body instead of the former attacks on one's own body as a felt enemy.

I will go into the other German term, 'niederkommen', with the double meaning of falling and giving birth, later.

The meaning of the biological and the erotic body

Another common feature of the three papers is the particular focus on the relationship between the maturation of the *biologically* sexual body and the integration of the *psychologically* sexual body into the adolescent's self and sense of self.

According to Dejours (2003), we are owners of two bodies: the biological body and the erotic body. To take up Laplanche's image: when the physical hormonal instinct pushes in during puberty, it finds the chair already occupied by the psychological sexual drive. I imagine that Laura Accetti has a similar relation in mind when she speaks of 'sexual difference' and states that 'gender needs to be embodied while sex needs to be symbolized'. All three papers show that a fragile, dyadic, and non-libidinal, non-triangular child's self can only experience the biological sexual maturation of its own body as an aggressive–destructive attack on the precarious balance of its own psychic drives and feelings. According to Solms (2022), the feeling is the drive. The sexual maturation leads to intolerable feelings! This happens even more, the less libidinal the previously internalized relationships between the self and its primary objects are. This includes the unconscious fantasies about the primal scene. If the primal scene fantasies are mainly associated with hate bonds in the sense of -H and lack of curiosity and rejection of erotic explorations in the sense of -K (Bion, 1962), the gradually sexually maturing body cannot be associated with psychic love bonds (+L). Instead, the enigmatic messages coming from within are now equated with a final overpowering by a foreign power. The fierceness of the sexual instincts meets a libidinally impoverished or not yet stimulated self, which – to return to Laplanche – clings anxiously to its chair or, to survive, must attack its own body as the aggressor. But this is also an unconscious *attempt at rescue*, and all three case histories illustrate the unconscious *attempts at rescue* that motivate the suicidal or masochistic risk-taking behavior. In the cases of Patricia Gherovici and Laura Accetti, a special connection between the attack on the original body sex and the desire for a mental self-constitution and autonomous psychosexual identity, different from the biological body, becomes clear, while in the case of Silvia Flechner, the patient's consistently masochistic aggressiveness contains his hidden libidinal desire: If he pleases his parents by confirming their projective death wishes and homicidal impulses through his risk-taking behavior, he is seeking their love. This dynamic becomes particularly touching when the patient sits at the bedside of his comatose father. The sad and tender hand holding between the two of them is a reversal of the original parent–child relationship, because it is only the unbreakable love of the son, branded as delinquent, for his father that allows him to express something loving without words.

In this context, I am also particularly interested in Patricia Gherovoci's emphasis on gender but also suicidal action as an *act*: when Jude jumps into the river, it is an 'act that speaks louder than words'. Patricia Gherovici describes Jude as 'only half-born' and at the same time feeling "oppressed because of gender" what leads to an exhausting battle between inside and outside. It is a moving scene when Jude declared to start their only interview in the middle, because they would know neither a beginning nor an end. The situation seemed similarly hopeless in the face of their struggle for a free and autonomous sexual identity, so that the desperate, real leap into the river also took on a symbolic meaning: to kill oneself to be reborn. Freud's patient Sidonie had also jumped, according to Freud because of the loss of her homosexual love object, not so much because of her struggle for sexual identity. Freud identified the unconscious symbolic meaning of the dramatic action of jumping with the help of the double meaning in the German word 'niederkommen'. In a concrete sense, it can mean 'to fall' but is used almost exclusively metaphorically in the sense "to give birth to a child." Patricia Gherovici emphasizes that Freud used this metaphor mainly in the realm of his Oedipal theory according to which Sidonie's leap in the sense of 'niederkommen' contained her unconscious wish to have a baby from her father. According to Freud, Sidonie's leap and suicide attempt was both a punitive act and a manifestation of her unconscious Oedipal desire. Freud remained object-centered in this way. By contrast, I find it very convincing that Patricia Gherovici takes up Freud's play on words but turns the unconscious desire away from the object and onto the subject: in her patient Jude, the desire to give birth is directed toward their own person, their own self. This is where there is a fundamental connection between all three papers.

Even if impulsive self-harm or suicidal behavior cannot be equated with a transgender identity and body-modifying gender reassignment, which also violates the original biological body, I consider it crucial that all three clinical papers make a connection between the active search for a possible annihilation of one's own physical and psychic existence and an at least unconscious wish to be reborn and to live differently than before. This paradox is an expression of a core conflict within the person. For a psychoanalytical understanding and the resulting therapy, it remains essential that both self-harming and potentially suicidal acts as well as body-modifying interventions are associated with the hope of a changed or new life, whereby the perceived hopelessness is certainly more pronounced in the area of suicidal acts. Gender modification seems to be associated with more conscious hope, despite all the suffering experienced. But as all three authors movingly show, it is not possible without the experience of psychic pain.

I want to exemplify this position by especially turning to Patricia Gherovici's reference to Schelling. I will not comment on her interesting and sophisticated ideas on femininity because this would transgress the limits of my discussion of all three papers. I will concentrate on her concept that the transformation of the body given at birth into another body is a creative act. She refers to Schelling and his definition of the act as a paradoxical formal structure with the retrograde alteration of its own preconditions for the possibility of changes in the present, and she also includes Lacan's 'Sinthome'. I see a potential connection to Freud's (1918) concept of *Nachträglichkeit (après-coup)*, but I repeat her central idea: After passing through a death, the transformation of the body given at birth into another body is a creative act that makes life livable, if the previous state was lacking psychic life. I see this as psychodynamic, and I very much agree with her call not to pathologize bodily changes and gender transformation. However, I would like to mention the dimension of suffering in this creative act. A trans-female teenager once told me during her transition: "Nobody does something like this voluntarily. It is always an inner suffering that leads to this decision." In my view, it is true that a sex change can be a creative act of revitalization and even lifesaving – a young transman once told me very clearly that he would have killed himself without the process of trans-formation. But if we as psychoanalysts put emphasis on the creative act and the potential psychic rescue that is coming from gender transformation, or also from attempted suicides with the unconscious aim to live differently, we must not forget the pain that is connected with these acts. In all the cases I know of, it was always important to give sufficient space in the analysis to the mourning of one's own losses that cannot be fully repaired by imaginative acts. We still have to think about the following question: What is the relationship between relief after the imagina-tive 'second birth' by changes of the sexual body and grieving recognition of the breaks in one's own life, even if the authorship of one' s life is so decisive?

I think that the case of Maria/Andrea that Laura Accetti described can also be seen from the point of view of the act. Laura Accetti hinted to the fact that the feeling of *being alive* has a psychosomatic matrix and that a *vital body* can only develop from this basis. Winnicott (1963) called it *indwelling* – again a reference to the inner home. And he referred to what had traumatically impinged on the self, but also to missing experiences in the sense of a lack of stimulation and mental forma-tion, or of "a potential semanticisation," as Laura Accetti calls it. She underlines the necessary "incursion of a deforming presence, that can be generative, creating modifications, alterations in the structuring of the thought." In her fascinating and detailed description of the clinical process – where she also mentions the transgen-erational transmission of the suicidal states of Maria's mother to Maria/Andrea –, *bodily action* (according to Aulagnier 2001) by repeated self-harming or contem-plating the void, with the intention of jumping from the fifth floor of her house, could be seen as this incursion of a deforming presence that, in the case of somatic survival, can become the beginning of a semanticization. This becomes particu-larly clear in the dreams that Andrea can now develop during the analysis with the analyst as a present third object. The pleasurable murder of the mother or of a part of herself becomes clear in the first dream, while the second dream also refers to falling and a new birth. With respect to wings and flying, I want to ask: is the gender transformation a life-saving solution, or is there a danger of a manic denial of the underlying depression? In her paper, Laura Accetti connects it with fantasies of infantile omnipotence in the patient. Of course, this would put the emphasis rather on the creative aspect than on the defense of depression. Nevertheless, I see the third dream with the spider as a reminder of this depression. It seems important to me that, as with the question of sufficient space for mourning, there is enough time to work through possible manic defenses, so that a lively interaction between a sense of creative departure and mourning can develop.

The analytic process

All three colleagues have shown, besides their emotional containment, how cru-cial it is to focus on working through the masochistic acts as an attempt at self-determination in the face of powerlessness. And I see a special commonality that all three colleagues have focused on a transformation of the patient's parentification. Patricia Gherovici had only one session, but Jude mentioned their adult responsibility, whereas Silvia Flechner and Laura Accetti could offer a longer period of healthy dependence that could link their patients' masochistic striving for autonomy with a growing libidinal experience in the transference. Identifying with the analyst as a witness to the traumas suffered and at the same time as a life-oriented interpreter of the self-harming actions could help the patients to stop fighting their own bodies as hated objects. As we saw, the recent trauma preceding a suicide attempt is usually a painful separation and loss of an idealized object, and that loss actualizes and represents the initial lack of an internalized protective parental couple. It is the analyst's challenge not to lose sight of the ambivalent search for protective internal objects despite all the hatred. I have mentioned the tragic but also moving scene where Silvia Flechner's patient Max holds the hand of his comatose father. I believe this scene takes up and transcends the earlier parentification. It shows how much Max was able to identify with Silvia Flechner's work of interpretation, which combined love and hate. To close: it became clear how much all three analysts were able to convey a feeling of hope that was not naive but life-affirming by working through their patients' self-destructive actions, hatred, and desperate love desires. For this, I would like to thank all three of them with great appreciation.

Notes

1 McGorry, P.D. et al. (2024). The Lancet Psychiatry Commission on youth mental health. The Lancet Psychiatry, Volume 11, Issue 9, 731–774.
2 Richmond, L.M. (2022). Surgeon General Calls for Action to Address Youth Mental Health Crisis. Psychiatric News, Volume 57, Issue 2, https://doi.org/10.1176/appi. pn.2022.2.11 (last accessed January 12, 2025).

References

Aulagnier, P. (2001). *The Violence of Interpretation.* London and New York: Routledge.
Bion, W.R. (1962). *Learning from Experience*. London: Karnac.
Dejours. (2003). *Le Corps, d'abord: Corps biologique, corps érotique et sens moral.* Paris: Éditions Payot & Rivages pour l'édition de poche.
Faimberg, H. (2005). *The Telescoping of Generations.* Listening to the Narcissistic Links between Generations. London and New York: Routledge.
Freud, S. (1918). *From the History of an Infantile Neurosis.* The Standard Edition of the Complete Psychological Works of Sigmund Freud (Vol 17, pp. 1–124). London: Hogarth Press.
Freud, S. (1919). *The 'Uncanny'.* The Standard Edition of the Complete Psychological Works of Sigmund Freud (Vol. 17, pp. 217–252). London: Hogarth Press.
Laplanche, J. (2014). *Sexual. La sexualité élargie aux sense freudien.* Paris: PUF.
Solms. (2022). Revision of Drive Theory. *Journal of the American Psychoanalytic Association*, 69(6), 1081–1107. https://doi.org/10.1177/00030651211057041
Winnicott, D.W. (1963). Fear of Breakdown. In: Caldwell, L., Joyce, A. (Eds., 2011) *Reading Winnicott* (pp. 200–208). London and New York: Routledge.

Chapter 20

Some reflections on the three papers of suicide and masochism in adolescence today

Paula Guadalupe Cerutti Agelet

Introduction

The articles by Silvia Flechner, Patricia Gherovici, and Laura Accetti address with the complex clinical challenges of adolescents, where the thanatic aspects of the drives manifest through risky behaviour and suicide attempts that threaten the life itself. The ongoing updating of psychoanalytic theory contributes to understand and treat this problem, expanding the clinical perspective while also considering the specificities of the social and cultural context that affects adolescents and their new forms of subjectivation. Including these dimensions is essential to reflecting on the future of future generations.

Through multicultural clinical vignettes, the authors illustrate psychic functioning during the turbulent stage of puberty and adolescence, reconstructing early histories that remain as a living memory and are updated in the adolescent, where the body takes a central focus. Understanding each case implies recognizing that the genesis of suicidal tendencies arises from a complex web of cultural, historical, intra- and inter-subjective factors, configuring a coexistence between primitive traces and the present experience.

The three presentations highlight the value of psychoanalysis as a research method (Freud, 1923), preserving its essence by formulating questions to develop hypotheses about how each subject copes with intolerable psychic pain.

Some reflections

Silvina Flechner explores the factors in the history of children and adolescents who engage in self-harm and suicidal acts, where experiences of abandonment—or, conversely, the intrusive environmental tendencies—play a central role. Early anxieties erupt and complicate those typical of adolescence, particularly with the reactivation of the Oedipal complex. A primitive psychic pain, difficult to represent, is mitigated through destructive ways: self-harm serves as a prelude to suicide, which constitutes a massive return of self-destruction in response to the impotence to effect any external change. Through self-harm, the patient attempts to dismantle the "apparatus of feeling and thinking." In "On Narcissism: An Introduction," Freud refers to

DOI: 10.4324/9781003647317-24

a libidinal distribution in which physical pain facilitates the withdrawal of investments from the external world (Freud, 1914). All three papers highlight a process where the transference bond with the analyst—anchored in the analyst's recognition of suffering—enables the possibility of introducing a new libidinal redistribution. This allows the "healthy part" of the patient can attach its interest to the available figure of the analyst, who offers alternative ways for expressing suffering beyond those already known. For example: "(…) as soon as the treatment began, she was able to express her deep distress and feelings of emptiness and loneliness" (Flechner); "In the first phase of the analysis, she shared some dreams that hinted at a deep understanding of our space and the specificity of our work" (Accetti); "(…) she shared the complexities of her life, including being trans, dealing with chronic Lyme disease, ADHD, and the challenges of being queer" (Gherovici).

Silvina Flechner asks: could self-harming be the symptomatic expression of our time? In a world marked by hostility and constant shifting, where "violent ideals" are promoted—wars, fanaticism, pandemics, massive technological access, among others—I agree with Heribert Blass in posing the question around mourning: What happens to the construction of adult identity and the mourning processes (Aberastury and Knobel, 1973) in this context, where the projection of a vital and creative insertion into adult life might be hindered? I ask: is it mourning or melancholy in relation to childhood?

In *Civilization and Its Discontents*, Freud states that human beings aim to attain happiness by avoiding displeasure and seeking the absence of pain (Freud, 1930). This tendency takes on different forms of subjective expression depending on the historical period. One could hypothesize that today's adolescent self-destructiveness reflects a cultural discontent—manifesting powerlessness and frustration—expressed through a prevailing inclination towards autoplastic responses (internal alterations) rather than alloplastic ones (transforming the external environment in a constructive way). Such suffering could also be understood as a defensive retreat into illness, which, in accordance with the pleasure principle, spares the ego from greater psychic labour. The resulting secondary gain may postpone a fuller integration into adult life in a society perceived as threatening and marked by high ideals of success and productivity, thus prolonging the adolescent moratorium. Where psychic processing takes place, powerlessness and frustration instead emerge, hindering the necessary psychic elaboration.

Patricia Gherovici emphasizes that the suicidal attempt itself may represent the search for a new birth. Death drives are not strictly opposed to life but rather appear as a condition for its possibility. She de-pathologizes the transgender experience and understands it as a possible way of existing—an act of self-creation that, as a kind of rebirth, makes life possible by allowing the patient to "feel alive." In her work with Jude, who feels "oppressed by gender", she highlights a "fall" from the position of child within the family system to that of caretaker for his siblings—a child-parent figure. A parallel appears in Flechner's paper: Max felt like a servant, hated by his mother and exposed to his father's violence. Laura Accetti, in discussing María/Andrea's case, describes maternal rejection and a reaction of strangeness from the very first intrauterine contact. Considering these elements as a "symbolic death of the child's position" led me to revisit Mauricio Knobel's ideas regarding "Filicide"—a concept developed by Argentine psychoanalyst Arnaldo Rascovsky— linked to adolescence aggression and suicidal tendencies, as possible identification with or enactment of unconscious parental fantasies (Knobel, 1986).

In relation to masochism, all three cases reveal depressive aspects underlying adolescent suffering and, in some instances, those of their parents as well. In melancholia, we can strikingly observe the psychic split in which the superego sadistically punishes the ego that has narcissistically identified with the object. This masochistic submission to the superego can lead to suicide as an attempt to kill the internalized object. This dynamic can be seen in Flechner's patient, who exclaims: "She is a psychiatric patient just like me."

Laura Accetti highlights the central role of the body in pubertal metamorphosis, linked to the fear of disintegration anxieties. She analyzes the impact of early wounds to the ego, resulting from the vicissitudes of the mother—child dyad—in this case, tied to maternal depression and suicide attempts, the primordial rejection of the bodily self, and the intrusion of unprocessed elements from the maternal psyche that resurface during the psychic work of puberty. Alongside this demand for psychic metabolization, an original maternal imprint is reactivated. In continuity with Flechner's paper, Accetti underscores the importance of a primitive pain that could not be represented through words and must be contained and transformed within the analytic process through a dialogue constructed with the patient. On this topic, Roosevelt Cassorla (2021) points out that in such cases—marked by potential acting-out and impulsivity, where words are lost—the analyst's work resembles that of a tightrope walker. The patient may masochistically attack the process in an ambivalent struggle that prevents them from receiving the relief and improvement that the analytic work could bring, potentially leading to self-destruction at its most extreme.

All three texts present the analyst facing the challenge of internalizing a new experience with the object within an asymmetry that holds and creates meaning through interpretive work. I believe that in cases dominated by self-destructive behaviours, attacks on the therapeutic bond, the reactivation of trauma, and distrust in the object, the value of the analyst lies in their experience of the transference scene and the anxieties it evokes. This requires a strenuous task of metabolizing the evoked affects, thoroughly analyzing countertransference and inferring the transference scenario the patient enacts and unfolds.

The "suicidal gesture," according to Laura Accetti, becomes a search to create an experience through a bodily act—an attempt to reestablish an intimate connection with the experience of disintegration in the primitive psychic life, in order to represent it. Patricia Gherovici, for her part, notes that from a place close to death, a "rebirth" is possible, where the transgender experience makes life livable. In this sense, how might we think about the mixing and unmixing of drives?

Conclusion

These psychoanalytic reflections on current adolescent problems reflect the rigorous and committed work of colleagues with the psychoanalytic method, not only as a research tool, but also as an effective therapeutic method to alleviate psychic pain in complex situations where life is at risk. This conviction is manifested in the analyst's vital commitment to open up new possibilities for the elaboration of suffering caused by highly intense thanatic aspects.

The deep identification with psychoanalytic thinking that sustains the singular process of each patient constitutes an anchor in chaotic times, marked by haste and promises of quick solutions. Relying on the foundations of our theory is the way forward amid the turbulence of our era, without losing the direction and specificity of our task as analysts.

References

Aberastury, A., & Knobel, M. (1973). "El síndrome de la adolescencia normal" en *La adolescencia norma*, pp. 35–44. Buenos Aires: Paidós.

Cassorla, R.M.S. (2021). "Configurações borderline y narcísica" en *Estudos sobre suicidio: Psicanálise e saúde mental*, pp. 95–113. Editora Edgard Blücher.

Freud, S. (1914). Introducción del narcisismo en *Obras completas* (Vol. XIV), p. 79. Buenos Aires: Amorrortu Editores.

Freud, S. (1923). "Dos artículos de enciclopedia: Psicoanálisis y Teoría de la libido" en *Obras completas* (Vol XVIII), p. 231. Buenos Aires: Amorrortu Editores.

Freud, S. (1930). El malestar en la cultura en *Obras completas* (Vol XXI), p.76. Buenos Aires: Amorrortu Editores.

Knobel, M. (1986). "Familia y sociedad: El filicidio en la adolescencia" en *La universalidad del filicidio*, p. 156. Buenos Aires: Legasa.

Index

For Product Safety Concerns and Information please contact our EU
representative GPSR@taylorandfrancis.com
Taylor & Francis Verlag GmbH, Kaufingerstraße 24, 80331 München, Germany

www.ingramcontent.com/pod-product-compliance
Lightning Source LLC
Chambersburg PA
CBHW050349270326
41926CB00016B/3659

9 7 8 1 0 4 1 0 8 8 7 8 3